Watersheds 3

Ten Cases in Environmental Ethics

LISA H. NEWTON
Fairfield University

CATHERINE K. DILLINGHAM
Fairfield University

WADSWORTH

™

THOMSON LEARNING

Australia • Canada • Mexico • Singapore • Spain • United Kingdom • United States

Publisher: Eve Howard
Philosophy Editor: Peter Adams
Assistant Editor: Kara Kindstrom
Editorial Assistant: Chalida Anusasananan
Marketing Manager: Dave Garrison
Development Consultant: Jake Warde
Marketing Assistant: Adam Hofmann
Print/Media Buyer: Robert King
Permissions Editor: Bob Kauser

Production Service: Buuji, Inc.
Copy Editor: Alan DeNiro
Cover Designer: Leslie Fitch
Cover Image: Monet, "Creuse Torrent," 1888 (detail) from Eyewire
Compositor: Buuji, Inc.
Text/Cover Printer: Webcom Ltd.

Library of Congress Cataloging-in-Publication Data

Newton, Lisa H., date.
  Watersheds 3 : ten cases in environmental ethics / Lisa H. Newton, Catherine K. Dillingham.
    p. cm.
  Includes bibliographical references and index.
  ISBN 0-534-51182-1
    1. Environmental ethics. 2. Environmental ethics—Case studies. I. Dillingham, Catherine K. II. Title.

GE42 .N48 2002
179'.1—dc21   2001026518

Wadsworth/Thomson Learning
10 Davis Drive
Belmont, CA 94002-3098
USA

For more information about our products, contact us:
Thomson Learning Academic Resource Center
1-800-423-0563
http://www.wadsworth.com

International Headquarters
Thomson Learning
International Division
290 Harbor Drive, 2nd Floor
Stamford, CT 06902-7477
USA

UK/Europe/Middle East/South Africa
Thomson Learning
Berkshire House
168-173 High Holborn
London WC1V 7AA
United Kingdom

Asia
Thomson Learning
60 Albert Street, #15-01
Albert Complex
Singapore 189969

Canada
Nelson Thomson Learning
1120 Birchmount Road
Toronto, Ontario M1K 5G4
Canada

To the land,
and to our grandchildren's future

Contents

CHAPTER 3   *LIFE IN THE GREENHOUSE*   45
          The Effects of Global Warming

CHAPTER 4   *THE EXTENDED FAMILY*   59
          The Saga of the Great Apes

CHAPTER 5   *A QUESTION OF RESPONSIBILITY*   78
          The Legacy of Bhopal

Preface

We would much rather read books than write them. The only reason to write a book is that you need something to teach with and there's nothing there, or it's there in such a scattered and inconvenient form that you can't use it for a large class. This is the issue with the classic cases of environmental ethics—the "defining moments" when human technology trips over itself and sprawls into an ungainly heap of poisoned soil, polluted water, human injury and death, with no one to explain it or pay for it. In such moments, we can focus the student's wandering attention on the real problems of environmental complexity: the biological, economic, and legal issues underscored by the damage irrevocably done to real people and the land they depend upon. For our own purposes alone, then, we had had to assemble the snippets of newsprint that hold the information for these cases; it was a short step to put the cases together in a book for our colleagues.

This edition reflects a new urgency about current events. The first edition focused in particular on the classic stories—Love Canal, the tropical rainforest, the Exxon *Valdez*—that had brought environmental consciousness to the fore in the 1970s. This edition includes genetically modified organisms (GMOs), antibiotic resistance, and the current slaughter of the great apes—all problems that have become issues only within the last few years. The latest emanations (emissions?) from the administration that assumed office on January 21, 2001 strongly suggest that citizen interest in the environment will be of crucial importance over the next four years.

We have found the use of cases an enormous help in the classroom. A case is a story. We deal with theories in our classrooms, but we anchor our theories in stories, for if a theory cannot find illustration in the things that actually happen to us, the theory is bound for the dustheap. Stories are easy to remember, fun to talk about, and the foundation of insight. In the case of these classic stories, known to all, that insight is generalizable, and will be good for the foreseeable future. Assembling them for practical use each semester has made our work considerably easier for us. We trust it will do the same for you.

Cases from the second edition not used in this edition are available to adopters of this book on the Wadsworth website. A passcode is registered and may be obtained by contacting you local Wadsworth/Thomson Learning representative.

We would like to thank our editor, Peter Adams, for his patience and helpful suggestions in the course of the preparation of this manuscript. We would also like to thank the following reviewers of this manuscript: Leslie Francis, University of Utah; Wendy Lee-Lampshire, Bloomsburg University; Charles Verharen, Howard University; and William Vitek, Clarkson University. Above all, we gratefully acknowledge the help and support of God and our families (especially Victor Newton and Bruce Dillingham), without whose forbearance and support the completion of this project would not have been possible.

Lisa H. Newton and Catherine K. Dillingham
March 19, 2001

THE NATURE OF
THE PROBLEM

The natural world seems to be deteriorating around us, and it seems to be our fault. We are uncertain about the extent of the deterioration, the means that would reverse it, and the prospects for human life in the future if those means are undertaken. We are not sure that we have the political will to pay what those means would cost, and we have more than a suspicion that the costs may be unthinkably high.

These have been bad times for environmental consciousness and conscience. When the first edition of *Watersheds* came out in 1992, we had just elected a Vice President for the United States who had written a book (that in itself worthy of note), and at that an excellent book, on the relation between civilization and the natural environment, strongly urging protection of our remaining natural resources and wiser policies on energy use and consumption.[1] Most recently (depending on how one reads the presidential election results in Florida) we apparently have elected a President whose first environmental act was to urge the opening of the Arctic National Wildlife Refuge for oil exploration. The environmental movement itself has been fragmented by self-indulgent "anarchist" actions staged by less responsible partisans, campaigns of dubious validity and scientific worth on the part of its most dedicated leadership, and frankly deceptive campaigns (with names like "Wildlife Studies Association" and "GreenWorld") funded by mining and utility companies. What seemed to be a determined and intelligent national movement stretching from the first Earth Day to the 1990s now seems lost. The very passion that newly converted environmentalists—or just alarmed citizens—bring to the discussion of environmental policy can work against effective action, by antagonizing the quieter sort of citizen and by encouraging cynicism if the worst predictions do not immediately come true. Attempts to produce good scientific proofs on the state of the environment for public conception run into the perpetual dilemma of popular science: when the projections are accurate and responsible, they tend to be misunderstood and distorted by press and politics; when they are simplified for popular consumption, they tend not to be strictly true, and often cause alarm. That alarm itself is new: it is a type of formless apprehension that may define the century to come. We are frightened, and we do not know how frightened we should be; this is not the best condition in which to formulate policy.

So the first assignment for any work on the environment is to clarify questions, sort out fact from judgment and opinion, analyze terrors into workable tasks, and focus emotion through the lens of logic into practical policy. That happens to be, since Socrates, the traditional assignment of the discipline of Philosophy. The question that lies before the people of the world, especially of the more developed parts, concerns the search for moral imperatives: what is to be done? What are our duties in this new and confusing age—to ourselves, our children, other nations, to all living things, to the planet? What policies should we adopt to promote the greatest happiness of the greatest number of human beings in the long run? Must that happiness be balanced against the welfare of the biosphere? May we put the happiness of our own countrymen in some privileged place in the calculation? What type of human being will we have to be to carry these new imperatives into practice? While we work to change the relationship between our very recently evolved civilization and a natural world that has been evolving over eons, how will we have to change our accounts of human virtue, aspiration, and self-realization?

These are the classic questions of ethics. The crises of the environment, the headline catastrophes, have posed new ethical questions, and those questions have spawned a new literature, indeed a whole new academic discipline. For although the first effect of environmental catastrophe, accomplished or impending, is to throw all policy and prudence into question, the second is to throw all philosophy into question. Let us take those questions one at a time.

First, disaster demands reevaluation of all policies effective at the time. Decisions that seemed prudent and cost-effective at the time they were made—decisions to build a school over an old dump (as happened at Love Canal), to prune excess manpower from a little-used oil-spill response team (that Alaska was supposed to maintain to clean up oil spills in Prince William Sound), to defer maintenance on some backup safety systems at the chemical factory (as happened in Bhopal)—suddenly seem terribly unwise, indeed criminally negligent. Our response is, appropriately, to develop more stringent and far–reaching policies, to introduce new probability calculations into business prudence, and, in effect, to transfer some of the costs of cleaning up a disaster to the safety preparations before it happens, hoping to avoid the balance of the costs entirely. The debate (if so polite a word is appropriate to describe the aftermath of an environmental catastrophe) is centrally ethical, a debate on the appropriate balance between individual rights and the common good, between short-term and long-term benefit, and among the interests of all parties to the activity. We have a field, Applied Ethics, that encompasses all such ethical inquiries in practical issues; a new field, Environmental Ethics, includes these inquiries as they extend to take into account the interests of the biosphere itself.

Second, that last modification raises conceptual problems that go beyond policy and prudence. The next effect of environmental catastrophe is philosophical inquiry—especially when the event is generalized to the ongoing catastrophe of the last days of the 20th century: an end to all frontiers, the threat to the last wilderness, the incredible rate of consumption of nonrenewable resources, the depletion of the ozone layer, and the extinction of species. While we always knew that we would make mistakes, and that accidents would happen, and that humans through carelessness or venality might cause isolated disasters, only recently has it occurred to us that our entire approach to the natural world could be a disaster in itself and a crime—not just imprudent but conceptually and morally wrong, like slavery. Maybe humans should not be treating Nature as a mere thing, to be exploited without limit. Maybe Nature is part of our community, like us, requiring respect and nurturance rather than mindless "use." It is beginning to dawn on us that resources are not unlimited; it is possible that they are not even "resources," in the sense of material available for use, for "taking." Maybe we will have to learn to live as a part of all life, subordinate to the natural workings of the natural world that sustains us, if we are to continue to live at all.

This philosophical doubt on the environmental front has occasioned some genuinely original inquiry. One of the most interesting moves in philosophy since the dawn of this newer, more acute, environmental consciousness, has been "ecofeminism," a fusion of environmentalism with feminism, which distinguishes approaches based on *life taking* (the exploitation of "resources") from those based on *life giving* (partnering with Nature), arguing for the superiority of the latter. Another interesting move identifies all living matter as part of the biosphere (occasionally personalized as "Gaia"), a nurturant, life-giving, superorganism, in which and as part of which we live, and only in which can we flourish as fully realized persons. Whatever destroys this organism destroys humanity; as long as we continue to imagine Nature as a "thing" to be commandeered to our purposes, and conceive of living organisms other than ourselves as "objects," the destruction will continue. The human imperative for survival therefore demands a total revision not only of our uses of nature, but of our imaging and conceptualizing of the natural world. This organic approach is one of several that presently form the "deep ecology" movement.

The field of philosophy has expanded, very recently, to include careful treatments of the new philosophical approaches to the natural environment. For this reason alone, these developments in philosophy, fascinating as they are, will receive very little attention in this book. Beyond the superfluity of one more theoretical analysis, it turns out to matter very little—when the cod disappear from Georges Banks and the cloud of poison rolls over Bhopal—whether we approach the problems from the perspective of ecofeminism or deep ecology, or, for that matter, from Kantian or Utilitarian perspectives. Sound policy—policy that brings the costs of predictable malfunctions forward, into the setting up of the economic arrangements in the first place—is what is needed, and rigorous enforcement of that policy. It should be noted, that in the course of developing that policy, we will have to go deeper than the immediate surface "causes" of the incident that has focused our attention, to examine the political and economic practices that made it eventually inevitable. These inquiries can be penetrating, even radical; for example, to develop a policy that will be effective in preventing the depletion of fisheries, we will have to reexamine our entire pattern of assault on natural resources, and the underlying attitude of disrespect that eventuates in the terrible waste of life in the natural world. Similarly, to develop a policy that will prevent the destruction of the ancient groves in the Pacific Northwest, we may have to bring into question the whole institution of private property in land.

Nothing should prevent the student, or instructor, from going beyond the concerns of public ethics raised by these cases to fundamental considerations of the moral and metaphysical status of Nature and its relation to the humans that, temporarily, inhabit it. While attempts to deal directly with the distortions of our national and international life caused by short-sighted energy policies will not be helped by bouncing the problem back to the conceptual level—indeed, they may be significantly hindered by such redirection—ultimately, we will have to engage in just such reconceptualization. As then Senator (later Vice President, now Professor) Al Gore put it in *Earth in the Balance*:

> The strategic nature of the threat now posed *by* human civilization to the global environment and the strategic nature of the threat *to* human civilization now posed by changes in the global environment present us with . . . challenges and false hopes. Some argue that a new ultimate technology, whether nuclear power or genetic

engineering, will solve the problem. Others hold that only a drastic reduction of our reliance on technology can improve the conditions of life—a simplistic notion at best. But the real solution will be found in reinventing and finally healing the relationship between civilization and the earth.

THE REASON AND PLAN FOR THIS BOOK

Al Gore's formulation raises the most serious aspect of the environmental crisis. We may be very good at developing new technologies, or at least new wrinkles on existing technologies, but there lies the problem: we have never thought of the earth as anything but the raw materials for our technologies, and we are total flops at reinventing and healing relationships, whether in our families, our communities, our nation, or the peoples of the world. Adding the planet Earth to our list of failed relationships only takes us further out of our depth. The question is not, yet, how to "solve" the problem of the environment, but how to get a handle on it, how to think about it, how to begin to comprehend its complexity.

That's where this book comes in. Faced with global dilemmas of indescribable complexity, demanding not new gadgets to solve immediate problems but new ways of relationship to the globe itself, we look for microcosms in which the dilemmas may be faithfully reproduced, but limited as to time and place, therefore becoming easier to grasp. Each one of these cases is a "defining moment," in Al Gore's formulation, that "focuses media coverage and political attention, not only on the environment itself, but also on the larger problems for which it is a metaphor. . ." When we debate environmental problems on the global level, we find we cannot agree on anything—not on the facts, nor the prospects for the future, nor on the ethical and political principles that should govern any solution. But on concrete cases, like the radioactive tanks at Hanford, the death of the fisheries, or the gas explosion at Bhopal, we can reach certain, very basic agreements—at least, that whatever happened is bad, and should not happen in the future—and we can use that agreement as the foundation for further explorations of the issues. If nothing else, a knowledge of the headline cases—the lunch table conversation cases, the cases that are broadly known—can supply a common coinage for an ongoing discussion.

The book aims to be useful to a variety of purposes, academic and otherwise. It is primarily designed as a supplement to all college and graduate level courses in Environmental Ethics, Business Ethics, Ecology, Environmental Law, Social and Legal Environment of Business, Energy and the Environment, and Environmental Economics. Five or six academic departments are represented right there; perhaps the cases will prove sufficiently interesting to extend that range. These stories are not, after all, the private property of any academic elite or theoretical approach. They are, for better or worse, the property of all of us, as unwitting and unwilling indirect agents of their occurrence; and as heirs, with our children, of their consequences. We had best get to know them well.

NOTES ON THE TEXT

We have tried to keep all chapters to a length convenient for reading and discussing in the course of a single class assignment, prefaced by some questions to focus the student's attention as the chapter is read, and concluded with some questions for reflection, which will encourage synthesis of the material, with more general insights on ethics and the environment, and a short list of books and articles for further reading. A more complete list of reading suggestions will be found after the Epilogue.

Note

1. Al Gore, *Earth in the Balance: Ecology and the Human Spirit* (Boston: Houghton Mifflin, 1992).

CHAPTER I

Frankenfood Meets the Greens

The Controversy over Genetically Altered Crops

QUESTIONS TO KEEP IN MIND

How are Genetically Modified Organisms (GMOs) different from ordinary hybridized farm plants?

What did Monsanto hope that its genetically modified crops would do?

What objections does Greenpeace have to genetically modified crops?

THE NEW SCIENTIFIC HORIZON

It all began quietly. That crops could be engineered to resist weed killers—saving farmers, in the case of genetically engineered tomatoes, potentially $30 per acre each season by reducing the need for hand or mechanical tilling—was announced in March, 1986, in a two-page article in *Science,* authored by Marjorie Sun. The Department of Agriculture was expected to announce very soon its approval of the first outdoor tests of the engineered plants. The article discussed the potential of such a development, especially the business opportunities that awaited the chemical companies who engineered seeds resistant to their own herbicides. There was some discussion of the risk of vertical monopolies as chemical companies acquired seed companies to create the fit they were looking for; there was some talk of the possible environmental problems if farmers became less careful with herbicides; there was a concern over regulation by the EPA.

None of the concerns seemed to be serious.[1] As for the concern that people might not want to eat foods known to be genetically modified—that did not come up. No one suspected that at the time.

The need for improvement in the world's agriculture was well known. Up to 40% of the world's crops are destroyed as they grow or before they leave the field. Right now it takes one hectare (2.5 acres) to feed four people, according to Maria Zimmerman, who is in charge of agricultural research for the sustainable development department of the United Nations Food and Agricultural Organization. Because of a projected increase in demand, stemming from a higher population living at a higher standard of living, that hectare will have to support six people in about twenty years. Working harder will not get the job done; technology has to help. We have the technology. "Scientists can now tell with precision which of 50,000 genes in a plant governs a particular trait. If it is beneficial, they can take that gene out of one species—something that wards off a common insect, for instance—copy it and stick it into another organism, to protect it. That organism, and its offspring, will then have a genetic structure that lets them resist such pests."[2]

By the end of that year, MIT's prestigious *Technology Review* had reported the development of new (at the time) and safer herbicides, especially Monsanto Company's glyphosate, with other contributions from DuPont and Cyanamid. But these are broad-spectrum herbicides, lethal to all plants, which had spurred research to engineer crop plants that will not suffer from the herbicide. The article notes a huge potential payoff should such plants be developed.[3] A year and a half later, Jane Brody reported new developments in hormone production: designer livestock, cows created by altering hormones produced by genetic engineering, have more beef and less fat.[4] The most impressive advance to date was announced a year after that—plants that contained their own insecticide. Understandable enthusiasm greeted the plants with *Bacillus thuringiensis* (Bt), a natural insect-killer, engineered into them. There were muted worries that there might be health and safety problems, both for humans and the environment, if more exotic forms of molecule were to be used and got loose; the danger that bugs might get immune to Bt surfaced even then.[5] Environmentalists fought the use of bioengineered Bt, in part on behalf of the organic farmers, who would use nothing else and were worried about acquired resistance. When it came to cotton, however, they had to concede that biotech was better than the alternative. *Forbes*, a business booster, treated the cotton issue as a success story. In a 1990 article (entitled, of course, "The Lesser of Two Weevils"), *Forbes* reported that cotton farmers in the United States had put 100 million pounds of agricultural chemicals on their crop each year for the last several years, most of it insecticide. Monsanto's cotton, with Bt engineered into it, resists bugs without all the spraying, saving the environment. The article noted signs that cotton pests were beginning to show resistance to the sprayed stuff; this fate may well await Bt.[6] But for the time being, agribusiness in the form of Monsanto, the cotton farmers, and the environment all profited from the new developments. Before entering controversial grounds, it should be noted that the progress continued from that point, and was widely accepted. "A decade ago," Michael Specter reported in April 2000, "no transgenic crops were commercially available anywhere on earth; in 1995, four million acres had been planted; by 1999, that number had grown to a hundred million. In the United States, half of the enormous soybean crop and more than a third of the corn are the products of biotechnology."[7]

UNEXPECTED CONTROVERSY

Tomatoes may have led the way to the present impasse. In 1993, John Seabrook, writing in the *New Yorker,* introduced the Flavr Savr, a tomato developed by Calgene. Almost everyone was enthusiastic about the long-lived tomato, especially Wall Street. Jeremy Rifkin, president of the Foundation on Economic Trends and an antitechnology activist of long standing, well-known in technological circles for unflagging opposition to biological research and change, was not. He was already organizing a boycott against it. Seabrook went on to mention that the Mycogen Corporation was even then developing a corn with Bt in it, and that that would be helpful in cutting the use of pesticides (which amounted to 25 million pounds of chemicals per year on corn alone in the United States). That development also was opposed by Jeremy Rifkin and by Environmental Defense (formerly The Environmental Defense Fund), citing the possibility of cultivating insect resistance to Bt. Rhone-Poulenc, meanwhile, wanted to make money selling its bromoxynil herbicide, so it was helping Calgene develop a bromoxynil-resistant cotton plant. That meant, in the activists' understanding, more herbicide use. (The growers disagreed, pointing out that if they didn't have to worry about the crop dying from the herbicide, they could use it once, thoroughly, and be done with it. The activists, most notably Rebecca Goldburg of the Environmental Defense Fund, pointed out that when the local weeds acquired the herbicide resistance, you'd have to use all kinds of *other* herbicides to get rid of them.)[8] Meanwhile, in the Flavr Savr, there is an antibiotic to cut down on bacterial attack. Just as regular exposure to an insecticide will lead to insecticide-resistant insects, regular exposure to an antibiotic will lead to antibiotic resistance among the microbes, and that development can be very costly in terms of human health. Jeremy Rifkin saw the whole development as a move to help the drug and chemical manufacturers cash in on the food business. "What we're seeing here is the conversion of DNA into a commodity, and it is in some ways the ideal corporate commodity—it's small, it's ownable, it's easily transportable,

and it lasts forever. . . . Genetic engineering is the final enclosure movement. It is the culmination of the enclosure of the village commons that
began five hundred years ago. As we have developed as a society and we
have moved from an agricultural to a pyrochemical to a biotechnical culture, we have seen that whoever controls the land or the fossil fuels or,
now, the DNA, controls society."[9]

By the middle of 1998, the battle was joined. Michael Specter wrote
an extensive and thoughtful article on the European rejection of
"Genetically Modified Organisms" (GMOs) in the summer of that year.
Beginning with a quote from a traditional farmer in Germany, denounc-
ing the U.S. attempts to "change the basic rules of life" by genetic engineering, he drew out the opposition's credo: "Here we are going to live
like God intended." Why is Europe so conservative about its food, he
wondered, and came up with three logically independent answers. First,
Europe has many small farmers, who are threatened by the new agribusiness crops; these farmers are too small to buy into the revolution, and
will be driven out of business if it is successful. Second, Europe has a
strong environmental movement, including involvement of the "Green
Party" in most European nations, especially Germany. This movement is
committed to the preservation of the natural species, and therefore
opposed to the introduction of new ones, especially species that, spreading through the wild, might threaten natural species; since they had their
birth opposing chemical pollution, they are reflexively antibusiness. The
third and most telling reason is "recent history": "The shadow of the
Holocaust is dense and incredibly powerful still," said Arthur Caplan,
the American ethicist now at the University of Pennsylvania. "It leaves
Europe terrified about the abuse of genetics. To them the potential to
abuse genetics is no theory. It is a historical fact."[10]

How big a deal is it really, Specter asked, to genetically engineer a
tomato, corn, or potato plant? Joseph Zak, under contract to the
American Soybean Association to calm Europeans, minimized the
change, putting it in the line of all advances in agriculture, for instance,
"when we moved to breeding to make a better product." Another
observer said that Europeans see it as "tampering with their food." And
the perception of manipulation "drives people crazy."[11]

In the fall of 1998, *The Ecologist* devoted an entire issue to the controversy. Entitled *The Monsanto Files: Can We Survive Genetic
Engineering?*, and featuring on its cover the skeleton of a horse half-
buried in the endless sand of a lifeless desert, it was a scathing attack on
business in general, and Monsanto in particular. "This is the company
that brought us Agent Orange, PCBs and Bovine Growth Hormone; the
same company that produces Roundup, the world's biggest selling herbicide, and the highly questionable 'Terminator Technology.' . . . Can we
allow corporations like Monsanto to gamble with the very future of life
on Earth?" The issue continues with allegations of threats to health from

every GMO on the market, hormone-produced milk, the herbicide Roundup, and all the dioxins and PCBs that Monsanto has sown into the environment from its varied operations. There are several direct attacks on Robert Shapiro, the CEO of Monsanto.[12]

Why this reaction? The connections between the provocation and the reaction don't always seem to match. Whatever it may be to insert Bt into the DNA of a corn plant, it surely is not to undertake the extermination of all the Jews and Gypsies of Europe. How does the Holocaust come to mind? Is "the very future of life on Earth" really at stake?

Also on the list of relevant objections to bioengineering is "Mad Cow disease," referring to an episode of bovine spongiform encephalopathy (BSE) in the U.K. some years ago. (The lastest European outbreaks of the disease were not foreseen when *The Ecologist* went to press.) BSE is a disease, not a product of genetic engineering (or genetic at all). What, then, does BSE have to do with it? First, that profit-oriented innovations had led farmers to include the offal of slaughtered animals in feed for their (normally herbivore) herds of beef cattle, and that is how (we think) the cows became infected in the first place; second, that even when infected cattle staggered and fell before the television cameras of three continents, scientists plausibly argued that such disease could not possibly affect humans, so British beef was quite safe; third, that after all the scientists promised it wouldn't happen, some people who ate that beef became very sick. What does this prove? It proves that reassuring scientists are not always right, and may not always be honest. BSE has no other role in this controversy, but it is a very strong supporting role: the BSE controversy served to undermine the authority of regulatory authority and scientific pronouncements, and that undermining turned out to be very important in the outcome of the GMO debate.[13] We'll see those cows again.

"We have eaten the apple and now we will have to live with the knowledge it gives us," said Gian Reto Plattner, a professor of physics at the University of Basel. ". . . If you look at this as a question of risks it's pretty clear that these crops are safe," Professor Plattner said. "Explosions and fire are far more dangerous, and we use them every day. But nobody is looking at the use of genetics that way. This is a religious discussion we are having. Many people feel nature is immutable. This work tells them they are wrong, and then they are being told to forget about their basic beliefs. It's really asking a lot."[14]

Of course the objections were answered. No less a personage than former President Jimmy Carter argued the safety and acceptability of genetically modified organisms, "everything from seeds to livestock." Protesting the regulations proposed for adoption by signatories to the Biodiversity Treaty forged at the 1992 Earth Summit at Rio de Janeiro, Carter argued that the requirement that recipient nations approve, item by item, the importation of any GMOs, would leave food and vaccines rotting on docks all over the world. A farmer himself, Carter points out that "for hundreds of years virtually all food has been improved genetically by plant breeders," by the simple techniques of selective breeding. There is no evidence of any harm from any genetically engineered products, some evidence of much benefit, and if the technology is halted at this point, the real losers will be the developing nations and the poor of the world.[15] But where science and regulators had not been totally effective, Jimmy Carter's influence added little; the controversy continued. In October 1998, Michael Pollan wrote an extensive account of a potato (New Leaf Superior), from development to planting in his own garden; the controversy that enveloped it, including a gripping account of his own uneasiness with this unregulated, unexplained organism, foreshadows all later problems with this technology.[16]

THE TERMINATORS AND THE LORDLY MONARCHS

In the middle of 1999, the volume of the war increased noticeably. Popular literature was beginning to notice the controversy, and the consumer movement checked in on the side of the environmental activists.[17] Meanwhile, a new controversy erupted. Monsanto had engineered a new kind of gene, instantly dubbed the "terminator gene," one that would make sure that its bioengineered plants had no progeny. Why do this? An unsigned editorial in *The Economist* explained: "Terminator is a set of genes that act as a series of molecular switches. These switches are set off by a chemical signal sprayed on genetically tinkered seed. Although the plant springing forth from that seed is healthy and can go about its business of producing grain, say, quite normally, the grain that it produced will not grow if planted, because the activated terminator gene has killed off the seed's reproductive bits. This means that farmers who want to grow a plant with the same genetically engineered traits next season have to go back to the company for more seeds."[18] A new uproar greeted the news. First, how mean of Monsanto to deprive poor farmers of the developing world the possibility of saving their seeds! More ominously, would these genes spread, by pollen, to the fields of neighboring farms? If they did, would they inject themselves into the seeds of traditional crops, making it impossible for farmers planting them to save their seeds from year to year? How would these farmers know that their seeds were contaminated until a new crop planted simply failed to germinate, and their family starved? What new death spores was science (for profit) loosing on the world?[19]

The publicity was immense. Still in development, and long in advance of being used anywhere, terminator genes were already being blamed for crop failures all over the world. The Rockefeller Foundation, which sponsors agricultural projects across the world, strongly objected to their use. Monsanto CEO Robert Shapiro, by now used to progress blowing up in his face, formally promised not to commercialize the genetic engineering of seed sterility. "Given its parlous public image, Monsanto must be hoping that its move will buy it a little goodwill. The terminator technology has raised such interest in the industry, and caused such an outcry in society, because it is a neat and potentially powerful way for biotechnology firms such as Monsanto to protect the intellectual property locked in genetically modified seeds . . ."[20] As Laura Tangley pointed out, "More than 1.4 billion people, most of them in poor, developing countries, rely on farm-saved seed as their primary seed source and are unable to afford repeated annual expenditures for new seeds." As a result, terminator seeds could be a real "threat to world food security," according to Hope Shand of the Rural Advancement Foundation International, a farmer's advocacy organization. Monsanto, Tangley points out, is not the only company working on them. "The battle highlights the difficulty of protecting intellectual property when the products are sophisticated genetic technologies. Monsanto and other firms have said the terminator is a legitimate way to recoup the billions of dollars they have poured into developing bioengineered crops with traits such as insect resistance."[21]

That's a good point. How *do* we protect real intellectual property? The controversy also underscores the difference between developed-world and undeveloped-world patterns of agriculture. Yearly buying of new seeds is the way farmers do business in the United States now. The hybrid seeds that farmers use to produce the wonder crops to which we have become accustomed do not breed true—do not produce the uniform crop we expect—so we have to buy new each year. But in poorer countries, they often recycle whatever seeds they have, hybrid or not. They have no choice.

In high-technology agriculture, in developed countries, terminator genes could have their uses. In experimental fields, where we are trying to introduce new hybrids, the use of a terminator could save the time and effort of "tasseling," removing the male pollen before the plant can self-fertilize. If we can get the formula specific enough, we can shut down genes (like the engineered gene to produce the pesticide Bt) when we don't need it, and turn it on when we do. The uses are tantalizing. But in the present world uproar, they are not open for discussion.[22]

The controversy rapidly elaborated. It did not stay in Europe: in the middle of 1999, Brazil suddenly discovered reasons to dawdle over the approvals needed for growers to plant genetically modified ("Roundup Ready") soybeans, and to build a Roundup herbicide factory. Why? European resistance was cited, that sort of fear being highly contagious. Brazil wanted to make sure that their farmers could sell their crops. Monsanto, which had just invested $550 million in Brazil, was less than happy; why not let growers make the decision?[23] In an article tellingly entitled "Tampering with the Natural Order," Mark Nichols told the story of a farmer who grows canola (rape) on his farm near Bruno, Saskatchewan, who never to the best of his knowledge bought seed from Monsanto, who now finds Roundup Ready (herbicide resistant) canola on his farm, and Monsanto suing him for the royalties. How did it get there? How much control over farmer's crops should Monsanto have? At this time there is little controversy in Canada or the United States about GM foods, but will Canada follow the example of the United Kingdom? Nichols suggests that the approval process for these crops (Monsanto and others voluntarily submit safety test results) is probably compromised, since Canada has poured $300 million into biotech research and development.[24]

What's the farmer to do? An editorial in *Farmers Guardian* in April 1999 groused that "in the middle of claims and counter-claims, speeches, demonstrations, and a High Court decision that environmental protestors could not be banned from interfering in GM crops, farmers were 'piggies-in-the-middle' in all of this," unable to plant competitive crops or rely on the government to protect their income if they didn't. This is essentially a PR battle, the *Farmers Guardian* commented, and if it were a soccer match, "the score so far is about 7–0 to the environmentalists and we haven't even got through the first quarter."[25]

In May of 1999, the soccer match turned even more decisively against Monsanto, as engineered corn was discovered (so it was claimed) to be dangerous to Monarch butterflies.[26] Suddenly, wrote John Carey, covering science from Washington for *Business Week,* "foes of bioengineering in the food supply have their own potent symbol: the beloved monarch butterfly. In mid-May, Cornell University researchers reported that pollen from corn altered to slay corn-borer pests can land on neighboring milkweed plants, where it can kill monarch butterfly caterpillars. The finding has biotech foes exulting. 'The monarch butterfly experiment is the smoking gun that will be the beginning of the unraveling of the industry,' says Jeremy Rifkin . . . The findings cast genetically altered food plants in a new light. They may benefit farmers and consumers, but now opponents have evidence that there could be worrisome ecological effects on other species." Both Greenpeace and the Union of Concerned Scientists are now asking the EPA to pull the seeds off the market.[27]

Monsanto and Novartis, Carey wrote, became worried that this sort of problem could cause the European fear of gene-altered food to cross the Atlantic. Right now the European Commission will not approve pest-resistant corn or other GM products. "The industry is in big trouble," according to agriculture consultant Charles Benbrook. "It misplayed its hand by overstating its command of the science and its knowledge of the consequences."[28] If biotech companies had considered unintended side effects years ago, they would not, he argued, be on the defensive now. "The industry 'asked for trouble, and they got it,' says monarch expert

Lincoln Brower of Sweet Briar College."[29] The judgment seems harsh; who could have suspected damage to monarchs? But that is just the point, of course.

"If the current British furor over genetically modified foods were a crop not a crisis," chortled *The Economist* in June 1999:

> . . . you can bet Monsanto or its competitors would have patented it. It has many of the traits that genetic engineers prize: it is incredibly fertile, thrives in inhospitable conditions, has tremendous consumer appeal and is easy to cross with other interests to create a hardy new hybrid. Moreover, it seems to resist anything that might kill it, from scientific evidence to official reassurance. Now it seems to be spreading to other parts of Europe, Australia and even America. There, regulators will face the same questions that confront the British government: how should the public be reassured, and how can the benefits of GM foods be reaped without harm, either to human beings or to the environment?

At least, U.K.-based *The Economist* consoled us, the United States doesn't have to deal with the Prince of Wales, who had taken a very public position against GMOs. The editorial went on to point out that this unforeseen consumer backlash "threatens to undermine both this new technology and the credibility of the agencies that regulate it." That, recall, was the major effect of the fallout from Mad Cow disease (those cows again).[30] By repeated infections of scandal, and general suspicion (fanned by nongovernmental organizations) that government is in league with the biotech industry, food fears seem to have developed a resistance to official reassurance, much as insect species develop resistance to pesticides.

Through the summer and fall of 1999, the media continued its barrage, tracking the continuing battles in Europe,[31] tracking the damage to U.S. farmers from the boycott,[32] studying the potential for GMOs to spread to the wild,[33] questioning the ability of bioengineered crops to feed the world as claimed,[34] chronicling the new kinds of crops and livestock being brought onto the GM line (including leaner pigs and extra-meaty hogs, and "Enviropig," a porker with replicated mouse genes that produces manure with less phosphorus),[35] and, most ominously, tracking the growing trend in the United States to demand proof that GM food is really safe.[36] By October, Monsanto found itself contending with claims that its central weed killer, Roundup (glyphosate), caused cancer. Apparently, a "confidential" EC report had concluded that it had "harmful effects" on mites and arthropods that consume harmful insects. Humans exposed to glyphosate, according the Channel 4 news report that broadcast the report, are three times as likely to get non-Hodgkin's lymphoma. The report was a low blow to Monsanto: general acceptance of Roundup is essential if the Roundup Ready crops are to be marketed.

Monsanto spokesmen dismissed the scientific basis of the studies, pointing out that they were conducted in 1995, were badly designed then, and had never been taken seriously.[37]

FIGHTING A NETWAR: THE LEGACY OF MAD COWS

Monsanto was doing something wrong, and nothing in the management manuals could tell them just what. They seemed to have science on their side, government regulatory agencies had been supportive, and they thought they could really improve the nutritional status of the world (while making money for their shareholders). Where did all this hostility come from? The major factor, as anyone could see by the fall of 1999, was that in none of their calculations had they anticipated the reaction to GMOs from the large privately funded, nongovernmental organizations (NGOs) like Greenpeace and Environmental Defense. After all, to whom is a business, a for-profit publicly held corporation, accountable? Two accounts dominate the literature.[38] One holds that the corporation is accountable only to its owners, the shareholders. This view is generally propounded by the Wall Street–oriented business commentary, and upheld by a significant stream of our legal tradition. The other, associated with the liberal reform movement that infused the corporate world in the 1970s and into the 1980s, holds that good management must weigh the claims of all the "stakeholders," all who will be affected by the decisions of the corporation.[39] Both views are logically consistent, and both are widely espoused. The latter is generally accorded, among business ethics academicians, some moral superiority to the former. But neither one of them include, in theory or in practice, the NGOs as parties who will demand an accounting, and so the NGOs, from case to case, continue to take corporations completely by surprise. Monsanto, Novartis, and the other players in the biotech farming industry were no exception. Eventually, the companies—especially Monsanto, the main target—realized that they had to talk to the NGOs directly.

Barry Came, of *Maclean's*, documents the resulting historic conversation between Robert Shapiro, CEO of Monsanto, and Peter Melchett, executive director of Greenpeace U.K., by transatlantic satellite. Melchett, in his glory, accused Shapiro of every form of insensitivity and monopolistic practice, and finally of "bullying" to force GM foods on Europe. Shapiro answered dourly that if he was a bully, he sure wasn't very successful at it. This was, according to Came, the "first high-profile acknowledgement that the world's biotech industry, based largely in the United States, is losing the global battle to convince the public of the benefits of genetic engineering." All their efforts had antagonized Europeans more than they persuaded. Shapiro identified his own sin: he forgot to listen. It was his fault, and the result was the public rejection of GM products. Canada, Came noted, may be next on the list of the boycott. Already items were being taken off the shelves for suspected GM content. Shapiro had already been forced to agree not to market the Terminator seeds. Investors were unhappy and the boycott was spreading:

> Increasingly, genetically "improved" crops are trading at deep discounts, while European processors have been willing to pay premiums of as much as $1.50 a bushel for non-GM crops. In September, the huge U.S. grain processing corporation, Archer Daniels Midland (ADM), advised American grain farmers to begin segregating GM and non-GM crops. At the same time, the two main U.S. baby food manufacturers, Gerber Products Co. and H. J. Heinz Co., declared they would no longer use genetically modified corn or soybeans in any of their products.

More problems were foreseen for canola farmers, who do not segregate their crop.[40]

"The problem is as much about public perceptions as it is about science," comments Came, echoing a theme that underlies the entire conflict:

> In Europe, the anti-GM battle has been waged against the backdrop of a series of European food scares that began with BSE, or "mad cow" disease, in Britain [there are the cows again], and has escalated with scandals over carcinogenic dioxins in Belgian poultry and dairy products, and the use in France and elsewhere of sewage slurry in animal feeds. The aggressive stance of U.S. based agribusiness giants has not helped. The U.S. government, responding to pressure from the powerful agribusiness lobby in Washington, has taken the Europeans to court at the World Trade Organization, winning successive decisions against Europe's restrictions on Caribbean bananas and growth hormone additives in beef. The Americans have threatened similar challenges to European resistance to the free import of genetically engineered grains . . . The combined effect has been to shatter Europeans' confidence in what they are eating and drinking as well as fostering deep resentment about the unrestrained power of U.S. multinational corporations. "There has been an unprecedented, permanent and irreversible shift in the political landscape," Greenpeace's Lord Melchett told Shapiro last week. "People are increasingly aware and mistrustful of the combination of big science and big business." . . .

Where will this go next? Newly elected president of the European Commission, Italy's Romano Prodi, singled out food safety as the top priority of his infant administration. He proposed a pan-European food agency to deal with issues such as those involving British beef, Belgian chickens, and U.S. genetic modifications. "We have to provide answers," he said, "to those who are wondering if official information can be trusted these days, or is it all being manipulated for economic and political purposes?"[41]

What do you do with a public relations disaster? Came pointed out that the problem was one of public perception, so Monsanto hired a "perception management" (public relations) firm to take care of the problem. Burson-Marsteller has been retained to pitch genetically modified foods as safe for people and nature. It is, indeed, a novel attempt to reach out to the critics. Shapiro recently "admitted that Monsanto's former hard-ball tactics with critics has backfired against the company, which has been called 'Monsatan' and 'Mutanto' by its biotech opponents. He now wants to establish a dialog . . ." In the name of dialogue, Shapiro has agreed to meet (privately) with Jeremy Rifkin at the Greenpeace London office. Ralph Nader will arrange the meeting. Meanwhile, no one at B-M will talk to reporters. B-M's job is to counter hysteria; now B-M is getting some hysterical picketing of its own, accused of "deception management," and aiding and abetting polluters.[42] There is a pattern here. All attempts to solve the problem, initiated by the target of the problem, are liable to instant condemnation by the targeters as part of the problem. We will see it again.

Rick Mullin, writing in *Chemical Week* in the last month of 1999, drew one clear lesson from the fracas: ". . . successful corporations will begin taking consumers and the public as seriously as they take Wall Street and shareholders. It shows that while U.S. consumers understand that the role of business is to make profits and create jobs, they also believe the most important goal for companies will be to help build a better society."[43]

"Any lawyer will tell you," he went on, "and any scientist will dispute— that perception is reality. In this case, the lawyers are right. If a majority of the U.K.'s population feels genetically modified seeds pose a threat as severe as eventual global famine, that concern had best be reckoned with. There are good examples of how to handle this, and how not to. While Monsanto fell on its sword by dismissing concerns as typical public ignorance of scientific fact, DuPont chairman and CEO Chad Holliday publicly avowed his company's need to respect public opinion. Addressing the Chief Executive's Club of Boston in September, Holliday said, 'We have to listen to the people who are raising alarms. We don't have all the answers, and to pretend we do, or to brush off concerns as unfounded, is to be arrogant and reckless.'" It took a little longer, but Monsanto eventually came to the same insight:

> David Morley, senior VP of plant sciences at Monsanto, admitted in a speech to the Commercial Development and Marketing Association that, "Greenpeace effectively made [genetic modification]

a consumer issue. We made it a science and regulatory issue. We were behind the curve." . . . Against a widely perceived threat, Monsanto's calculated efforts to gain trust based on its mastery of science failed. In essence, Monsanto repeated the fatal public relations error made by the nuclear energy industry in the 1970s.[44]

Mullin is not alone in drawing that analogy. Paul Magnusson and his coauthors had made the same comparison to the nuclear industry in *Business Week* in October 1999. They go on to point out that the huge PR war is not without consequences on the land. To avoid the EC boycott, Archer Daniels Midland had demanded that all its suppliers segregate GM grain from "natural" grain. Consider the dilemma of farmer Dave Boettger: he has 280 acres, half in GM crops. ADM will pay eight cents a bushel more for the natural product. But if testing reveals even a tiny amount of altered genes in the higher priced shipment, he has to pay ADM to dump the whole load. Pollen blows over all his fields; he can make no guarantees that none of the GM pollen blew into a natural field. Now, how does he sell his crop?[45]

Those GM crops were sold to the farmers, after all, as an "agricultural revolution: The new corn, soybeans, potatoes, oilseeds, and cotton promised to fight pests, boost yields, and cut chemical use. . . . Now they find that the fierce backlash in Europe . . . is cutting off billions of dollars in export sales." Even as the battle goes on, with everyone swearing the GM foods are safe, all food processors are going back to buying conventional foods.[46] This retreat from the new crops hurts farmers, and incidentally undermines the battle against protectionism in world trade. We could, after all, retaliate for this irrational prejudice against our crops more than we have. We could demand "safety guarantees" for French wine and cheese, after all. What about the French practice of "using animal blood to draw solids from its red wines"? "Allowing public sensitivities to decide these highly technical issues is a very dangerous slope," said Clinton administration chief agricultural negotiator Peter L. Scher. The demand for "labeling," as far as Scher was concerned, was a nonstarter: it's like placing a skull-and-crossbones on each package, and invites exclusion.

The stakes are high. Overseas shipments of U.S. crops came to $46 billion in 1998, giving us a $5 billion trade surplus in farm products. Half of U.S. soybeans and one-third of U.S. corn are genetically modified. About 60% of processed food, and virtually all candy, syrup, salad dressing, and chocolate, have GM material in them. Monsanto had hoped to reap $881 million by 2003 in licensing fees for its high-tech seeds. It appears that they will fall far short of that target.[47]

This is not just a matter of anti-U.S. sentiment, although that contributes. Activists go after European companies too, like Switzerland's

Novartis. The companies, scientists, and governments agree that GM food is safe. The FDA has ruled that no special labels on GM food are needed since the new strains are not different from hybrids developed by cross-breeding. The World Health Organization (WHO) also has approved GM food. "But science is no match for public opinion in Europe, where debacles such as Britain's mad cow disease [those cows again] and other food-contamination problems have eroded confidence in government regulators. Now, the bio-food phobia is catching on in Japan. Brewers have sworn off GM corn, and the government is mandating labeling for 28 different products containing GM food. Japanese tofu makers, responding to public sentiment, are switching to non-GM soybeans, jeopardizing some 500,000 tons of imports, most of them from the U.S." U.S. companies, by now, approve of Romano Prodi's suggestion for an EU equivalent of the FDA, on grounds that it might restore government credibility.[48]

As the battle continued through winter and spring, a measured defense of biotechnology was heard. John Carey and others presented a solid examination of the whole topic in *Business Week* toward the end of 1999;[49] Margaret Kriz did the same in *The National Journal*.[50]

Both pieces pointed out that genetically engineered foods had indeed been tested, certainly much more than conventional foods were ever tested, and that time and again, the proof of the pudding had been in the safe eating. Paul Krugman, a columnist for the *New York Times*, poured contempt on the whole biotech protest, pointing out that GM foods have indeed been tested, had been shown to be safe and really useful, while the "dietary supplement" industry, which retails without prescription all kinds of megavitamins and the like, is entirely unregulated, unwatched, and potentially really dangerous.[51] But the trend was still strongly the other way. Carey Goldberg reported a huge protest march in Boston that raises serious questions about the level of information available to activists. The protest was timed to coincide with Bio2000, a meeting of biotechnology scientists and business promoters (7,000 participants were expected in Boston for five days). The businessmen and scientists did their best to contain the uproar: "In a pre-emptive salvo against the protesters, about 2,000 scientists from around the world, including two Nobel laureates, signed a 'Declaration in Support of Agricultural Biotechnology,' said AgBioWorld.com, an advocacy group that released the declaration on Thursday. It quoted the declaration's organizer, Dr. C. S. Prakash of Tuskegee University, as saying that 'biotech crops allow farmers to grow more food on less land with less synthetic pesticides and herbicides.'"[52]

But he was outnumbered. "Protesters argued today that the agricultural biotechnology industry, fueled by greed, was placing human health—possibly the health of the biosphere—at risk. 'These are the people who gave us thalidomide babies,' Sarah Seeds, a protester who also trains others to protest nonviolently, said of the participants in the Bio2000 convention. 'Now they want to give us genetically modified food.'"[53] Thalidomide? If 2,000 scientists are ineffective, can the "perception management" firm do any better? The spring of 2000 blossomed with truly lovely full-page full-color ads in the newspapers ("Biotechnology gives her a better way to protect her crop—and her grandchildren's planet"), and a wonderful, well-written brochure, "Good Ideas Are Growing," in bright color, sponsored by the industry association, the Council for Biotechnology Information. Will this campaign work? Ross S. Irvine, in a special article in *O'Dwyer's* PR Services Report, thinks the whole campaign is ridiculous. "The Council for Biotechnology Information is spending more than $50 million for an advertising campaign to convince consumers that biotech food is safe to eat and not a threat to the environment," in an effort, probably useless, to keep Frankenfood fear out of the United States. "They are basically throwing the money away because feel-good image ads just don't make it in the era of the Internet. Corporate PR people need to engage in a 'netwar' to succeed in today's fast-paced communications arena." There is nothing wrong with biotechnology, he points out; it holds out great hope for the world. But this isn't the way to defend it. "It's hard to believe that the corporate PR people who are supposed to be laying the foundation for public and regulatory acceptance of biotechnology stubbornly rely on communication strategies and tactics that were effective 20 years ago. Corporate PR pros who want to update their PR effectiveness should look at the strategies and tactics used by activist groups. The challenge is to adapt those strategies for the corporate world. . . . reliance on traditional communications tools such as brochures, toll-free phone lines, and advertising is out-of-date in cyberspace. It's worth noting that anti-biotech activists and other non-governmental organizations have gained the upper hand in the biotech debate without the use of paid advertising. They have mastered the power of the Internet to make their argument and forge alliances."[54]

How do they do that? "'Information is power' is the lesson learned by NGOs during the past fifteen years. They learned that if they provided their supporters with information, those supporters felt knowledgeable and empowered. With that sense of empowerment, supporters were comfortable taking a public stand on issues. The NGOs also learned that as supporters were given more information, they became increasingly autonomous and took the initiative to undertake their own PR campaigns. Through the use of the Internet—and its ability to distribute vast amounts of information quickly and inexpensively—local grassroots groups have enormous resources at their disposal. In any community, a small group of activists with an Internet connection could become an informed, effective, and powerful champion of a cause. . ."[55]

For example, there's the NGO that Monsanto should have known well: the Pesticide Action Network of North America (PANNA). Its mission is to replace pesticides with environmentally friendly, less dangerous means of pest control. By now it links "over 100 affiliated health, consumer, labor, environment, progressive agriculture and public interest groups in Canada, Mexico and the U.S. with thousands of supporters worldwide to promote healthier, more effective pest management through research, policy development, education, media, demonstrations of alternatives and international advocacy campaigns." (This is from the PANNA Web site, http://www.panna.org.)All those organizations in that coalition can reinforce each other re pesticides or re their home cause; with the level of communication they have, they can easily take on any new related cause, constructing links to the home interests of all their affiliates. Biotechnology does admirably as such a new cause.

As far as activism is concerned, the move to the net is a paradigm shift, which has already attracted the attention of the American military:

> In the early and mid-1990s, RAND, the American military think tank, started looking at the Internet and its impact on modern conflicts, including those involving social activists and NGOs. Biotech opponents are a recent example of the type of social activists RAND discusses. RAND notes: "The information revolution is leading to the rise of network forms of organization, whereby small, previously isolated groups can communicate, link up, and conduct coordinated joint actions as never before. This, in turn, is leading to a new mode of conflict—netwar—in which the protagonists depend on using network forms of organization, doctrine, strategy, and technology. Many actors across the spectrum of conflict from terrorists, guerillas, and criminals—who pose security threats—to social activists-who do not—are developing netwar designs and capabilities." From the concept of netwar, RAND coined the word "netwarrior," which can be either an individual or an NGO. At the heart of a netwar is the dense, free, and broad distribution of information to a variety of activists who have an interest in an issue. . . . [56]
>
> The heart of the NGOs' success is blindingly simple: "The keys are to share information freely and to let the situation evolve from there. This is a difficult lesson for corporate PR folks to accept. . . . Corporate PR is about control. It's about centralized crafting and distribution of information. It's about designating spokespeople. It's about ensuring that all parts of the corporate hierarchy, whether it be an individual company or a trade association, are 'singing from the same page.' It's about organizing a coordinated response to the guerrilla tactics of opponents, oblivious to the fact that those guerrilla tactics have been more effective and powerful than traditional corporate PR methods. The biotech industry's PR campaign reflects this traditional command-and-control approach to corporate

communications. In the age of netwars, these strategies and tactics are outdated, ineffective and wasteful."

The corporation's traditional functional hierarchy, it turns out, is its worst enemy:

> RAND has this to say about netwars which are now an established and recognized form of social conflict: "The information revolution favors and strengthens networks, while it erodes hierarchies. Hierarchies have a difficult time fighting networks. It takes networks to fight networks. Whoever masters the network form first will gain major advantages."

The messages to the controllers of the biotech industry's campaign are clear, Irvine concludes:

> Enter the 21st century. Learn from past and ongoing netwars in which you have been defeated in the battle for public understanding and acceptance. Give up your hierarchical, command-and-control approach to communications. Adapt to the realities of the Internet. Master the network form of organization. Become net-warriors![57]

The Council for Biotechnology Information ("Good Ideas Are Growing") now has a Web site, http://www.whybiotech.com, in addition to its full-page ads, booklets, and an 800 number (1-800-980-8660). Maybe it will do the industry some good. But it will be catch-up ball all the way.

PRODUCTIVE COWS AND FRANKENFISH: TWO MINIATURES OF THE CONTROVERSY

In the middle of the debate on GM foods generally, side consideration was given to two instructive miniatures. The issues are the same: the same doubts, reassurances, and ultimate activist boycotts attend milk whose production has been enhanced by hormones, and salmon genetically engineered to grow more quickly. The instructive detail is that both of these pertain to an area of agriculture where abundance, even surplus, gives the human race an unaccustomed luxury of picking and choosing.

An unsigned item in *The Economist* in July 1999 reported on a meeting of the Codex Alimentarius Commission, a joint body of the Food and Agriculture Organization (FAO) and the World Health Organization (WHO). "At issue is a genetically engineered version of bovine growth hormone called rbGH, known in Europe as rbST. According to its manufacturer, Monsanto, approximately 30% of American dairy cattle are injected with rbGH at some stage in their lives, raising their milk yields by roughly 10%. Although both America's Food and Drug Administration (FDA) and Codex's scientific advisory committee on food additives (JECFA) consider it safe, many national governments and consumer groups beg to differ." The same pattern—of reassurance by all appropriate scientific bodies, and of rejection of that reassurance by activist groups that no one could have anticipated—shows up here, with the same result. There has been a moratorium on hormone-enhanced milk products in Europe since 1990. Canada joined in this one, in January 1999. What's wrong with the hormone? Veterinaries cite side effects for the cows—lameness, fertility problems. And there is a 25% greater chance of developing mastitis. The mastitis worries public-health experts, not because it causes pain to the cow but because it is treated with antibiotics, which get into the milk and therefore into us, "leading to worries about allergic reactions and antibiotic resistance."[58]

The September issue of *Consumer Reports* underscored the warning. Not just corn and potatoes are genetically engineered, they pointed out. Milk "may come from cows injected with Monsanto's recombinant bovine growth hormone, Posilac, to boost milk production. Monsanto says that roughly 30% of the nation's cows are in herds that get this hormone, produced by genetically engineered bacteria. And 60% of all hard-cheese products today are made with Chymogen, a biotech version of an enzyme from calves' stomachs that helps separate curds from whey."[59]

This time the U.N. was not on Monsanto's side. In August of 1999 the United Nations Food Safety Agency endorsed the European Union's (EU) moratorium on Monsanto's genetically engineered bovine somatotropin (BST). The FDA had ruled in 1993 that BST is safe. But Europe and Canada disagree.[60] Prominent in this issue is the offhand remark in *The Economist,* that there was plenty of milk to go around (for those who could afford to buy it). What is the possibility that this whole food fight is a product of generous times in the developed world, where no real need for more food is felt and we can afford to be fastidious?

In the summer of 1998 Dr. Rebecca Goldburg of Environmental Defense raised the issue of "transgenic" fish. AquaBounty Farms, of Waltham, Massachusetts, was preparing to commercialize a kind of Atlantic salmon with an engineered growth hormone. Genetic engineering seemed a logical next step in the phenomenal growth of aquaculture; as the demand for fish worldwide increases, and the wild fisheries deteriorate under the pressure of overfishing, we will have to depend on the fish farms to get the fish to the table. And AquaBounty "claims that its transgenic Atlantic salmon can grow as much as 400 to 600% faster than the nontransgenic ones."[61]

That's the good news. The bad news, Goldburg insists, comes when the transgenic fish escape from the rearing facilities and join the native fish. What could go wrong? Her list is interesting: ". . . fish containing a new growth hormone gene might displace wild fish if they outcompete the natives for food or spawning sites, since the transgenic fish would be larger and grow faster than wild fish at a given age. Genes for freezing tolerance might expand the geographic range of engineered fish, allowing them to compete with new, more northerly (or southerly) species and potentially reducing populations of these fish."[62] Why is this bad news? Our transgenic fish turn out to be bigger, stronger, and better in the evolutionary competition, so they displace some of the weaklings. Why is this wrong? It is wrong not on any anthropocentric ethic (centered on human rights and interests), but on the "Land Ethic" first put forward by Aldo Leopold in *A Sand County Almanac*.[63] The ecocentric (as opposed to anthropocentric) value is that of the integrity of the ecosystem—its ability to persist in its natural way, undisturbed by the introduction of alien organisms. The introduction of transgenic organisms into the mix is like introducing kudzu, or zebra mussels—an exotic species likely to destroy the ecosystem by displacement of its natural residents, who have lived in symbiotic harmony for eons. That is why it is wrong.

At least in this piece, Goldburg does not take on the other scenarios that are entirely possible with the untested transgenic species. Others do. If wild females preferred genetically engineered males (as Goldburg argues, since they seem to prefer larger mates) and if young engineered fish are unable to survive in the wild, escape could wipe out the entire wild species.[64] It is also entirely possible that there is some virus out there that the wild species are immune to by now, but that the transgenics will be susceptible to—again, if they mate with the wild females, wiping out the species. In any case, it is not expected that salmon will be the last fish to be commercialized in transgenic form, nor that the trip of the transgenics from the breeding pen to the table will be free of controversy.[65]

THE WALL STREET WAFFLE

Investors look at matters from a narrow, but very well focused, perspective. Is this company, this industry, a good investment? If I add these shares to my portfolio, will they make money for me? The answers to this question, where genetically engineered agricultural products are concerned, has been one large ambivalence. It is not possible to pick a time before which all accounts were bullish on biotech stocks, and after which they were bearish. Rather, enthusiasm and disenchantment seem to coexist in the same financial universe, with the latter holding a distinct edge.

The bulls make a convincing case, for instance, through Tim Stevens, in "Sowing Seeds of Success," appearing in *Industry Week* in September 1999. Stevens is enthusiastic about the emergence of the "industry of life science. . . . a convergence of chemistry, pharmaceuticals, biotechnology, agrobusiness, and nutrition." Its value comes from synergy among those enterprises, all of which are working with DNA, recombinant processes, the very stuff of life itself. Of course the industry will have "growth spurts and growing pains. . . . divestitures and myriad acquisitions . . ." and the like, but with a strong technology base, this very diverse enterprise presents an "enormous" opportunity for value creation (according to Gary Pfeiffer, CFO of DuPont, Wilmington, DE.)[66] This sentiment is echoed in a substantial account of the industry by Ray A. Goldberg, writing on "Transforming Life, Transforming Business: The Life-Science Revolution," for the March/April 2000 issue of the *Harvard Business Review*. While generally enthusiastic about the new "life-science industries," Goldberg emphasized the transition problems that it would have to confront. Essentially, a life-science company merges a pharmaceutical enterprise (drugs) with an agricultural enterprise (seeds). Both will be using recombinant DNA technology, so the combination makes sense. But drug companies moving into agriculture must remember that they are moving from a very high profit industry with no cycles to a cyclical industry with a much lower return. The corporate cultures of the industries are very different. Monsanto and Novartis are cited in the article as examples of life-science companies that ran into financial difficulties that they had not foreseen. For some reason there are problems gaining the foreseen efficiencies in marketing and distribution. Goldberg acknowledges that the major problem seems to be overcoming resistance to the product.[67]

While the bulls are formal and tentative, the bears are scathing. Wall Street has little patience with corporations that cannot manage their public relations problems. As early as April 1999, Amy Barrett was warning investors not to "sow their seeds too soon" in the emerging life-science industry. Monsanto was praised as a good investment individually, only because of its new drug, Celebrex, selling in the infinitely rich market of remedies for arthritis. But as for the rest of the industry, ". . . . life-sciences business has limitless potential. But for those looking for an opportunity to invest, the key word is "potential"—the big payoff from biotech agriculture will likely be years in coming."[68]

By the end of the summer, Deutsche Bank was advising investors to get out of the industry: ". . . the public's rejection of genetically modified foods in Europe may lead to a share price collapse for genetically modified seeds firms," such as Pioneer Hi-Bred and Monsanto. "Today, the term genetically modified organism has become a liability," says Timothy S. Ramey, analyst at Deutsche Bank (New York). "We predict that genetically modified crops, once perceived as the driver of the bull-case for this sector, will now be perceived as the pariah."[69] At that point, Shapiro apparently gave up, not for the first or last time, and started looking for a good buyer to sell the company to.[70]

After listening to both sides, *The Economist* joined the bears. "The world's leading 'life-sciences' firms, among them Novartis, AstraZeneca and Monsanto, which have put together agricultural products and drugs, are wondering if they got their cross right. Much-vaunted exchanges of technologies and joint development have yet to materialize. Compared with agriculture, making drugs is so profitable that many life-sciences firms find agrochemical divisions a drag on their share prices." With Monsanto, many life-science companies were planning to sell off the agricultural division. The life-science combination, *The Economist* observed, should have worked: both need recombinant DNA information and processes. But basic research is only one-fifth of the development cost; the rest is field trials and marketing, and at that point the two industries are very different. "As Tray Thomas, head of Context Consulting, points out, consumers will pay the earth for a new medication, but farmers balk at a new, expensive chemical. Agriculture is inherently less profitable than pharmaceuticals, with profit margins of around 10%, about a third of what drugs earn. Few pesticides fetch more than a billion dollars; and indeed the worldwide market in chemical pesticides and seeds is $35 billion, roughly a tenth of global drug sales." The present slump in commodity prices due to years of good harvests hurts more; the consumer backlash against GM foods makes matters worse. The American market may be next. And there may be crossover boycotts: Some German doctors have threatened to boycott Novartis' drugs because of its GM crops. Under those circumstances, it is wise to break up these companies. Matters are not helped by a financial backlash, as once-enthusiastic investors are urged to the door.[71]

By December 1999, GMO enthusiasm was under full attack. "If you're making up your New Year's tally of what's in and what's out, add the once-trendy term 'life-sciences company' to the latter list," wrote Amy Barrett in *Business Week*. Novartis and Monsanto were once stars in any portfolio of businesses. "These days, however, many of those same companies are scrambling to cast off the life-sciences moniker." They're all shedding their agricultural divisions to concentrate on their pharmaceutical divisions. Monsanto is obviously trying to do the same. "Why the sudden reversal? For one thing, the consumer backlash against genetically engineered foods continues to grow in Europe, and it shows signs of gaining traction in the U.S. That makes the business of marketing genetically engineered seeds a tricky one. At the same time, the U.S. farm economy remains in the dumps, hurting sales of traditional herbicides and pesticides." The vaunted "synergy" never really materialized.[72]

An article in *The Economist* chronicled Robert Shapiro's fall from grace with scornful wonder. "How could a master of marketing and an exponent of business ethics get things so spectacularly wrong?" By that time, Monsanto had merged with Pharmacia & Upjohn, and *The Economist* confidently expected that soon the agribusiness would be history, as would Shapiro. To his defenders, he was a visionary trying to save the world's environment and feed the world's people. To his detractors, he was blind. "He failed to understand the nature or the magnitude of the mess that Monsanto is in, or the way to extricate it, until it was too late." There was some bad luck, the article conceded. After all, he wasn't responsible for Mad Cow disease. But he failed as a businessman. He moved too fast buying up seed companies "to have a lock on the science from laboratory to farm." As a result, he paid too much, he got the company in much too much debt, and simultaneously attracted the attention of farmers, activists, and the Justice Department for monopolistic tendencies. When he withdrew Monsanto's offer for the last seed company, they were $6 billion in debt, which would have been all right if the biotech industry had taken off as it was supposed to do, which it did not. Investors deserted him all the more quickly.[73]

Shapiro's major mistake, according to *The Economist,* was to attempt to carry on business as usual when the NGO attacks began. He and his managers:

> were convinced that those whose ignorance led them to reject biotechnology would eventually be swayed by Monsanto's assurances of safety and its research, which is highly praised in both industry and academia. Company officials have doggedly defended the firm's genetically tinkered seeds and high-tech agrochemicals by trotting out studies on increased crop yields and falling pesticide outlays. *Yet the public wants to talk about social values, not soyabean statistics.* Mr. Shapiro now acknowledges that he was naïve, especially when it came to fighting the criticism of pressure groups and the press by scientific arguments alone. What Mr. Shapiro seemed to forget was that scientific certainty often sounds like corporate arrogance.[74]

The message is significant. We have tried everything to get the owners and managers of very large corporations to listen to messages of consumer need, morality, caution, and attention to the environment. We have tried persuasion, and persuasion usually lands on deaf ears. We have tried regulation, and watched corporate campaign contributions distract legislators from taking regulation seriously. We tried in desperation tying ourselves to trees. Now, finally, here is a successful effort. It is no shining model: the activists know much less about the science than we could have wished, their targets are not always well chosen, and this whole debate has *nothing at all to do with Mad Cow disease.* Meanwhile, they may have poisoned the atmosphere so that later developments that might bring real good, especially to the poor of the world, will not be brought to market. But they have, finally, succeeded in convincing the business press and at least one industry that environmental concerns must be taken seriously or the consequences may be disastrous for the market, the corporation, and the investor.

The conclusion, as far as the business world is concerned at this point, was articulated in June 2000, again in *Business Week*. Shapiro had failed at Monsanto. The company had changed focus from limitless visions to cutting costs. All revenue was threatened by "global backlash against genetically engineered foods." The $30 billion deal that had merged Monsanto with Pharmacia & Upjohn in March had spun off Monsanto as the agribusiness section. Should investors consider putting their money into that agribusiness spinoff from the new company? "Our overall view is to stay away," advised a portfolio manager at Dresdner RCM Global Investors. Especially since the backlash seems to be spreading to Brazil, Monsanto must prove that it can deliver solid earnings growth now before investors will be interested in it again.[75]

PRECAUTIONARY PRINCIPLE VERSUS RISK BENEFIT RATIO: WHY PUBLIC RELATIONS IS NOT THE ONLY PROBLEM

Is there more here than meets the eye? Europeans are not normally less rational than Americans; there is no *a priori* reason why Europeans should be terrified of food that we have been eating for years without apparent harm. Three other factors in the profoundly hostile European reaction are worth mentioning before we pass to the future.

First, there is the possibility that Europeans have a preference for what is known as the "precautionary principle": the conservative principle according to which no new thing is to be accepted until it has been proved beyond a reasonable doubt to be safe and better than the present products. Americans, on the other hand, more trusting of novelty, may be inclined to go with a risk-benefit calculation, placing the new idea (or product) on a par with the old and comparing them for safety and advantage. So Americans may shrug off an unknown innovation while Europeans greet it with skepticism.

Second, even if Europe had in this case decided to go with a risk-benefit calculation, weighing whatever risks there might be with the benefits of genetically altered food, no one ever suggested to them that there were any consumer benefits. Monsanto did not think any risks were associated with the foods. But were there any benefits? All the benefits mentioned were for the growers, who could cut dramatically their costs for chemicals and labor, and so make a bigger profit. Presumably some of the savings would be passed on to consumers, but the GM corn went mostly to hog and cattle feed (to other producers, not to consumers), and the rape plants were all ground up for canola oil which went into processed food, not to be sold on the shelves. At no point did the consumer get in on the cost savings, and no one ever suggested that these GM foods were healthier, safer, or better tasting.[76]

Third, there is the question of the small farmer. Europe has many of them, and they make up a powerful political force. GM crops, with the high expense for seed and the economies to be realized in savings on tillage, are not for the small farmer. Their profit is in volume. GM crops, like all large-scale agribusiness, do best in depopulated areas like the Great Plains in the United States, where small towns turn to ghost towns as the Atlantic and Pacific coasts gain population. In the United States, the small farmer is not a political force; the "farm vote" is cast by the enormous automated farms that have inherited the heartland. Is this move to agribusiness, away from the small farmer, a good idea? The question has force in the United States, where sentiment at least remembers the Family Farm, and political weight in Europe, but is of terrible moment in the developing world. Over India, the Philippines, and other nations of Africa, Asia, and South America, the search for "market access" has given priority to huge plantings of single crops for export only. Ironically, these large farms, owned by multinational corporations, often share the region with the farmers they displaced, now without enough food to feed their children.[77] Ultimately, the issue of whether it is better for the environment, for the consumer, and for the farm family, to carry on agriculture through small local farms providing local markets with a variety of crops, or through huge monocultures supplying global markets through worldwide transportation networks, is larger than we can consider here. But it's worth thinking about.[78]

WHERE WE GO FROM HERE

What future can we expect for genetically modified food? As we write, both sides of the dispute are in motion. A cover story in *TIME* on the new "golden rice," genetically modified to contain beta-carotene (vitamin A) proclaims, "This rice could save a million kids a year," and proceeds to present a convincing argument for the assertion, based on the extent and consequences of malnutrition in the developing nations. The article rehearses the by now familiar arguments against uncritical acceptance of genetic modifications, and does a nice job of capturing the European suspicions of multinational companies bearing gifts of new products.[79] But its focus on Ingo Potrykus, professor of plant science at the Swiss Federal Institute of Technology, who worked for years to develop the rice, puts a human face on the development of transgenic organisms for the first time. Potrykus really does want to save the world, or at least to feed a significant portion of its children with a more nutritious diet. Before the world writes off GMOs as an idea whose time will not come, someone has to explain why it is not necessary to save those children from blindness and depressed immune systems.[80]

On the other side, the opposition mutates as fast as a microbe. A lawsuit against Monsanto and others was launched in December by Jeremy Rifkin and several small farmers, alleging that Monsanto "forced" genetically altered seeds on to the market, misled farmers and generally engaged in anticompetitive practices. Monsanto lawyers call the suit a "stunt," but who can tell how these actions may end?[81] Meanwhile, all the controversy has finally stirred the regulatory agencies into action; we may expect more attention to the testing and marketing of GMOs in the United States.[82] Until recently, the controversy faced off European GMO-opponents and U.S. GMO-supporters; now reports of "ecoterrorism" on Long Island suggest that the battle may be crossing the pond more quickly than we thought.[83] The campaign to require labels on all genetically modified foods continues to sputter. "If biotechnology products are so safe, why can't the consumer know when a particular food product contains modified ingredients?" asked a letter to the *New York Times* on June 8, 2000. Henry Miller, recent head of the FDA's Office of Biotechnology, had earlier asserted that there is no "right to know" where there is no health or safety issue. A federal appeals court had invalidated a Vermont law that required milk labels to disclose the use of bovine somatotropin, he pointed out, because the labels were a constitutional violation of commercial free speech. Charles Margulis, genetic engineering specialist at Greenpeace, pointed out in the same column that the same court decision indicated general FDA incompetence in the area.[84]

Meanwhile the industry continues to develop new technologies, possibly in hopes of finding one that will not arouse the ire of the activists; as of July 1, 2000, U.S. farmers were still planting genetically modified crops on their farms.[85] By now cotton and corn, protected by Bt, are widely grown, Canola and Roundup Ready soybeans are still popular, and in many circles, new transgenic crops are defended. When a ringspot virus attack on Hawaiian papayas in 1994 almost destroyed the orchards, with no chemical or "natural" remedy available, only the introduction of transgenic papaya saved the crop. Hawaiian papaya growers are now very enthusiastic supporters of GMOs. Similar viruses afflict many crops in Africa, according to Kenyan plant scientist Florence Wambugu. She hopes that the introduction of a transgenic sweet potato that is resistant to the feathery mottle virus will help Africa double its sweet potato harvest. There seems to be no other option. Bananas may be next. In Africa, nearly half the fruit and vegetable harvest is lost because it rots on the way to market; bananas that ripened more slowly could yield 40% more bananas. Herbicide-resistant plants would improve education: "We could liberate so many people if our crops were resistant to herbicides that we could then spray on the surrounding weeds. Weeding enslaves Africans; it keeps children from school."[86] Wambugu's opinion of the European flap on "frankenfood"? "Ludicrous."[87]

And for all our doubts, our policies on buying, using, and even think-ing about GMOs are substantially inconsistent. There is still no satis-factory explanation for the fact that GMOs have been a nonissue in the U.S. and anathema in Europe. And why is it such a problem in Japan, even with trace amounts previously unsuspected?[88] There is no separat-ing worries about food safety and worries about public relations. Genetically modified crops are now widely grown (52% of soybeans are modified), even as the conflicts multiply. Novartis, a Swiss pharmaceu-tical giant, makes and sells genetically modified corn and soybean seeds, while Gerber Products, one of its subsidiaries, has virtuously banned all genetically modified ingredients from its baby-food formulas. Heinz has banned GMOs from its baby foods but not its other products. McDonald's will not accept genetically modified potatoes for its fries, but it cooks them in vegetable oil made from modified corn and soy-beans. Pepsi Cola uses corn syrup made from genetically modified corn, but Pepsico's Frito-Lay division won't use that corn in its chips. But for a company to maintain even a limited ban successfully, it must have extraordinary knowledge of its sources. Most companies buy products on the open market, and most food suppliers have no idea whether or not there are GMOs in the mix. The "labeling" agenda would be very hard to carry out even if everyone thought it was a good idea.[89]

The last straw, or blade of grass, in the controversy, is surely the genetically engineered suburban lawn. Among its catalog of future developments ("Tech2010") suggested by the *New York Times* in its June 11, 2000, Magazine Section is a lawn "that never needs mowing," because of the introduction of a gene that breaks down steroids and inhibits growth. That is not all; more recently, Scotts Company announced that it is working on a lawn that resists weedkillers, another that is drought resistant, another that flourishes in winter. Maybe we'll even have lawns in many different colors. Just please don't call it "Frankenlawn."[90]

QUESTIONS FOR REFLECTION

+ Does genetic modification constitute "tampering with nature" in some way that our other nonnatural practices (from wearing clothes to selective breeding of cocker spaniels) do not? Why or why not?

+ Are companies obligated to take into account organizations like Greenpeace, no matter how mistaken or self-serving they may be?

+ Why would it be wrong to introduce a transgenic species into the wild? Or would it?

+ Think of examples on both sides.

Notes

1. Marjorie Sun, "Engineering Crops to Resist Weed Killers," *Science* 231 (21 March 1986): pp. 1360–1361.

2. Michael Specter, "Europe, Bucking Trend in U.S., Blocks Genetically Altered Food," *New York Times* (20 July 1998): pp. A1, A8.

3. Charles M. Benbrook and Phyllis B. Moses, "Engineering Crops to Resist Herbicides," *Technology Review* (November/December 1986): pp. 55ff.

4. Jane E. Brody, "Quest for Lean Meat Prompts New Approach," *New York Times* (12 April 1988): pp. C1, C4.

5. Amal Kumar Naj, "Can Biotechnology Control Farm Pests? Specialty Plants May Cut Need For Chemicals," *Wall Street Journal* (May 11, 1989): p. B1.

6. Gary Slutsker, "The Lesser of Two Weevils," *Forbes* (15 October 1990): pp. 202–203.

7. Michael Specter, "The Pharmageddon Riddle," *New Yorker* (10 April 2000): pp. 58–71.

8. Rebecca Goldburg, "Biotechnology's Bitter Harvest: Herbicide-Tolerant Crops and the Threat to Sustainable Agriculture," *Biotechnology Working Group* of the Environmental Defense Fund, internal report, 1990.

9. John Seabrook, "Tremors in the Hothouse: The Battle Lines Are Being Drawn for the Soul of the American Consumer as Agribusiness Launches the First Genetically Altered Supermarket Tomato," *New Yorker* (19 July 1993): pp. 32–41.

10. Michael Specter, "Europe, Bucking Trend in U.S., Blocks Genetically Altered Food," *New York Times* (20 July 1998): pp. A1, A8.

11. Ibid.

12. See the entire issue of *The Ecologist: Rethinking Basic Assumptions* 28, no. 5 (September/October 1998).

13. The Mad Cows have given birth to a floating panic about such mysterious brain diseases. Consider U.S. government plans to destroy nearly 400 sheep because there was a chance that they *may* have been exposed to Belgian sheep that *may* be infected with some variant of BSE (as opposed to scrapie, a disease of the same family which often shows up in sheep and is not transmissible to humans). See Carey Goldberg, "U.S. Planning to Destroy Sheep at Risk of an Infection," *New York Times* (18 July 2000): p. A12. If that's not enough, consider "mad squirrel disease," the flap over which is chronicled by Burkhard Bilger in "Letter from Kentucky: Squirrel and Man," *New Yorker* (17 July 2000): pp. 59–67.

14. Michael Specter, "Europe, Bucking Trend in U.S."

15. Jimmy Carter, "Who's Afraid of Genetic Engineering?", *New York Times* (26 August 1998): Op-Ed.

16. Michael Pollan, "Playing God in the Garden," *New York Times Magazine* (25 October 1998): pp. 46ff.

17. Ralph Nader, foreword to *Genetically Engineered Foods: Changing the Nature of Nature (What You Need to Know to Protect Yourself, Your Family, and Our Planet)*, by Martin Teitel and Kimberly Wilson (Rochester, VT: Inner Traditions International, 1999).

18. "Fertility Rights," *The Economist* (9 October 1999): Editorial.

19. Barnaby J. Feder, "Plant Sterility Research Inflames Debate on Biotechnology's Role in Farming," *New York Times* (19 April 1999): p. 18.

20. "Fertility Rights," *The Economist*.

21. *U.S. News and World Report* (18 October 1999): p. 83.

22. "Fertility Rights," *The Economist*; "Terminator Terminated," *Farm Industry News* (November 1999).

23. Kara Sissell, "European Consumers Stunt Brazilian Crops," *Chemical Week* (21 April 1999): p. 48.

24. Mark Nichols, "Tampering with the Natural Order: Genetically Altered Foods Are Filling North American Shelves with Startling Speed—and Scant Publicity," *Maclean's* (17 May 1999): p. 59; John Micklethwait, "Europe's Profound Fear of Food," *New York Times* (7 June, 1999): Op-Ed.

25. "Red Faces over Genes in Greens," *Farmers Guardian* (23 April 1999): p. 10.

26. Carol Kaesuk Yoon, "Altered Corn May Imperil Butterfly, Researchers Say," *New York Times* (20 May 1999): pp. A1, A25; "A Warning From the Butterflies," *New York Times* (21 May 1999): Editorial.

27. John Carey, "Imperiled Monarchs Alter the Biotech Landscape," *Business Week* (7 June 1999): p. 36.

28. Ibid.

29. Ibid.

30. "Who's Afraid?", *The Economist* (19 June 1999): Editorial.

31. Diane Johnson, "France's Fickle Appetite," *New York Times* (2 August 1999): Op-Ed.; Warren Hoge, "Britons Skirmish Over Genetically Modified Crops," *New York Times* (23 August 1999): p. A15.

32. Melody Petersen, "New Trade Threat for U.S. Farmers," *New York Times* (29 August 1999): pp. 1, 28.

33. Charles C. Mann, "Biotech Goes Wild," *Technology Review* (July–August 1999): pp. 36ff. Solid coverage of the whole issue, beginning with the concerns that engineered crops might spontaneously breed with wild relatives, creating superweeds. See also: Carol Kaesuk Yoon, "Squash With Altered Genes Raises Fears of 'Superweeds,'" *New York Times* (3 November 1999): pp. A1, A18; Letters to the Editor, *New York Times* (8 November 1999).

34. Peter Rosset, "Why Genetically Altered Food Won't Conquer Hunger," *New York Times* (1 September 1999): Op-Ed.

35. "Seeds of Change: In the U.S. and Elsewhere, the Food Supply Is Being Genetically Altered. Here's Why You Should Care," *Consumer Reports* (September 1999): p. 41.

36. Marian Burros, "U.S. Plans Long-Term Studies on Safety of Genetically Altered Foods," *New York Times* (14 July 1999): p. A18; Jeffrey Kluger, "Food Fight," *TIME* (13 September 1999): pp. 42–44.

37. "Monsanto Denies Cancer Threat from Weedkiller," *Farmers Guardian* (15 October 1999): p. 7.

38. For purposes of this essay, the accounts will be essentially filed by title. A rich literature awaits those who would enter the discussion.

39. The term was coined, and the theory developed, by R. Edward Freeman, primarily in *Strategic Management: A Stakeholder Approach* (Boston, MA: Pitman, 1984).

40. Barry Came, "The Food Fight," *Maclean's* (18 October 1999): p. 44.

41. Ibid.

42. Kevin McCauley, "B-M engineers biotech PR drive by Monsanto," *O'Dwyer's* PR Services Report (December 1999): p. 1.

43. Rick Mullin, "Mob Rule," *Chemical Week* (8 December 1999), p. 5.

44. Ibid.

45. Paul Magnusson, Ann Therese Palmer, and Kerry Capell, "Furor Over 'Frankenfood,'" *Business Week* (18 October 1999): p. 50.

46. Ibid.

47. Ibid.

48. Ibid.

49. John Carey, Ellen Licking, and Amy Barrett, "Are Bio-Foods Safe?", *Business Week* (20 December 1999): p. 70.

50. Margaret Kriz, "Global Food Fights," *National Journal* (4 March 2000): p. 688.

51. Paul Krugman, "Natural Born Killers," *New York Times* (22 March 2000): Op-Ed.

52. Carey Goldberg, "1,500 March in Boston to Protest Biotech Food," *New York Times* (27 March 2000): p. A14.

53. Ibid.

54. Ross S. Irvine, "'Netwarriors' Fight Way to Top in Corporate PR," *O'Dwyer's* PR Services Report (May 2000): p. 1.

55. Ibid.

56. Ibid.

57. Ibid.

58. "Udder confusion," *The Economist* (3 July 1999): Editorial.

59. "Seeds of Change," *Consumer Reports* (September 1999): p. 41.

60. "U.N. Rules on BST," *Chemical Week* (25 August 1999/1 September 1999): p. 60.

61. Rebecca Goldburg, "Something Fishy," *Gene Exchange,* Environmental Defense, 1998 (updated May 2000).

62. Ibid.

63. Aldo Leopold, "The Land Ethic," in *A Sand County Almanac* (New York: Oxford University Press, 1949): pp. 201ff. See especially p. 224: "A thing is right when it tends to preserve the integrity, stability, and beauty of the biotic community. It is wrong when it tends otherwise."

64. Carol Kaesuk Yoon, "Altered Salmon Leading Way to Dinner Plates, But Rules Lag," *New York Times* (1 May 2000): pp. A1, A20.

65. Frederic Golden, "Make Way for Frankenfish!", *TIME* (6 March 2000): pp. 62–63.

66. Tim Stevens, "Sowing Seeds of Success," *Industry Week* (6 September 1999): p. 68.

67. Ray A. Goldberg, "Transforming Life, Transforming Business: The Life-Science Revolution," *Harvard Business Review* (March/April 2000): p. 94.

68. Amy Barrett, "Investors, Don't Sow Your Seeds Too Soon," *Business Week* (12 April 1999): p. 74.

69. Alex Scott, "Deutsche Bank Advises Investors to Sell Crop Companies' Shares," *Chemical Week* (25 August 1999/1 September 1999): p. 32.

70. Robert Westervelt, "Monsanto Back on the Block," *Chemical Week* (25 August 1999/1 September 1999): p. 9.

71. "Hybrid Rigour," *The Economist* (11 September 1999): Editorial.

72. Amy Barrett, "Gene is a Four-Letter Word on Wall Street," *Business Week* (20 December 1999): p. 76. See also "The De-merging of Life Sciences," *Farm Industry News* (January 2000): Editorial.

73. "Grim Reaper," *The Economist* (25 December 1999): Editorial.

74. Ibid. Emphasis added.

75. Amy Barrett, "Rocky Ground for Monsanto?", *Business Week* (12 June 2000): p. 72.

76. Ray A. Goldberg, "Transforming Life, Transforming Business: The Life-Science Revolution," *Harvard Business Review* (March/April 2000): p. 94.

77. Vandana Shiva, "Small Scale Farming: A Global Perspective (South)," *The Ecologist* 30, no. 4 (June 2000): p. 37.

78. A fair amount of such thinking is found in "Facing the Farm Crisis," a special supplement to *The Ecologist* 30, no. 4 (June 2000): pp. 28ff.

79. "Trojan Horse" is what that golden grain is usually called. See Andrew Pollack, "A Food Fight for High Stakes," *New York Times* (4 February 2001): p. 6.

80. J. Madeleine Nash, "Grains of Hope: Genetically Engineered Crops Could Revolutionize Farming. Protesters Fear They Could Also Destroy the Ecosystem. You Decide," *TIME* (31 July 2000): pp. 38–46.

81. David Barboza, "Monsanto Sued Over Use of Biotechnology in Developing Seeds," *New York Times* (15 December 1999): p. C1; Marian Burros, "Documents Show Officials Disagreed on Altered Food," *New York Times* (1 December 1999): p. A18; Mark Frankel, "Monsanto Faces a Fierce Food Fight," *Business Week* (27 December 1999): p. 66.

82. Melody Petersen, "U.S. to Keep a Closer Watch on Genetically Altered Crops," *New York Times* (4 May 2000): p. A23.

83. Michael Cooper, "Wave of 'Eco-Terrorism' Appears to Hit Experimental Cornfield," *New York Times* (21 July 2000): pp. B1, B8.

84. "Altered Food: To Label or Not?", *New York Times* (11 May 2000): Letters to the Editor; "Tell the Truth About Altered Food," *New York Times* (8 June 2000): Letters to the Editor.

85. "New Gene-altering Strategy Tested on Corn," *Science News* 157 (6 May 2000): pp. 294–295; David Barboza, "U.S. Farmers Still Planting Biotech Crops: Only a Slight Dip in Use of Gene-Altered Seeds," *New York Times* (1 July 2000): p. C1.

86. Madeleine Nash, "Grains of Hope,"p. 46.

87. Ibid.

88. Stephanie Strom, "Altered U.S. Corn Found in Samples Sent to Japan," *New York Times* (18 January 2001): p. W1.

89. David Barboza, "Modified Foods Put Companies in a Quandary: Science Is Called Sound But Public Is Not Sure," *New York Times* (4 June 2000): pp. 1, 34.

90. Brian Farnham, "The Lawn That Never Needs Mowing," *New York Times* (11 June 2000): p. 55, magazine section; David Barboza, "Suburban Genetics: Scientists Searching for a Perfect Lawn," *New York Times* (9 July 2000): pp. 1, 20.

CHAPTER 2

The Human Family Grows

Population as a Problem

INTRODUCTION

"We entered the 20th Century with a population of less than 2 billion. And left it with a population of 6 billion."[1] In 100 years, we added more than 4 billion people to our planet. But in 1650, only 350 years ago, our population was only 500 million. If we look at selected years and the length of time it took the population to double, from then to now, we get a better picture (see Table 2.1).

TABLE 2.1   Population Growth

Year (A.D.)	Population		Doubling Time
1650	500	million	200 years
1850	1	billion	80 years
1930	2	billion	
1950	2.5	billion	35 years
1985	5	billion	

Or, look at it this way:

It took from all human history to 1804 to reach 1 billion;

123 years to 1927 to reach 2 billion;

33 years to 1960 to reach 3 billion;

14 years to 1974 to reach 4 billion;

13 years to 1987 to reach 5 billion; and

12 years to 1999 to reach 6 billion[2]

There are, at this writing, 6.067 billion members of our species inhabiting planet Earth.[3]

QUESTIONS TO KEEP IN MIND

Why is the population growing so quickly now?

Why are we worried about it? People are good, aren't they?

What measures do we think will help the situation?

Take another look at the figures above. By now, those of you who are mathematically inclined have recognized the distinct characteristics of exponential growth—a long period of slow growth followed by very rapid growth over a very short period of time. There are lots of analogous situations. Here are just two:

I'll give you a dollar a day, $2 the second day, $3 the third, and so on, for a month. Or. I'll give you a penny on the first day and I'll double it each day of the month. Which do you want?

A farmer's pond had a tiny lily pad that was doubling in size every day. He was warned that it would choke the pond in 30 days. He didn't worry about it for 28 days because it seemed so small. On the 29th day it covered half the pond. He had to solve the problem in one day.

Population growth is usually described by two statistics:

1. *The growth rate:* The difference between the birthrate and the death rate; that is, between those born per thousand population and those died per thousand. This is usually expressed as a percentage—if 80 people were born to a population of 1,000, and 60 people died, the growth rate in one year would be 20 per 1000, or 2%.

2. *The fertility rate:* The average number of children born per woman over her lifetime in a given country.

But "it's more than just numbers," as described in the Population Reference Bureau's 1999 booklet by that name. Think of it this way: there have never been as many people on earth as there are now. People are living longer than ever (there are more old people), and at the same time, there have never been so many young people. The changes are not just in numbers: women's lives have changed more than men's; people are increasingly on the move, migrating across regions; and human activity, intensifying, has much more of an effect on the natural environment than it ever has.

WHAT HAPPENED?
THE DEMOGRAPHIC TRANSITION

Why did our population grow at such a rapid rate over such a short period of time? As we've seen above, the doubling time has grown shorter and shorter, consistent with exponential growth. The generally accepted explanation lies especially in the events of the Industrial Revolution, in the North,[5] resulting in a reduced need for many children; and what might be called the Health, Sanitation, and Medical Revolution in both the North and the South, resulting in a decline in the death rate. There is also the time element of the "demographic transition," a generalized rule of thumb, to take into consideration: it takes about a generation for a fall in the birth rate to follow the death rate decline.[6]

In the industrialized North in the early- to mid-1800s, the Industrial Revolution brought about an increase in per capita income and increase in life expectancy due to factory jobs, improved sanitation, clean drinking water, a reduction in disease with better health care, and eventually vaccines and antibiotics. These, and probably many other factors, contributed to the decline in the death rate over a relatively long period of time, with a concurrent rise in the rate of population growth. Then, as farm hands moved to the city, there was less need to bear more children to tend the crops, women became (a bit) more independent, and eventually the drop in the birthrate also occurred, resulting in a declining population growth rate.

Essentially the same thing happened in the nonindustrialized South, much later, given all of the other social, geopolitical, cultural, and economic considerations beyond this discourse. Yet it was (and is) those countries that contained the largest percentage of the population in the first place.

But there was a big difference between the North and the South in the timing of the transition. In the South, the advances in health care and sanitation occurred abruptly, primarily post-World War II, with the spread of vaccines and antibiotics. Robert Kates notes that "it took 100 years for deaths to drop in Europe compared to the drop in 30 years in the developing world." That rapid decline in death rates in the South "brought unheard of population growth rates to Africa, Asia, and Latin America."[7] While fertility rates remained as they had been, averaging about six children per woman in a lifetime, actual survival increased dramatically, resulting in the possibility of population doubling every 20 years, accompanied by all the social and economic implications, such as food supply, education, jobs, and environmental degradation.

Because improved living conditions—resulting in increased life expectancy in the North—spanned many generations, the social changes leading to fewer children per couple happened gradually. But the South has been confronted with the economic and social necessity to defuse the population explosion or face pretty extreme consequences. That is easier said than done in a democracy with reproductive freedom, such as India, with a population of 1.002 billion, a fertility rate of 3.3, and a population doubling time of 39 years; versus an authoritarian government, where population control is more easily achieved, such as China, with a population of 1.264 billion, a fertility rate that has dropped from 5.5 to 1.8 in 40 years, and a population doubling time of 79 years.[8]

ENVIRONMENTAL IMPACTS OF HUMAN POPULATION GROWTH

The Optimists and the Pessimists

"There is a basic philosophical division in the study of population and the environment that is often characterized, or perhaps caricatured, as a debate between optimists and pessimists. Optimists believe that people have the creative capacity to overcome potential environmental harm from a growing population and intense economic activity. Pessimists foresee potential political, social, and environmental deterioration and collapse."[9]

The optimists point to improvements in health care, increased per capita income, increased life expectancy, increased economic opportunity, and technological innovation—all of which we've seen not only in the North, but certainly in many countries in the South over the past decades. The pessimists see more people causing more resource depletion, more pollution, and more energy use. This, in their view, leads to more burning of fossil fuels and wood, which produces more carbon dioxide, which further exacerbates global warming—with all *those* implications.[10]

The "I = PAT" Equation

The environmental effect of the growing human population is not related only to numbers. It's inevitably linked to how people live: what resources they use, how much energy they expend, and how much pollution they produce. To determine the environmental impact of humans, John

Holdren and Paul and Anne Ehrlich have proposed the I = PAT (or just IPAT) equation, where I = environmental impact, P = population, A = affluence per capita, and T = the damage caused by the technology that supports that affluence, or the good created by innovative energy and industrial technologies. By these measurements, obviously, one American with his energy intensive and consumptive ways causes much more degradation than that of a Masai herder in Kenya. In fact, using this equation, one American has the impact of:

70 Ugandans and Laotians;

50 Bangladeshis;

20 Indians;

10 Chinese;

and 2 Japanese, Brits, Frenchmen, Swedes, and Aussies.

"Viewed in this light, the United States is the world's most over-populated nation."[11]

One study found significant differences in the influence of each of these impact variables in different countries. For instance, population growth was considered the most important factor in increasing carbon dioxide emissions in Mexico and in Ghana (where the affluence actually decreased during the time period); in the United States, although population and affluence increased, carbon dioxide emissions were constant (due to improved technology); and in Poland and China, affluence was considered the most important factor having an environmental impact.[12] But while the IPAT equation is by no means precise, it has been used and quoted by many students of environmental issues.

Regardless of equations or measurements used, it's obvious to most that population growth is inexorably entwined with a number of other human predicaments as well: poverty, famine, women's rights, the distribution of wealth and land, and even newly appearing viruses. All of these issues are interrelated. In the pamphlet *Population Change, Resources, and the Environment*, the authors list the following as all related to population growth: urbanization, poverty and wealth, poverty and migration, poverty and resource subsidies, wealth and waste, wealth and motor vehicles, agricultural resources, water quality, oceans, health, biodiversity, and energy.

Population and Consumption

The relationship between the number of people populating a given country and the types of resources used by each person is one that has been given considerable attention recently, especially on the international scene at United Nations Conferences. Population growth has been well-studied, but the meaning and influence of consumption is less well-understood.

Robert Kates, in his article "Population and Consumption," gives the following definitions of consumption, according to the definer:

Physicist: What happens when you transform matter/energy

Ecologist: What big fish do to little fish

Economist: What consumers do with their money

Sociologist: What you do to keep up with the Joneses

And he goes on with a quote from a National Research Council report:

> For over two decades the same frustrating exchange has been repeated countless times in international policy circles: A government official or scientist from a wealthy country would make the following argument: The world is threatened with environmental disaster because of the depletion of natural resources (or climate change or the loss of biodiversity), and it cannot continue for long to support its rapidly growing population. To preserve the environment for future generations we need to move quickly to control global population growth, and we must concentrate the effort on the world's poorer countries, where the vast majority of population growth is occurring. Government officials and scientists from low-income countries would typically respond:
>
> > If the world is facing environmental disaster, it is not the fault of the poor who use few resources. The fault must lie with the world's most wealthy countries, where people consume the great bulk of the world's natural resources and energy and cause the great bulk of its environmental degradation. We need to curtail overconsumption in the rich countries which use far more than their share, both to preserve the environment and to allow the poorest people on earth to achieve an acceptable standard of living.
>
> This argument has being going on, in one form or another, for years.[13]

Obviously, the more people there are to share the planetary pie, the smaller the piece per person will be. But the North—with 25% of the world's population—uses 80% of the world's resources; the United States alone, with 5% of the world's population, uses 30% of its resources.[14] In 1992, 15% of the world's population controlled 79% of the world's wealth.[15] And it's the women in the developing world that have suffered the most from these inequities (although some would say it's the children). Many women in Africa, Asia, and Latin America not only cook the food; in a majority of the cases, it is they who produce it. They work longer than men—in some instances, spending 8 hours a day collecting fuel and water—but are denied education, health care, land ownership, monetary credit, and outside employment.[16]

Population and Poverty

The connection between population growth and poverty is well defined and fairly obvious. But here are a few statistics from a *Popline* issue:

> About 1.2 billion people live on less than one dollar a day
>
> . . . approximately 57% of the world's population in the 63 poorest countries live on less than two dollars a day
>
> . . . 1/6 of the world's population [about 16.6%]—mainly in Europe, North America and Japan—enjoy 80% of the world's income and live on an average of $70 a day [Report from World Bank]"[17]

Julian Bond, at a commencement address at Washington University in St. Louis, quoted a fairly well known analogy that reduces the world's population to a small village of 100 people, and describes them as follows:

> 57 Asians, 12 Europeans, 10 from the Western Hemisphere—North and South, 21 Africans
>
> 70 non-white, 30 white
>
> 70 non-Christian, 30 Christian
>
> 6 would own 59% of all the wealth in the community, and they'd all live in the United States
>
> 80 would live in substandard housing
>
> 70 would be illiterate
>
> 50 would be malnourished

CHINA AND INDIA

As the world's two most populous nations (followed by the United States at 276 million and Indonesia at 212 million), India (1.002 billion) and China (1.264 billion) deserve a special mention.

In the late 1970s, India instituted a population control policy that offered transistor radios to men who had vasectomies and financial rewards to doctors who performed them. The policy backfired and is considered by some to be partially to blame for the downfall of Indira Gandhi's government. Today, India is considering free health insurance for those in poverty that agree to sterilization after having two children. "In another 15 years India's population is projected to be larger than all of the industrialized countries combined . . ."[18]

China proclaimed a "One-Child Policy" 20 years ago, and it certainly did raise an international ruckus, especially in the United States. The policy was aggressively enforced, primarily by extensive propaganda that extolled the benefits to the country that would result from a stabilized or reduced population. But the local enforcers were rewarded with perks and prestige, which led—in some cases, at least—to draconian measures, ranging from women being forced to have their IUDs checked regularly, to violence perpetrated on couples that broke the rules and had a second child, to forced abortions being performed on women who were in their second pregnancy—sometimes during the third trimester. "When the one-child policy was initiated, the apparent consensus was that it was too harsh, even draconian. Many demographers today, however, feel the policy has rescued China from a demographic disaster that would have resulted from an additional 300–800 million children." Now China is phasing out the policy as its population policy officials have concluded that "there will not be enough adult children to care for aging parents. . . ." With the phase-out, adults who have no siblings because of the policy will be allowed to have two children when they marry.[19] China's fertility rate has declined from 5.5 in 1960 to 1.8 in 2000.

U.N. CONFERENCES

Population issues were given a thorough airing at the U.N. conferences on population, in 1994 (Cairo); and on women, in 1995 (Beijing). A complete discussion of these events is beyond the scope of this chapter; however, it was apparent in both conferences that women were necessary actors in solving global problems—a point driven home arguably for the first time in the history of international conferences.

At the first U.N. conference on population held in Bucharest in 1974, the North pressed the South to control their population, while the South argued for equitable distribution of resources. It was here that the North came up with the slogan that "development is the best contraceptive," which became a mantra for policy makers from industrialized countries in following years. Ten years later at the Mexico City conference, the United States, embroiled in abortion controversy at home, declared that population was a "neutral issue," that market forces would solve population problems. But in Cairo, the Clinton administration reversed the U.S. stand, supporting feminist and environmental advocates. From this conference came support for improved women's education, improved health care for women and children, improved prenatal care, access to reproductive services, empowerment of women, support for adolescent needs, and support for sustainable development.[20] There was a general consensus that family planning programs by themselves would not solve the problem of population growth. Addressing underlying social problems, such as illiteracy and women's status, was an essential element of the solution.[21]

The 1994 agreement that the "most appropriate and effective way to stabilize population growth" is to reduce poverty, improve health care,

promote education, and "raise the status of women" was indeed unprecedented, as opposed to older ideas of just concentrating on family planning.[22] But the 1999 U.N. meeting to assess the progress towards the
1994 goals went considerably further, recommending "unrestricted
access to safe abortions in countries where it is legal," sex education at
all school levels, and "contraceptive advice" to sexually active
teenagers.[23] Predictably, there were objections from some Muslim and
Roman Catholic countries. The conference also addressed the AIDS pan-
demic and the need "for access to preventative [sic] measures," especially
for adolescents, as well as recognizing parental rights, "cultural values,
and religious beliefs."[24]

U.S. POSITION ON POPULATION POLICIES

Controversy over population policy in the United States manifests itself
in U.S. government funding for agencies that provide family planning aid
around the world because of the abortion controversy, and has resulted
in unbelievable bickering between congressional conservatives and the
White House, ranging from imposing a "gag rule," to holding up U.S.
payment of its dues to the United Nations, to holding foreign-operations
bills hostage, to denying dues to the International Monetary Fund.
During the Reagan and Bush administrations, the so-called "gag rule"
was imposed on funding for nongovernmental organizations that
"engage in activities to either promote or deter abortions," even when
private funds were used. It went as far as banning funding to any organization that virtually even mentioned the word "abortion."[25] President
Clinton rescinded the rule by executive memorandum in 1997, but ever
since then a group in Congress immediately undertook to revive it; in
March 2001, President George W. Bush reinstated the gag rule. In
addressing the abortion argument in the United States at that time, Dr.
Nafis Sadik, Executive Director of the United Nations Population Fund,
said, "By harnessing the energy expended in debating abortion and using
it to prevent unintended pregnancies, we can make enormous progress
toward ending the debate altogether."[26]

The other aspect to the controversy is United States funding for the
United Nations Fund for Population Activities (UNFPA), which is
staunchly opposed by the same group of anti-abortionists in Congress.
The reasoning behind the opposition has been that some UNFPA money
goes for reproductive assistance in China where there had been reports of
forced abortions. In 1998, they succeeded in cutting U.S. funding,
prompting Rep. Carolyn Maloney to claim that "1,200 women and more
than 22,000 infants will die" because of the decision she "maintained
that 'UNFPA is in no way connected to abortion' but rather 'provides
health care counseling and contributes to women who otherwise remain

ignorant about their own health as well as that of their children.'"[27] And U.S. Representative John Porter called it "'nonsensical' to deny funding to United Nations population efforts in 160 countries because of allegations of forced abortion in China. (Under the law then) "no U.S. population assistance can go to UNFPA as long as it has programs in China.")[28]

Since then, some funding has been restored, but not before restrictions were included; fights over U.N. dues and other appropriation bills ensued.[29] At this writing, a bill has been introduced to the House by Representative Maloney that would restore all international family planning assistance to 1995 levels—funding now is $200 million less than the 1995 funding.[30]

But surely, the bickering will go on.

PREDICTIONS AND SOLUTIONS

As of February, 2001, the world's population stood at 6.116 billion, increasing at a rate of 1.4%. Global population will double at that rate in 51 years. The projected population for the year 2050, using the medium fertility scenario (2 children per woman), is 8.9 billion; using the low fertility scenario (1.6), it is 7.3 billion; and using the high fertility scenario, it is 10.7 billion.[31]

In the booklet *More Than Just Numbers,* the Population Reference Bureau (among the most respected among population research nongovernmental organizations) listed a number of "certainties" about population growth in the next century:

+ "Population will continue to grow—we will add at least another billion people to the world's population by 2020.
+ Virtually all population growth will take place in the less developed regions of the world.
+ The eventual size of the world's population will depend in large part upon how many children today's youth decide to have, and when they decide to have them.
+ Birth rates will continue to decline worldwide."

The booklet also suggests a new vision has appeared: "to improve the quality of people's lives and to stabilize population growth, improve the natural environment, and promote sustainable economic development, that calls for:

+ greater equality between men and women
+ stronger partnerships between governments and the private sector
+ greater involvement by communities
+ more efforts to help children, adolescents, women, the elderly and people at high risks for HIV/AIDS."[32]

However, other observers have noted that 97% of growth occurs "in developing nations where funds for access to reproductive health services are limited," and the U.S. Agency for International Development has found that many women in the developing world do want to limit pregnancies but do not have access to reproductive services, including contraception.[33]

Indeed, one of the follow-ups to the 1994 U.N. Conference on Population and Development (ICPD) found "resources lagging for the goals of . . . reproductive health care; increased educational, economic and decision making opportunities for women and girls; and universal access to family planning services by 2015."[34]

For years, the generally accepted solution to population problems in the Third World, at least among policy makers in the North, has been, simply, access to contraception,[35] and/or that "development is the best contraceptive," the phrase bandied about at the 1974 population conference. Since then, numerous studies have demonstrated declining fertility rates in countries that have not necessarily had economic growth, but have had improved population planning programs and increased services to women. The authors of one article on fertility decline concluded, rather wryly, "contraceptives are the best contraceptive."[36]

Recently, some dramatic drops in fertility rates have been recorded (see Table 2.2 for declines between 1960, 1995, and 2000). (Once again, the fertility rate is the average number of children born to a woman in her lifetime in a given country.)

The fertility rate in the United States in 2000 is 2.1.

Evidence mounts that economic development may be a less important factor in reducing population than societal factors. A study reported by the World Watch Institute surveyed the effect of various social and economic factors on fertility rates in 80 countries between 1960 and 1980. Among the indicators looked at were literacy rate, health care, life expectancy, family planning programs, urbanization, per capita income, and energy use. They found that ". . . fertility levels were much more closely related to the social indicators of literacy, life expectancy, and family planning effort than to any measure of economic development."[37]

TABLE 2.2   Fertility Rates for Selected Countries, 1960–2000

	1960	*1995*	*2000*
Singapore	6.3	1.8	1.5
S. Korea	6.0	1.6	1.5
Taiwan	6.5	1.8	1.5
Brazil	6.2	2.9	2.4
Mexico	7.2	3.1	2.7
Costa Rica	7.4	3.1	3.2

Nevertheless, it appears that social advancements *alone* are not the cure. Countries that have strong birth control programs such as China, Indonesia, Thailand, and South Korea have also seen dramatic drops in birthrates. In Indonesia, for example, a family planning program was instituted that includes 40,000 village centers from which free contraceptives are distributed, and where reproductive information and services are provided. The slogan that "families should be small, happy and prosperous" is promulgated. Religious leaders favor contraception, there are family planning jingles broadcast, and evening sirens go off to remind women to take their pills. The fertility rate is down from 5.6 in 1972, to 3.5 in 1989, to 2.8 in 2000; contraceptive use is up from 400,000 couples in 1972 to 18,600,000 couples in 1989, with 55% of all married women using contraception in 2000 (it's 71 in the United States, and 39% in the less developed world, excluding China). And abortion is illegal.[38]

There are some who contend that there is no population problem. The evidence appears to deny that. There are some who still believe that "industrialization is the best contraceptive." The evidence appears to deny that also; and even if it were so, given the mathematics, we wouldn't have time for rapid industrialization-as-contraceptive. Emphasis on social programs, as well as the availability of reproductive services, appears to be the best hope for maintaining the human population at numbers that are commensurate with the survival of our own species at a reasonable standard of living, as well as all of the rest of the living planet. To quote Henry Kendall of MIT, "If we don't control the population with justice, humanity, and mercy, it will be done for us by nature—brutally."[39]

Let us conclude with a final speculation. Try as we will to improve the condition of the poor of the earth, nothing else can be done while the population continues to run out of control. We can stop population growth now, but only with very great difficulty, with draconian means of enforcement. We probably won't do it; there is not the political will on this earth. Meanwhile, we can halt the runaway spread of AIDS, tuberculosis, and malaria, but again, only with very great expense and difficulty. AIDS especially threatens to wipe out large portions of Africa during this decade, unless very vigorous methods are undertaken to halt the spread and to prolong the lives of the HIV-positive. Halting the spread of the HIV virus means changing the sexual habits of a continent, and we are not likely to succeed at that without terrible implications for foreign policy. In the next decade, the epicenter of AIDS will probably move to India; in the following decade to China. All these places are being halted in their economic progress by overpopulation, and none of them are friendly to Americans telling them what to do. They would not mind receiving the drugs needed to prolong the lives of HIV-positive patients, but it would be very expensive to get them enough, and they are unwilling and unable to pay for them. A full-blown AIDS epidemic will not help economic progress at first, because it wipes out the workers. But it also wipes out those most likely to conceive and bear children, so eventually it will reduce the population. In the long run, that may be the best thing for economic progress. Shall we just let AIDS run its course?

QUESTIONS FOR REFLECTION

+ Is there any acceptable way to lower the population? What would you suggest?
+ Is there any acceptable way to require the use of birth control, the procuring of abortions, or limitation on family size?
+ Is it acceptable to adopt different policies on disease control for countries that have, as opposed to countries that have not, a population problem?

Notes

1. *World Population: "More Than Just Numbers"* (Washington, DC: Population Reference Bureau, 1999).

2. David Foster, "Billions More Will Leave Century Than Entered It," *Albany Times Union* (27 June 1999).

3. *2000 World Population Data Sheet* (Washington, DC: Population Reference Bureau, June 2000).

4. *World Population: "More Than Just Numbers."*

5. As we proceed, we will be using the geographical term "North" to represent the world's less populated, industrialized, rich countries, generally located north of the equator (i.e., the United States, Canada, Western Europe, Japan, and Australia; and "South" to represent the more populated, less industrialized, poorer countries, generally located south of the equator (i.e., much of South America, Asia, and Africa).

6. See Alene Gelbard, Carl Haub, and Mary M. Kent, "World Population Beyond Six Billion," *Population Bulletin* (March 1999): pp. 4ff., for a more detailed explanation of the demographic transition.

7. Robert W. Kates, "Population and Consumption," *Environment* (April 2000): p. 13.

8. "The Century of Population," *1999 World Population Data Sheet* (Washington, DC: Population Reference Bureau): p. 1; *2000 World Population Data Sheet,* p. 6.

9. Robert Livernash and Eric Rodenburg, "Population Change, Resources, and the Environment," *Population Bulletin* vol. 53, no. 1 (March 1998): p. 2.

10. Ibid., p. 2.

11. Paul R. Ehrlich and Anne H. Ehrlich, *Healing the Planet* (New York: Addison-Wesley, 1991): pp. 7ff.

12. Livernash and Rodenburg, "Population Change, Resources, and the Environment," p. 8.

13. Robert W. Kates, "Population and Consumption," *Environment* (April 2000): pp. 10, 12.

14. Brian Donahue, "Putting Population in Perspective," *Friends of the Earth* (September/October 1994): p. 7.

15. Ibid.

16. Ibid.

17. "1.2 Billion Live in Absolute Poverty," *Popline* (May/June 2000): p. 7.

18. "India's Population Reaches One Billion," *Popline* (July/August, 1999); "India Considers Adopting Family Planning Incentives," *Popline* (March/April 2000).

19. "China Phasing Out One-Child Policy," *Popline* (May/June 2000).

20. Lincoln C. Cen, Winifred M. Fitzgerald, and Lisa Bates, "Women, Politics and Global Management," *Environment* (January/February 1995), p. 4.

21. Worldwatch Institute, *State of the World 1995* (New York: W.W. Norton, 1995): p. 177.

22. "UN Assesses the Success of ICPD (International Conference on Population and Development)," *Population Today* (January 1999): p. 4.

23. Paul Lewis, "Conference Adopts Plan On Limiting Population," *New York Times* (3 July 1999).

24. Ibid.

25. "Committee To Deliberate Mexico City Policy," *Popline* (September/October 1997).

26. "Informed Choice, Not Inflamed Rhetoric," *Popline* (May/June 1997).

27. "U.S. Funding for UNFPA Is Sacrificed," *Popline* (September/October 1998).

28. "State Dept. Prioritizes Funding for UNFPA," *Popline* (November/December 1998).

29. Eric Schmitt, "Deal on UN Dues Breaks an Impasse and Draws Critics," *New York Times* (16 November 1999).

30. "Bill Would Restore US Population Funds," *Popline* (March/April 2000).

31. 2000 *World Population Data Sheet; World Population: "More Than Just Numbers."*

32. 2000 *World Population Data Sheet; World Population: "More Than Just Numbers."*

33. Katie Molgelgaard, "Six Billion and Counting," *Nucleus* (Union of Concerned Scientists), (Fall 1999).

34. Ibid.

35. Donahue, "Putting Population in Perspective."

36. Bryant Robey, et al., "The Fertility Decline in Developing Countries," *Scientific American* (December 1993): p. 60; 2000 *World Population Data Sheet.*

37. *Planning the Global Family,* World Watch Paper #80, 1987.

38. Nathan Keyfitz, "The Growing Human Population," *Scientific American* (September 1989): pp. 66–67; 2000 *World Population Data Sheet.*

39. "Birthrates and Earth's Fate," *Boston Globe* (10 July 1994): Editorial.

CHAPTER 3

Life in the Greenhouse
The Effects of Global Warming

QUESTIONS TO KEEP IN MIND

In January of 1996, a climatologist speculated that El Niño, an odd-ball current in the Pacific Ocean, may have prolonged its stay in 1994 because of global warming.[1] How would we ever know? How could the observation ever be repeated?

What do we mean by "Science has proved . . .?" Why is that always a persuasive line in advertisements for new products? Why is "science" more certain than other disciplines (say, philosophy)?

Why does there seem to be so much uncertainty about "global warming," or "the ozone hole"?

How do policymakers usually proceed when they really are not sure of the facts? How do you think they should proceed? Does inaction have as many consequences as action? How would you balance the relative advantages and disadvantages between decisions to do nothing and decisions to do something?

BACKGROUND FOR THE TOPIC

The "greenhouse effect" is the (imperfect) analogy used to explain the atmospheric phenomena that keep our planet warm enough to sustain life. Our atmosphere allows about half the incoming solar radiation to reach the earth's surface. The balance is either directly reflected back into space or absorbed and held (for a while). The energy that does get through is either bounced back as heat or is used to do work (e.g., photosynthesis, evaporation, fuel our climate), and degraded to heat energy, and returned to the atmosphere. Here is where the greenhouse effect kicks in: some gases in the atmosphere, notably water vapor and carbon dioxide, have the capacity to hold onto that heat for a while, just as the glass panes in a greenhouse do. Without this heat-holding action, the earth's surface would cool to about -18° C (-4° F), instead of maintaining an average temperature of 14° C (57° F), and there would be no life as we know it.

The current concern is not that the greenhouse effect exists—we wouldn't be here if it didn't-but that it may be being exacerbated by anthropogenic increases in the effective gases, threatening a disruption to the equilibrium between incoming and outgoing energy, and a resulting average global warming. Since the start of the industrial revolution, humankind has been adding to the natural amounts of carbon dioxide entering the atmosphere, primarily through the burning of fossil fuels. Additionally, we have caused increases in other "greenhouse gases," among them methane from rice paddies and cattle flatulence; and nitrogen oxides from fertilizers, combustion, and other activities.

Sometimes a page of history is worth a volume of logic. If we go back just 100 million years ago, during the age of the dinosaurs, the temperature was about 10-14° F warmer than today. About 65 million years ago, the dinosaurs became extinct. We once assumed that the extinction was caused by a gradual cooling brought on by the oncoming Ice Age, but the theory of choice among scientists now is that the climate change was more sudden, brought about by the dust from a huge meteor impact. Whether the change was sudden or gradual, the dinosaurs didn't make it; the climate got colder, the mammals survived, and the primates, eventually including homo sapiens, evolved.

Agriculture and civilization began in the warming interglacial period that started about 15,000 years ago. Paleontologists tell us we should be on the verge of another Ice Age; therefore, shouldn't we expect the earth to be getting colder, even though it's not?

ON NOT REALLY KNOWING

Summing up the worst dilemmas of our discipline, one of my colleagues posted a cartoon on his office door: two worried men pace the executive suite, as one concedes to the other, "It's really still too early to know if it's too late to do anything about it." Global warming is like that—as is pollution of the oceans, coral reef bleaching, and, until recently, the deterioration of the ozone layer. We are still not really sure what we are seeing, and by the time we can be sure that the effect is there, that there really is damage from pollution and unsound use of resources, it will be much too late to reverse that effect and save ourselves and that sector of our planet. On the other hand, we must be very wary about acting *without* being sure of the effect. When we have only suspicions, an untested logic, and computer projections to go on, we may be able to justify advancing hypotheses and scheduling symposia in the annual conventions of learned societies—but can we justify suspending economically beneficial activities, throwing people out of work, and damaging the economic infrastructure of whole regions, solely on computer-projected horror scenarios? After all, the jobs lost are real, and the poverty endured for lack of them is very real, but the computer's fantasies are not, certainly not yet. Where putatively preventive measures cause no disruption, of course they may be recommended. But may we sacrifice the real present welfare of real people for the future possible welfare of future possible people? What ethical obligations obtain between metaphysically disparate generations?

JIM HANSEN BLOWS THE WHISTLE

On June 23, 1988, Dr. James Hansen, Director of the National Aeronautics and Space Administration's (NASA) Goddard Institute for Space Studies, testified before the U.S. Senate Committee on Energy and Natural Resources that "It's time to stop waffling so much and say that this evidence is pretty strong that the greenhouse effect is here."[2] This testimony was given in Washington, D.C., which was always steamy in summer, but this was the beginning of a summer that was to be the hottest on record (warmer ones were yet to come) and to produce one of the worst droughts in U.S. history. There were banner headlines the next day, and many scientists were shocked at such an unequivocal statement coming from a scientist with impeccable credentials. For this was the first time that a member of the club, as it were, exhibited such candor before a public, highly visible forum. Many of his colleagues felt he had been too absolute; others agreed with him but wished that he had hedged his bets a bit, or had given more attention to the imperfections of computer climate models. Nevertheless, six years later, he is still credited as the single most effective witness—the first voice that cried out in the wilderness near enough to be heard. Jim Hansen's testimony may well be the event that raised, in the public eye, the distinct possibility that humankind is changing the planet's climate.[3]

Controversy still exists over the implications of global warming, as well as the actions that need to be taken, but they are more political than scientific. The Intergovernmental Panel on Climate Change (IPCC), comprised of 2,500 scientists from around the world, published a report in

1995, stating in essence that global warming is here and is caused, at least in part, by human activity. And in January 2001 the same panel stated that "most of the observed warming over the last 50 years is likely to have been due to greenhouse gas concentrations," and predicted "warming by 2100 to range from 1.4° C to 5.8° C [approx. 3–10° F]."[4] Although nothing will ever quiet all the doubters, these reports, probably as much as anything else, has solidified the mainstream scientific opinion on this subject.

MORE EVIDENCE OF WARMING

Since Jim Hansen's warning, evidence has been pouring in that the planet is warming, possibly at a scary rate. A report by the scientists at the University of Massachusetts and the University of Arizona, using analyses of recorded temperatures, tree rings, sediments, and ice cores, concludes that the planet's northern hemisphere has been warmer during the past century than at anytime during the last thousand years.[5] Michael E. Mann, one of the authors of the report, conceded that there were some uncertainties in the data for the earlier years, yet found the "current warmth . . . unprecedented . . . The numbers for 1998 are so unusual. They push it up to the ballpark of 99% certainty that 1998 is the warmest year in the reconstruction." But others, at the Lamont-Doherty Earth Observatory, found some flaws in the study.[6]

Nevertheless, the trend continued into 1999, when November was the warmest ever in the contiguous 48 states since record keeping started 105 years ago. The temperatures there, as well as in Europe and Asia, put 1999 with 1998 as "the two warmest years on record." These data from the National Climatic Data Center are especially interesting because, while 1998 was influenced by the warming effect of El Niño, 1999 was under the cooling effect of La Niña. The latter sparked predictions of considerable cooling in 1999 compared to 1998. It didn't happen. Now, analysis of the yearly data indicates a warming rate over the last 25 years that is double that of the 20th century average.[7] Along the same line, Thomas R. Karl (also of the National Climatic Data Center) posits that the "sharply rising temperatures" of the last quarter of the last century, especially the last 10 years, "may mark a 'change point' in the rate of global warming." He cites a rate of growth of warming *prior to* the last 25 year as being 1.5° C per century, whereas the rate of the *last 25 years* has been 2° C per century. He concludes that there is only a 5% chance that the rate will stay at 2° C per century—it is much more likely that it will go to 3° C per century. But Tom Wigley at the National Center for Atmospheric Research dismissed this calculation as "quite an interesting little statistical analysis."[8]

Despite these and other quite compelling statistics, not all the "Doubting Thomases" of global warming have been convinced. One of their most effective pieces of ammunition has been the discrepancy between temperature measurements at the earth's surface and by satellite. Analysis by James K. Angell at the National Oceanic and Atmospheric Administration describes the differences as measured *by balloon since 1958* as follows:

Rate of temperature increase at the surface = 0.14° C per decade

Rate of temperature increase in the atmosphere = 0.10° C per decade

But since satellites have been used to measure the temperature, over the last 20 years, the discrepancy has grown to:

Surface rate of increase = 0.14° C

Atmospheric rate of increase = 0.4° C

The difference has been explained as the result of the air at the surface and in the upper atmosphere responding differently to events such as volcanoes, El Niños, La Niñas, and so on that have occurred over the last 20 years; yet the nay-sayers continue to point to the satellite data as proof that no warming has occurred.[9]

Other skeptics claim warming as a purely urban phenomenon, but National Climatic Data Center meteorologists have found the average temperature in rural areas to be same as in urban settings, showing an 0.8° C increase since 1880.[10]

PREDICTIONS AND VARIABLES

The predicted consequences of global warming are, by now, pretty well-known:

Flooded coastal areas due to melting glaciers and increase in ocean volume (the world's island nations are the most vociferous advocates of reducing greenhouse gases; 25% of the world's population live less than 1.1 meters above sea level);

Increased frequency and severity of storms (are we living it?); Droughts, heat waves, changes in precipitation causing floods (are we living it?); Increase in tropical diseases in temperate zones due to migration of insect vectors; Changes in ecosystems, species extinctions due to changes to habitat;

Bleached coral reefs (we are living it);

. . .and so forth.

But predictions and forecasts about climate are difficult, some say impossible, because of its complexity and natural variability. For example, the data for the late-1990s is certainly complicated by the El Niño and La Niña effects on temperature. Also, consider the consequences of positive feedbacks, such as warmer temperature = more evaporation = more water vapor (potent greenhouse influence) = more warming. D. Rind, in the journal *Science* comments, "Climate, like weather, will likely always be complex: determinism in the midst of chaos, unpredictability in the midst of understanding."[11]

However, evidence is mounting. Coral reefs are bleaching around the world. One of the healthiest reefs off the Dutch Island Bonaire, near Venezuela, is now bleached; and the International Society for Reef Studies has found the "most geographically widespread bleaching ever recorded", and has observed coral reef bleaching "all over the Caribbean."[12]

And ecosystem changes are being noted, in terms of populations and behavior of species:

> Frog populations are declining in Costa Rica;
>
> 59 bird species in southern Britain have changed their range;
>
> 34 butterfly species in Europe have changed their range;
>
> The Mexican Jay in Arizona has an earlier breeding season;
>
> Michigan wolf and moose populations are in decline; and
>
> Reindeer, moose, deer, and caribou populations are declining in Canada, Norway, United Kingdom, United States and Greenland.

Additionally, there are reports that disease in the oceans is increasing, "from sardines to seals."[13]

Of course, the trick is to prove that these events are caused by an increase in greenhouse gases and resultant warming, rather than by naturally occurring events. One lab experiment does support coral bleaching due to carbon dioxide buildup, as increased concentration of the gas resulted in slowing their growth, thereby making them more vulnerable to other threats.[14]

One of the most influential studies about the consequences of global warming to the United States was released in June 2000. The study, commissioned by Congress, was conducted by scientists from government agencies, universities, private organizations, and industry; and had 300 independent reviewers. Predictions included Atlanta summers in New York City and Houston summers in Atlanta, increased crops in some farmlands and decreased in others, decreased salmon migration, less snow in California, increased storms and coastal erosion, and a longer shipping period in Alaska for lanes stay open.[15]

Nevertheless, many uncertainties remain, says Thomas Karl, cochair of the committee of experts: "We don't say we *know* there's going to be catastrophic drought in Kansas. . . . What we do say is 'Here's the range of our uncertainties.'" Indeed, one climate model used in the study predicted drier soil in the Midwest over the next century, another predicted wetter soil.[16]

An even more recent study by a geologist at Texas A&M found that only 25% of the temperature increase since 1900 can be attributed to natural causes. The rest "can be attributed to human influences, particularly to rising levels of carbon dioxide and other . . . greenhouse gases that come from the burning of fuels and forests."[17] How politicians and policy makers respond to these studies remains to be seen.

WHAT'S GOING ON AT THE POLES?

Climatologists have long predicted that global warming would be most evident at the Poles, and the data have supported that. Antarctica (South Pole) has gotten the most attention over the years, presumably because it was already in the public eye due to the yearly appearance of the "ozone hole" (more than 50% ozone depletion due to manmade chemicals during the Antarctic spring—but that's another story. See *Watersheds II*). And sure enough, while the global average temperature has increased by more than 1° F since the Industrial Revolution, the average temperature in Antarctica has risen 5° F in the last 50 years.[18] Large chunks of ice have been breaking off glacial shelves over the last decade (including one in 1998 that was as large as Rhode Island). Such events do not affect sea level rise, because these ice masses are already in the water, but the West Antarctic Ice Sheet is considered unstable, and this could break into the ocean, the thought of which causes grave concern about sea level rise and coastal flooding.[19]

Changes in the Antarctic scene are not limited to ice cover, however. In the last 25 years, the Adelies penguins have declined from 15,200 breeding pairs to 9,200. Their prey, as well as the prey of whales and seals, is krill, the larvae of which live at the bottom of the ice. The loss of krill due to diminishing ice could wreak havoc to the food chain that goes from algae to krill to penguins, seals, and whales.[20]

Meanwhile, at the North Pole (the Arctic), the ice is getting thinner and the water warmer. An old-hand Arctic researcher is reported to have exclaimed, "Oh my God where did all the ice go?" when his research vessel arrived at the expected ice latitude. It should have been at 71 to 72° N, and they didn't see it until they reached 75° N.[21] NASA Goddard Space Flight Center reports that the Arctic sea ice has declined by more than 5% between 1978 and 1998. One concern, as an example of positive feedbacks, is the ice albedo feedback, the reflection of sunlight by the ice. With melting ice and more exposed ocean, the oceans absorb more of the light and warms accordingly, affecting currents, weather, and increasing the melting.[22] Another concern is the "Arctic Oscillation," pressure changes over the North Pole that result in increased winds, which tend to break up more ice. John Wallace, a meteorologist at the University of Washington, predicts that if the trend continues "we may be on the verge of an ice free Arctic Ocean in the summer."[23] A number of observers doubt that the Arctic changes can be due to natural causes. One states that the probability of the ice decrease being caused by natural variability is less than 2% for the last 20 years; another found that the chance of ice loss since 1993 being of natural origin is 0.1%.[24]

MISSING WARMING, MISSING CARBON DIOXIDE, CARBON SINKS

From the beginning of global-warming awareness, there have been discrepancies between the amount of carbon dioxide we produce through burning fossil fuels, the amount of carbon dioxide in the atmosphere, and the amount of warming that should have been produced because of the accumulating greenhouse gases.

Given the amount of carbon dioxide and other greenhouse gases that we pump into the atmosphere, there's been very little observed atmospheric warming—only a little more than 1° F. Climate modelers have hypothesized that much of the warming has been trapped in the oceans, but that's hard to prove. Now, a definitive study of millions of ocean measurements taken over many years has demonstrated that the world's ocean basins have warmed an average of 0.06° C between 1955 and 1995, close to the increase that had been predicted. These findings imply that that heat stored in the oceans will eventually reach the atmosphere, perhaps resulting in an increase of the upper level of predictions to 4.5° C by the year 2100.[25]

And where has all the carbon dioxide gone? One estimate is that less than half the carbon dioxide emitted by human activity remains in the atmosphere; the rest is stored either in the land or the water. There is evidence that land use in the U.S. accounts for the absorption of between 10-30% of our emissions. The amount of carbon that is stored on the land becomes important in terms of international agreements to reduce emissions; for example, if we plant more trees, do we get credit for reducing emissions?[26]

ENERGY

The global warming controversy, if it is that, boils down to energy use; and energy use, at least in the United States, boils down to the automobile. Carbon dioxide is the greenhouse gas that is the greatest contributor to increased atmospheric temperature; carbon dioxide comes from burning fossil fuels such as petroleum; gasoline comes from petroleum; and the gasoline that fuels our cars accounts for a large part of our being the largest greenhouse gas emitter in the world.

The "Partnership for a New Generation of Vehicles" was formed in 1993. Its goal was an 80 mile-per-gallon automobile, produced by the "Big Three" auto makers, with federal aid. Unfortunately, the 80 mpg goal appeared to be unrealistic just as Sports Utility Vehicles, with their 13-17 mpg efficiency, became popular. Meanwhile, Toyota produced a gasoline/electric hybrid that gets 50-60 mpg that's on the market now. The "Big 3" now predict a prototype efficient car by 2004.[27]

Although the U.S. automakers seem merely to be paying lip service to the goal of more efficient automobiles and using alternative fuels (Detroit continues to fight environmental regulations at the same time that they research electric, hybrids, and fuel cell vehicles),[28] but the rest of the world is moving ahead. Among other differences, most industrialized countries pay dearly for a gallon of gas, as compared to the United States. As of March 20, 2000, the cost per gallon in the following countries was:

Britain: $4.66

France: $4.06

Germany: $3.93

United States: $1.71

Gary Ross, the CEO of the PIRA Energy Group, comments on U.S. gasoline use: "Because of this addiction . . . Americans drive almost 50% more than Europe [sic], and its cars are less efficient. . . . It has cost the United States dearly . . . Europeans have long driven cars so small and so fuel thrifty that they would be laughed off the American road by any self-respecting owner of a Sport Utility Vehicle."[29]

As with the automobile industry, U.S. energy companies fall behind their counterparts in other industrialized countries. Although renewable energy sources are getting more attention here since the deregulation of energy markets, we're still way behind other countries. Germany and the Netherlands have been researching renewables for decades, but the United States just got started in 1973, and then had research funds slashed in the 1980s. More recently, the Senate cut 20% of the budget for renewable energy research and development. Japan spends three times as much as we do on solar photovoltaic cell research, and Germany has captured one-third of the world's wind powered energy growth.[30] For comparison, the United States spends, as a percent of net sales, the following for research and development in selected sectors:

Drugs: 10%

Transportation: 6%

Chemicals: 4%

Energy: less than 1%[31]

But there are some bright lights on the horizon, even the U.S. horizon. John Turner believes that even though the United States consumes 50%

of the world's energy, and even though converting to renewables "would require a change in U.S. production and consumption," it is possible. He presents a plan that demonstrates the "ability of photovoltaic technology alone to provide all the energy needs of the United States."[32]

On the other hand, the European goal of cutting greenhouse gas emissions includes limiting any temperature increase to 2° C, and limiting carbon dioxide emissions to a doubling of what they were in preindustrial times. According to Steve Fetter in the *The Bulletin of Atomic Scientists*, this would require much greater reductions in fossil-fuel use than even contemplated now, as well as an increase in carbon-free energy sources by 10 times from now to 2050.[33]

We are moving, albeit slowly, in that direction. The trend in the United States is towards lower carbon emissions per unit of energy produced—since 1950, we have halved the amount of carbon produced per unit of energy—but with increased population and economic growth, energy use increases, and so on, our carbon dioxide emissions continue to increase.[34]

Perhaps the most encouraging sign came from an advertising supplement appearing in the *New York Times* on June 19, 2000—Robert Shaw, a venture capitalist, predicted a hydrogen-based (noncarbon) global economy 20 years hence.

GLOBAL GEOPOLITICS: THE U.N. CONFERENCES

The U.N. Conferences on Global Climate Change, started in 1992 at Rio de Janeiro, and continued in 2000 in The Hague, have all featured some general common denominators:

1. Various pledges by nations to cap or reduce carbon dioxide emissions according to various formulae;

2. Pledges to "meet again" at given dates, to resolve disagreements (as opposed to a general throwing up of hands in disgust, and just giving up on any international effort to control global warming);

3. Managing conflict between the "North" and the "South"; in other words, industrialized nations versus developing nations, with the United States accused by many of being the biggest "foot dragger." Industrialized nations (excepting the United States) have generally been willing to accepting binding controls on carbon dioxide emissions, but also expected pledges from developing nations for future action on emissions. Developing nations, however, have held firm on no binding commitment until they see *action* on the part of the industrialized nations (especially the United States). Lurking in the background is the industrialized nations fear of population growth

combined with economic development in the South; thus causing them to look for some commitment to population control;

4. The U.S. Congress expressing adamant objections to any binding commitment without developing nations cooperation, making any signing of documents meaningless, given virtually no hope of Senate ratification;

5. Some disagreements among industrialized nations as to the consequences of reducing carbon dioxide emissions; with some nations seeing economic opportunity in developing energy efficient technologies, while others, especially the United States, predicting economic disaster accompanying any reduction in burning fossil fuels;

6. General agreement that funds should be created to help poorer nations develop energy efficient technologies, and that such technologies should be shared.

Specifically, at the Kyoto, Japan conference in December 1997, industrialized nations (overall) were required to drop carbon emissions to 5.2% below 1990 emissions by 2012. This created a furor among some U.S. senators,[35] as well a comment from the Global Climate Coalition, an industry group, that "business, labor and agriculture will campaign and will defeat the treaty if it is submitted to the Senate for ratification."[36]

Commentary from other constituencies was more diverse. Malawi's Minister of Finance and Environmental Affairs stated that the poor "are being asked to do more than our fair share to clean up."[37] Jerry Mahlman, of Geophysical Fluid Dynamics Laboratory noted, "Even if Kyoto cuts are observed, they "won't prevent total greenhouse emissions . . . it might take another 30 Kyotos over the next century to cut global warming down to size."[38] And the President of Navru, a small atoll in the South Pacific, warned that if action wasn't taken by industrialized countries to prevent global warming (and thus sea rise), his country would face "a terrifying rising flood of biblical proportions", and that "willful destruction of entire countries and cultures would represent an unspeakable crime against humanity"[39]

Meanwhile, while diplomats dither, Costa Rica, Honduras, Nicaragua, Belize, and Panama have become "emission entrepreneurs," and Argentina has pledged compliance with emission controls.[40] Since Kyoto, British Petroleum announced plans to reduce emissions and invest in solar energy, Toyota has produced a hybrid car, and Denmark is producing 8% of its electricity from wind power.[41]

The fourth Conference of the Parties to the United Nations Framework Convention on Climate Change met in late 1998 in Buenos Aires, during which details on compliance, flexibility, reporting, and other issues were discussed, and plans were made to meet in 2000 in The Hague to hammer out unresolved issues. These include using carbon sinks (such as planting trees) for credits towards reducing emissions, and counting a transfer of energy efficient technology from rich nations to poor nations as a reduction of the rich country's emissions—both issues favored by the United States.[42]

At least we're talking.

QUESTIONS FOR REFLECTION

Which of the following do you think are appropriate responses to the threat of global warming?

+ Get all nonelectric automobiles off the road
+ Require all power plants to cut emissions to zero
+ Significantly upgrade emissions controls on all automobiles
+ Encourage industries to collaborate in seeking ways to lower emissions
+ Nothing; there's nothing we can do about it anyway.

Defend your answer.

Notes

1. William K. Stevens, "Song of the Millennium: Cool Prelude and a Fiery Coda," *New York Times* (9 March 1999): p. F5.

2. Richard Monastersky, "1998: Warmest Year of Past Millennium," *Science News* 155 (20 March 1999): p. 191.

3. William K. Stevens, "1999 Continues Warming Trend Around Globe," *New York Times* (19 December 1999).

4. News Item, *Science* 291 (26 January 2001): p. 566.

5. William K. Stevens, "Song of the Millennium."

6. Richard Monastersky, "1998: Warmest Year."

7. William K. Stevens, "1999 Continues Warming Trend."

8. T. Hesman, "Recent Heat May Indicate Faster Warming," *Science News* 157 (4 March 2000): p. 148.

9. Richard Monastersky, "Weather Balloons Deflate Climate Blow-up," *Science News* 156 (4 September 1999): p.150; "As Globe Warms Atmosphere Keeps It Cool," *Science News* 157 (22 January 2000): p. 53.

10. Richard Monastersky, "Global Warming: No Urban Myth," *Science News* 155 (13 February 1999): p. 107.

11. D. Rind, "Complexity and Climate," *Science* 284 (2 April 1999): p. 105; Richard Monastersky, "Fickle Climate Thwarts Future Forecasts," *Science News* 155 (27 February 1999): p. 133; and Richard Kerr, "Big El Ninos Ride the Back of Slower Climate Change," *Science* 283 (19 February 1999): p. 1108.

12. Janet Raloff, "Sea Sickness," *Science News* 155 (30 January 1999): p. 72; and "Whiteout," *Scientific American* (April 1999): p. 30.

13. Ibid.

14. Richard Monastersky, "Carbon Dioxide Buildup Harms Coral Reefs," *Science News* 155 (3 April 1999): p. 214.

15. Andrew C. Revkin, "Warming's Effects to Permeate U.S." *New York Times* (12 June 2000): p. A1.

16. Richard A. Kerr, "Dueling Models: Future U.S. Climate Uncertain," *Science* 288 (23 June 2000): p. 2113.

17. Andrew C. Revkin, "Study Faults Humans for Large Share of Global Warming," *New York Times* (14 July 2000): p. A12.

18. David Helvarg, "On Thin Ice," *Sierra* (November/December 1999): p. 38.

19. Richard Monastersky, "Disappearing Ice Down South," *Science News* 155 (24 April 1999): p. 271; and "Plumbing Antarctica for Climate Clues," *Science News* 156 (27 November 1999). (For detailed discussion of the West Antarctic Ice Sheet, see Michael Oppenheimer, "Global Warming and the stability of the West Antarctic Ice Sheet," *Nature* 393 (28 April 1998): p. 325.

20. Henry Fountain, "Two Gigantic Icebergs Break Free from the Antarctic Ice Cap," *New York Times* (11 April 2000).

21. Richard Monastersky, "Sea Change in the Arctic," *Science News* 155 (13 February 1999): p. 104.

22. Ibid.

23. Richard A. Kerr, "A New Force in High-Latitude Climate," *Science* 284 (9 April 1999): p. 241.

24. "Skating on Thinning Ice," *Science* 286 (3 December 1999): p. 1813; Richard A. Kerr, "A New Force in High-Latitude Climate," *Science* 284 (9 April 1999).

25. Richard A. Kerr, "Globe's 'Missing Warming' Found in the Ocean," *Science* 287 (24 March 2000): p. 2126.

26. Christopher B. Field, and Inez Y. Fung, "The Not-So-Big U.S. Carbon Sink," *Science* 285 (23 July 1999): p. 544.

27. Glenn Zorpette, "Waiting for the Supercar," *Scientific American* (April 1999): p. 46.

28. Will Nixon, "Back to the Future," *The Amicus Journal* (Fall 1999): p. 17.

29. Edmund L. Andrews, "At $4 a Gallon, Finding Joy on the Road Not Taken," *New York Times* March 24, 2000.

30. Kathryn S. Brown, "Bright Future or Brief Flare—for Renewable Energy?", *Science* 285 (30 July 1999): p. 678.

31. Robert M. Margolis, and Daniel M. Kammen, "Underinvestment: The Energy Technology and R and D Challenge," *Science* 285 (30 July 1999): p. 690.

32. John A. Turner, "A Realizable Renewable Energy Future," *Science* 285 (30 July 1999): p. 687.

33. Steve Fetter, "Energy 2050," *The Bulletin of Atomic Scientists* (July/August 2000): p. 28.

34. William K. Stevens, "Global Economy Slowly Cuts Use of Fuels Rich in Carbon," *New York Times* (31 October 1999).

35. Janet Raloff, "Nations Draft Kyoto Climate Treaty," *Science News* 152 (20 and 27 December 1997): p. 388; Joseph Room et al., "A Road Map for U.S. Carbon Reductions," *Science* 279 (30 January 1998): p. 669.

36. William K. Stevens, "Kyoto Meeting Moves Closer to Agreement to Cut Greenhouse Gases," *New York Times* (10 December 1997).

37. Calvin Sims, "Poor Nations Reject Role on Warming," *New York Times* (13 December 1997).

38. David Malakoff, "Thirty Kyotos Needed to Control Warming," *Science* 278 (19 December 1997): p. 2048.

39. Seth Dunn, "Can the North and South Get in Step?", *Worldwatch* (November/December 1998): p. 19.

40. Ibid.

41. Christopher Flavin, "Last Tango in Buenos Aires," *Worldwatch* (November/December 1998).

42. Joanna Depledge, "Coming of Age at Buenos Aires", *Worldwatch* (November/December 1998): p. 53.

The Extended Family
The Saga of the Great Apes

QUESTIONS TO KEEP IN MIND

In what ways are the great apes like us? In what ways are they different?

What is the biggest threat to the great apes at this point?

What means are available to us to preserve the great apes in the wild?

BUSHMEAT

"In a clearing in the jungle of the Congo river basin," Laura Spinney writes, "local hunters hold an illegal market twice a month with workers from a nearby logging concession to trade bushmeat for ammunition, clothes and medicine. Among the carcasses that change hands are chimpanzees, gorillas and bonobos (pygmy chimpanzees), all of which are protected species."[1] That is not the only market. All over the tropical forests of West and Central Africa, Latin America and Asia, increasing numbers of commercial hunters are slaughtering the primates, especially the great apes, for food and also for export. Conservationist Jane Goodall, the world's foremost expert on the chimpanzee, has stated that unless this hunting is stopped, "In 50 years there will be no viable populations of great apes left in the wild."[2]

It is not easy to tell people in poverty not to hunt monkeys and apes. They are traditional food in Central Africa, and to the hunters, "They're just animals."[3] A hunter will get $60 for an adult gorilla, and a full-grown chimpanzee would bring almost as much. (Since gorillas bring a better price than chimpanzee, chimpanzee meat is often sold as gorilla.) Concerned observers in the area often have reservations about the practice, but end by defending the hunting. As David Brown of the British government's delegation to the Convention on Trade in Endangered Species put it, bushmeat is "a major component of the economies of much of equatorial Africa. It is a primary source of animal protein and the main export commodity for the inhabitants."[4] He therefore thinks that the "industry" should be "managed, not stigmatised and criminalised."

Hunting is now a greater threat than habitat loss to ape populations already strained to the breaking point. "The World Wide Fund for Nature estimates that there are no more than 200,000 chimps, 111,000 western lowland gorillas, 10,000 eastern lowland gorillas and 620 mountain gorillas left in the wild." With respect to bonobos, their "numbers are thought to have halved in the past 20 years. . . ."[5] Why has the hunting of primates increased so dramatically, especially in Africa? In all probability, the hunting is triggered by the African population explosion of the last 20 years, which has increased the density of human population all through the forest and countryside, and left a hungry population in the burgeoning cities. In Congo and Cameroon, for instance, the pygmies used to eat anything that moved in the forest with no fear of impacting the species: there was one pygmy per 10 square kilometers, and with their poisoned arrows, at that density, they could do no real harm. They would probably do no harm at ten times that density, at one person per one square kilometer.[6] But now there are many more people than that, not only pygmies but participants in the new extractive industries.

The trigger for the crisis was clearly the logging industry. In efforts to pay off their debts and develop their nations, West Africa governments have contracted with foreign companies to log the remaining rainforests. According to Jeff Dupain of Belgium's Royal Zoological Society in Antwerp, the companies usher hunters into previously inaccessible forest land when they make the logging roads; they "make it easier for hunters to get to the wildlife and transport carcasses back to towns, often using the loggers' lorries and boats."[7] Worse yet, as it happens, is their technique of driving roads deep into the bush to divide the forest into sectors to be worked. Where the forest is fragmented, the ability of a forest species to reconstitute itself after hunting is severely compromised, probably destroyed. As if to ensure the maximum destruction of wildlife, the companies issue the loggers rifles ("to protect themselves"), and don't send in enough food, expecting the workers to live off the land.[8] In one logging camp alone, in one year, according to a report released by the Wildlife Conservation Society, more than 1,100 animals were killed, totaling 29 metric tons.[9] The hunting of wild game is three to six times higher in communities adjacent to logging roads. The WCS estimates that the annual harvest of bushmeat in equatorial Africa exceeds one million metric tons.

In 1998, a coalition of 34 conservation organizations and ape specialists called the "Ape Alliance" estimated that in the Congo, up to 600 lowland gorillas are killed each year for their meat. While the initial exchanges of that meat take place in the bush, the bulk of the meat is sold in the cities. The railway station at Yaounde, the capital of Cameroon, houses a bushmeat market that does not close; one ton of smoked bushmeat, largely chimpanzees and gorilla, is unloaded there on a daily basis.[10] It is no secret. "It's a 500-foot stretch of sidewalk only a few blocks from the presidential offices and the $200-a-night Hilton Hotel...." Behind the antelope stalls are "piles from which long arm bones protrude, obviously those of chimpanzees and gorillas. At the fetish stalls, you can buy chimpanzee hands, gorilla skulls, round slices of elephant trunk or the bright red tails of endangered gray parrots."[11] (If you boil the finger of a gorilla, the people believe, and add the water to the baby's bath, the baby will be strong like a gorilla.)[12] Thousands of chimpanzees are killed each year. Chimpanzees reproduce at the rate of one baby every four years, gorillas usually more slowly than that. The apes do not have the reproductive capacity to bounce back from this kind of assault.[13]

There can be no doubt of the West's reaction to the facts as we have discovered them. A World Wide Web query on the subject of "bushmeat" yielded "about" (the search engine's word) 2,170 entries in .17 seconds, and every single one of them linked to an organization determined to stop the slaughter and protect the apes. In April 1999, the same month that the WCS report came out, 28 organizations and agencies, led by the Jane Goodall Institute, came out with a major statement on the protection of the apes. The consensus statement enumerated the measures that would have to be taken immediately if the apes were to survive, calling on educators, governments, and corporations in general—especially the logging, mining, and other extractive industries—to take immediate action to protect the apes.[14] A year later, the situation had not improved. Writing in the *Washington Post*, Jane Goodall estimated that the number of chimpanzees had declined to 150,000 from the million and more when she began her chimpanzee research in 1960.[15] Six months later, the 2500 delegates to an eight-day environment meeting in Amman, Jordan, ended with a request to the World Conservation Union (IUCN) to put all possible pressure on governments to take steps to curtail the trade in bushmeat. By that time the hunting was "a commercialised industry where automatic weapons have replaced bows and arrows," an industry worth $350 million a year in Ghana, $121 million annually in the Ivory Coast.[16] The directors of the represented environment groups talked grimly of "strong conservation solutions" that had to be adopted immediately.[17]

Yet there is clearly no unanimity with the developing world. The sense of revulsion that attends the contemplation of the market in ape hands and fingers, shared by so many in the nations of Europe and North America, is obviously not shared by the hunters, the loggers, or even by the African and Asian governments nominally in charge of the hunting grounds. How come we feel it? Before we go any further with this controversial subject, let us take a closer look at the great apes and see if we can discover first who these apes are, and from that, possibly, the source of our conviction that the bushmeat harvest is fundamentally wrong.

THE QUARRY IN THE GREAT BUSHMEAT HUNT

Who are the great apes? At one point, a variety of species of large tailless apes lived in large numbers in equatorial Africa and Southeast Asia, but those populations have been reduced to fragmented pockets. As above, we count the individuals in the four remaining species in the hundreds and the thousands, knowing that the number is so low that a new virus could wipe out them all. In our generation, we may see the end of the wild apes. What are they—quick, before they are gone?

First of all, as we all know, they are our relatives. Furthest from us in the family are the "lesser apes," the gibbons (*hylobates*) of Southeast Asia, who show amazing dexterity and acrobatic skill, but who are distinguished from monkeys only by their tendency to walk upright. The "great apes," our closest relatives, are the orangutan, the gorilla, and the chimpanzee. We'll take a quick look at them, and then go on to the enormous ethical dilemma they pose for us.

The Orangutans (*Pongo Pygmaeus*), native to Borneo and Sumatra, live in solitary splendor in the canopy of the Asian rainforest, from which they rarely descend to the ground. They are not bipedal (disposed to walk on two feet) at all, tending toward the bibrachial—their major mode of locomotion is swinging through the trees. Males are about twice the size of females, and have overlapping territories of about 40 square kilometers. They do not tolerate each other, and tend to harass and kill any males they meet in the course of their day's foraging.[18] In the wild and in normal times, they have little use for humans. These are not normal times. Their habitat has been invaded by war, agriculture, and logging; their numbers were down to 20,000 in 1992, and are much smaller today. They will not survive, even now, without human help. According to a *National Geographic* report on orangutans published in August of 1998, the apes may reproduce only once in an eight-year interval; the mothers nurse their infants for about six years, and older siblings can hang around for several more years. As habitat shrinks, male violence increases, and the death rate of males rises. The prospects for the survival of the species in the wild are not good.[19]

The African apes are closer to us. The bonobos (*pan paniscus*), native to central Congo, are simply smaller chimpanzees, recognized as a separate species only since the 1930s. The chimpanzee (*pan troglodytes*) is probably our closest relative, sharing 98.5% of our DNA. (Does that make the consumer of bushmeat 98.5% a cannibal? Karl Ammann would contend that indeed it does.[20]) The gorilla (*gorilla gorilla,* as named by a biologist fresh out of imagination) is the largest of the apes; the male averages 400 lbs. None of the apes are truly bipedal, suggesting to some anthropologists that bipedalism made the 1.5% difference between the ape and the human; the mechanisms by which the change occurred are still under scrutiny.

The extensive similarities between us and the apes raise serious moral questions about the great bushmeat hunt. The chimpanzees, for instance, use tools. They extract termites from their mounds with straws and sticks, and they crack nuts with hammers. They pick out "anvils," depressed knotholes of harder wood where a nut can be positioned securely; find "hammers," pieces of hard wood or stones for the tougher cases; bring their piles of nuts to the anvils; and start hammering.[21] The behavior is in no way instinctive. It is learned, taught to each new generation by the last. Further, it is cultural; in different areas, different groups of chimpanzees have learned different ways of cracking nuts, and use different tools to catch termites.[22] The gorillas, for another example, live in foraging tribes much like our own hunting-gathering forebears, where dominant males protect and lead the troop and gentle females painstakingly rear their widely spaced infants. The chimpanzees hunt in groups; the gorillas forage in family tribes. They communicate complex messages; we do not know how. Language, as we know it, is impossible for them because of the placement of the structures of their throat; they cannot guide air over a voicebox as can we. But they can learn language: chimps have been taught American Sign language, lexigrams, and token languages. They can communicate with us when we are willing to use these languages, not at any high intellectual level, but at least at the level of a young child.[23]

How do we know what we know about the apes? Because of their similarities to us, they have attracted many of the best students to observe and inform us of their ways. Louis Leakey, the great anthropologist of early humanoids, specifically sent three of his best students to study the apes.

The careers of those students—all women (Leakey thought that women would develop better rapport with wild apes)—are instructive. "Leakey's Angels," as they were called, followed identical paths. They went to the apes to study them, to advance the science of zoology by collecting and publishing data on these fascinating animals. Later graduate students came to join them, also to study. Then, as they became alarmed at the pressures on the habitat and on the numbers of their "subject matter," they turned their emphasis to public education, hoping to influence more enlightened policies that would be to the long term benefit of both animals and humans. Then, caught up in the campaign with an inevitability explained best by that 98.5% identity, they became advocates for their subjects, set up orphanages and hospitals for the surviving victims of the bushmeat and black market rare animals trade. By this time, they had dropped all pretense of seeing them only as beasts. They had taken up their posts to study the apes, but they stayed to protect them.

Dian Fossey, who chose the mountain gorillas, achieved the dubious and quite unexpected fame of martyrdom. She arrived in Africa in 1963, determined to study the mountain gorillas of Rwanda. With the support of Louis Leakey and financial help from the National Geographic Society, she set up permanent residence in the Karisoke Research Center in Rwanda in 1967. During her 18 years of studying the mountain gorillas at Karisoke, she became, effectively, a part of a gorilla group. She was able to watch youngsters be born, grow, mature, and become responsible adults in the group; one of her favorites, Digit, became a head of a family as she observed. Then Digit was killed by poachers (his head taken as a totem, his hands cut off to be made into ashtrays), and Fossey was galvanized into action. She wrote a book, *Gorillas in the Mist,* to popularize her cause, and turned her research center into a refuge as she became a crusader for the cause of protection of the gorillas. Eventually she made herself disagreeable enough to be killed (in 1985) by the poachers whose prey she was trying to protect. The story made a good read, and the scenery was dramatic, so in 1987 a movie was made of her book to track her career and (not incidentally) to publicize the cause of protection of the animals who had become her friends. It is through that movie that most of us know of her.

Birute Galdikas, possibly the least known of the Angels, chose the most remote setting for her work—Borneo, one of the last habitats of the orangutan. She met Leakey in 1968, and with his support and that of the National Geographic Society she set up a research camp in Borneo (Camp Leakey, of course). She has been there ever since. In 1995 she published her autobiography, *Reflections of Eden: My Years with the Orangutans of Borneo,*[24] which describes her education, scientific career, and the establishment of Camp Leakey. By then the camp had become not so much a research center as a refuge, where wild orangutans, rescued from the poachers, are rehabilitated and integrated eventually back into the wild. With a coauthor, she published another book in 1999, rich with photographs of the orangutans, for the sole purpose of raising money for her center.[25]

But for the dramatic movie about Dian Fossey, Jane Goodall, who has spent 40 years studying the chimpanzees in Gombe National Park in Tanzania, would surely be the best known. Goodall spent the first 30 years following a midsized group of chimpanzees as they hunted, socialized, and squabbled on a mountain within the park. Eventually, they got used to the zoologist following them around, and she was able to document their lives in some detail. As she studied she wrote, and presented to the world a picture of omnivorous and versatile personalities of animals very like ourselves; it was she who first documented the use of tools and the possibility of culture among the chimpanzees.[26] She went through the same mutations as the others: from spending time in Africa to study the chimpanzees, she now spends most of her time on the lecture circuit trying to raise money for them.

Goodall also brought us the most startling and disturbing revelations about the lives of the great apes. She had studied the chimps for years, raised her child among them, and learned their social structures, customs, laws, as well as the distinct and quirky personalities of the troop she chose to follow. But then she sent in new and alarming reports, this time of psychosis among the chimpanzees. A female who had no infants of her own started to steal infants from weaker females. Since she could not care for them, she ate them. Others started accompanying her on her kidnap raids, and begged infant flesh for themselves. A terrible pattern of psychotic murder and cannibalism played itself out before Goodall's eyes, hitherto unseen in the animal world. Apparently the behavior had a physical origin, and stopped when the female herself became pregnant.

Worse yet were the implications of vicious intergroup violence. After many years of group living, her troop split, a small band of them taking up residence on the other side of the mountain. Then the smaller group began to die off, one by one, killed by some beast or beasts. Troubled, Goodall began closer observations to see what was killing them. To her surprise and horror, she found that the killers were groups of raiders from the other half of the group. Chimpanzees were attacking other chimpanzees, in a way that she had never seen. Violence was not unusual among the chimpanzees: males often fought each other for dominance in the group. But in those ordinary conflicts, no one died (or got seriously hurt). In these new conflicts, the victim always died, or was left for dead. The attacks were planned, organized, and directed for maximal effectiveness, isolating a single member of the victim group and ambushing him. The strongest chimps led the attack; youngsters followed along and gleefully pounced on the victim when he was almost dead.

There was no reason for the attacks. There was no rivalry over food—there was plenty for all on both sides of the mountain. There was no rivalry over land, females, or any other goods. There was no threat (except to the victims after the raids started). There was no question that the hunt and the killing were deliberate: the night before a raid, the raiding party would take up their positions in a tree near the normal territory of the other group, and spend the night in very untypical silence. The hunt itself would be carried out silently, clearly in order that the victim might not have warning to get away. It was deliberate killing of another of their own species and acquaintance, for no reason but that he was of a different group. It was, in the words of one observer, a clear case of genocide. And the killers clearly enjoyed it, very much.

Far from challenging the conclusion above, the psychotic and genocidal behavior reinforces it: the great apes are all too human, alarmingly human. Their lives are much like ours in our foraging period, 30,000–50,000 years ago. Their families are much like ours. They sin. They have rituals of forgiveness for individual sin and are totally unconscious of group sin. They are just like us. When we look into the eyes of the ape, we look at our own not-so-distant past.

Is it that fact primarily that grounds our conviction that we must somehow protect the apes from slaughter? For we are so convinced; as of October, 2000, even the tightfisted U.S. Congress had voted $5 million for the Interior Department, "to use for grants to organizations involved in efforts to protect the great apes."[27] On what is our conviction based? Where, ethically speaking, are the apes? There are different, and occasionally incompatible, ethical grounds advanced for our determination that they must be protected. We will take these up in what follows.

APES IN THE WILD: THE PRESERVATION OF ENDANGERED ECOSYSTEMS

In the objections to the uses of apes for meat, one of the first points always noted is that apes, as species, are "protected." What is this "protection"? What is the rationale for "protecting" species?

First, let us be clear that it is not the "species," in the sense of a certain pattern of DNA that is being protected—we could freeze a few tissue samples and preserve the species forever, in that sense. Nor is it, except in desperation, the individuals that we want to save. The entire ecosystem itself is always the object of conservation activity (the forest, in this case) in which the species operates. We may think of every species as a unique tract, a text from nature, a storehouse of information, infinitely valuable; each species is a chapter in the book of its own ecosystem. The species and the ecosystem evolved together and must be preserved together.

We should bear in mind that the movement to protect the great apes in the wild plays two roles, roles in tension, in the worldwide initiative to preserve the environment. The first role is as keystone of the ecosystem, the animal near the top of the food chain without whose presence the balance would not be kept. The New England ecosystem was for all intents and purposes destroyed, for instance, when for good and sufficient reason the cougars and wolves were killed or driven out. By now accustomed to the overpopulation of white-tailed deer and rabbits, and to the impoverishment of the woods and fields caused by overgrazing, we shall never know how that ecosystem functioned when it was in balance. Similarly, the tropical forest cannot be saved unless we can save it with all its species flourishing. And the danger is real: with the slow rate of reproduction of the great apes, these species are under significant threat. The second role played by the apes is as symbol of the ecosystem, much as the northern spotted owl symbolizes the redwood forest in the battle to save the giant sequoias of California's northern coast. The apes are known to gather sympathy on their own, because they are so like us, and portraying the apes as endangered will win sympathy for the effort to preserve the ecosystem, without which they cannot live in the wild. The first role is described as part of ecology, the second is frankly part of preservation strategy. When the environmentalists mix the two, the result can be ethically ambivalent.

The same ambivalence is found in the assaults on the apes. When the forest fires broke out over the West and Central Kalimantan provinces of Indonesia some four years ago, primatologist Barita Manullang, head of the World Wide Fund for Nature's Orangutan Conservation Project in Jakarta, went to Central Kalimantan to see how the orangutans were faring. The result horrified him.

> In each [village] he found a baby orangutan held in a crude cage. He knew immediately that animals' mothers were dead: a mother orangutan would never abandon her young. When pressed, the farmers in each village told Manullang the same gruesome tale. A mother with the baby clinging to its long reddish hair had fled from the nearby smoking forest into the village's gardens in search of food. Barking dogs had alerted the villagers to the presence of the animals. As the dogs attacked, farmers wielding machetes and sharpened sticks hacked and stabbed the mothers to death. The babies were taken captive—to be sold for up to $100 apiece as pets or to illicit wildlife traders. The dead mothers were skinned and eaten.[28]

The habitat problem is particularly severe for the orangutans, who are found only in the wilderness of Sumatra and Borneo. The rich tropical forest in which they make their homes provides abundantly if left alone. But agribusiness is making constant inroads on the forest, and the 1997 fires made their situation much worse. There is strong suspicion that the fires were not accidental. International proposals (including an environmental impact study in 1996) had recommended conserving 70% of the Central Kalimantan orangutan habitat as environmental reserve. But Jakarta (including President Suharto's powerful family) saw more profit in a Mega-Rice Project that would require massive deforestation of that habitat. Deforestation went forward regardless of environmental impact, and the burning finished the job. The fires drove the animals out of the woods, making life easier for the poachers, and simultaneously made e areas not worth preserving as forest habitat. Agribusiness and poachers alike profited from the fires.[29]

Yet Manullang found it difficult to condemn the small farmers who had killed the orangutans, even as contemporary observers find it difficult to condemn all killing of gorillas for bushmeat. The farmers have no choice in their approach to the orangutans. They live by subsistence farming, close to the edge of survival, and cannot afford to let the hungry apes, driven out of the forest, demolish their gardens. Indeed, the meat of the adult orangutans killed in this latest slaughter probably added significantly to the annual protein intake of the farmers.

The same ambivalence attends the situation of the Karisoke gorillas. Rwanda, neighboring Burundi, and several other central African nations have been involved in terrible civil wars, genocide (especially between the Tutsis and the Hutus, who are ancient rivals), revolutions, and military coups. The planting cycles have been disrupted, and often the people do not have enough to eat. The wars and the genocide have severely compromised the ability of Rwandans to preserve their gorillas. Their occupations wiped out, the people have had to occupy the land wherever possible, demolishing the forest for food, fuel, wood, and building materials. They have no choice.[30] How can we tell them that the gorilla's life is more valuable than their own—even if, in the grand sweep of history, it's true?

APES IN THE LABORATORY: UTILITARIAN BENEFITS AND TROUBLING CLAIMS OF RIGHT

If the chimpanzee shares 98.5% of our genetic endowment, then why does it not get asthma, rheumatoid arthritis, acne, or—especially—AIDS, even when the virus is clearly present in the bloodstream? How can the apes harbor a similar virus harmlessly? What can we learn about human diseases, now and in the future, from experimentation with these animals? There is a call on now to sequence the chimpanzee genome, and study the chimps' resistance to diseases.[31] But even now, the poachers have lowered the number of wild chimpanzees available, to the point of hindering research. With all the human benefits at stake from a multiyear study of the immune system of chimpanzees, is there no way we can keep them out of the cooking pots?

And after the uses of chimpanzees' bodies for medical research, what else may we learn from that overwhelmingly similar genome? Since the great apes can learn language, and seem to experience all emotions that we know, they may provide an irreplaceable subject for the study of language acquisition and human psychology. As above, we also find (or rather, Jane Goodall found) the same psychopathologies in the chimpanzee, even the tendency to genocide.[32] Might we not study that? We cannot do research at all on sophisticated human criminal behavior, not only because of certain problems with informed consent, but also because it becomes impossible to conceal from the subject what is being studied. Yet chimpanzees, who exhibit all the psychopathological behavior that we do, are not able to understand the hypotheses of the research. Perpetually naïve subjects, they may well be able to give us pure results about very impure behavior. Maybe, from this research, we could even learn to control it ourselves.

What limitations attend our use of the apes in the laboratory? There is a growing movement to end all animal research, or at least regulate it much more strictly. In the past, animals of all kinds have been beaten, tortured (not as part of the research but for the amusement of the staff), abused, neglected, caged without fresh air or exercise, starved, and left to die of infection in uncleaned cages. Clearly such treatment is wrong, and wrong for reasons that have nothing to do with the special qualities of the apes. We acknowledge an obligation to treat all animals *humanely*— not "humanly," but gently, so as not to cause them pain or distress. That general obligation entails at least that animals should be fed and watered properly, allowed adequate exercise and companionship, and kept in clean and well-lighted quarters. The obligation applies to our pets, dogs and cats, and to our farm animals, as well as to the monkeys and apes we keep in captivity for research or for the amusement of our children. (The imperative for the "humane" treatment of animals actually first applied to our horses, and was much encouraged by nineteenth century English books for girls, like Anna Sewell's *Black Beauty*.) The humane perspective asks only that we show mercy and consideration to creatures that share with us the capacity for pain.

Because of the history of, and propensity for, abuse, scientific research that uses animals for its subjects lies under special obligations, enforced by federal regulation. Regulation has not prevented studies of unimaginable cruelty—one of which, Thomas Gennarelli's University of Pennsylvania study on head injuries, came to national attention when the Animal Liberation Front "liberated" a particularly damaging set of videotapes from the laboratory and gave them national exposure.[33]

Some of the rules developed in the name of humane treatment grate against the scientific purposes for which the study is done. If the higher mammals are to be used for experimental surgery, for instance, and if there is a strong likelihood that the animal will be in pain should it be allowed to regain consciousness, the rules call for the animal to be humanely killed before it wakes up. It is not always possible to do that and be absolutely sure that the surgery was a success.

But humane treatment is not the only issue with the apes. With chimpanzees in particular, their very similarity to us raises questions about the way we do our research. In the major studies of chimpanzee research, especially Roger Fouts's semiautobiographical account of his life with the chimpanzees,[34] questions of right and humane treatment tumble over each other. He abhors the "prison-like" setting of most experimental labs, roundly condemns the scientists who do research for their own professional purposes, and ends up suggesting that no matter how useful it is, we ought to abandon animal research altogether.[35]

APES IN COURT: SHOULD THEY HAVE THE RIGHTS OF PERSONS?

We may grant that it is important to preserve ecosystems, for good environmental reasons. We may also grant that it is important to preserve animals that are useful for research, and to treat those animals humanely. But there seems to be more to the apes question than those provisos. In many respects, outlined above, they are *human:* they have culture, they react to suffering as humans do, they are very like us. Should apes be treated as humans? This is the final and great question.

The stories always start off the argument. Anecdotes of ape behavior continually catch us where our human sympathy lives. Eugene Linden tells us one of them:

> Twenty years ago I met a chimpanzee named Bruno. He was one of a group of chimps being taught American Sign Language to determine if apes could communicate with humans. Last year I went to see him again. The experiment is long past, and Bruno was moved in 1982 to a medical laboratory, *but he is still using the signs* . . .[36]

Encouraged by his community, as he thought, he had learned how to talk in the community in which he found himself. Then, the experiment over, his ability to talk was of no further use to the members of the group, who had never thought of him as more than an animal, so they had shipped him off to someplace where he could be used as an oversized lab rat to test vaccines or new drugs. But he still wants to talk, to communicate. He is not content with the secure and well-fed life. He is like humans, and he wants to reach out to humans as they once reached out to him. What right have we to impose such isolation?

Bruno seems human. Shall we extend to him, and to his species, the rights of humans? John Blatchford, a British zoologist, suggested as much in 1997.[37] David Pearson, of the Great Ape Project (a systematic international campaign for rights for the great apes, founded in 1993) took up Blatchford's suggestion in January of 1998, calling attention to a "paradigm shift over the past 20 years or so in our understanding of the complex emotional and mental lives of the great apes—a complexity that demands we confer the basic rights of life, individual liberty and freedom from torture on all great apes."[38] By 1999, the Great Ape Project joined the New Zealand campaign for full "human rights" to apes: to ensure that New Zealand's Animal Welfare bill contained a "clause making non-human great apes the first animals in the world with individual, fundamental rights that will stand up in a court of law: the right to life, the right not to suffer cruel or degrading treatment, and the right not to take part in all but the most benign experiments."[39] The campaign failed, voted down in the New Zealand parliament in May of that year.[40] Parliament did, however, recommend an end to all experiments involving apes except for the benefit of the apes themselves.

The campaign continues, calling for a United Nations Declaration of the Rights of Great Apes. This Declaration would include all the above rights as well as the right not to be "imprisoned" without due process. Due process? The language necessarily causes nervousness, not only among the zookeepers, but also among those who carry on research designed to protect the welfare of apes. Must they obtain informed consent in the future?

Primatologist Frans de Waal of the Yerkes Regional Primate Research Center in Atlanta argues that according rights to the apes puts us on a "slippery slope" toward the absurd. "[I]f you argue for rights on the basis of continuity between us and the great apes, then you have to argue continuity between apes and monkeys," and so on down to the laboratory rats.[41] Philosopher Peter Singer, author of *Animal Liberation,* is less worried about rats obtaining legal rights, and wonders if the slippery slope can't be tilted the other way: "[I]f you deny chimps certain rights, then logically you have to deny intellectually disabled children too."[42] Do we?

Insight magazine decided that the topic was worth a debate, and just prior to the New Zealand vote, asked Steven Wise, author of *Rattling the Cage: Toward Legal Rights for Animals,* to defend the affirmative, and David Wagner, professor of constitutional law at Regent University, to defend the negative, on the question, "Should great apes have some of the legal rights of persons?" Wagner's opposition rests flatly on the assertion that:

> Humans are nonarbitrarily different. There is a remarkable consensus of both religion and philosophy on this uniqueness. . . .Judaism was the first to proclaim that God made man in His image and that He revealed Himself to mankind. Later on, Christianity proclaimed a radical redemption for all humankind, rooted in the claim that God Himself had taken on human nature . . . Kant . . . taught that the capacity of human beings to give and demand reasons for their actions was the basis of their rights and duties. And finally, our Founding Fathers declared that the American experiment was based on certain self-evident truths, beginning with the truth that all men are created equal, that they are endowed by their Creator with certain unalienable rights. Notice the constant copackaging of certain ideas: human uniqueness, capacity for reason-giving and special divine creation.[43]

The claim is reinforced with abundant quotation from Scripture and Shakespeare.

Steven Wise rests his position on the extensive similarities between humans and great apes, and the appropriateness of including rights for apes in the wave of rights—consciousness that has come into being across the world in the last half-century. The circle of rights has expanded inexorably and irreversibly. At one point we (of Western civilization) were willing to confine political rights to a small circle of propertied white men—the "men," by the way, of the quote from Jefferson in Wagner's piece. The natural expansion now includes the whole human race, including those who have no capacity whatsoever for reason-giving. There is no inconsistency, he insists, between arguing that the great apes should be accorded certain rights of persons now, but that not every life form need be given the same rights. The ultimate limits of equal justice will have to be determined by the legal and political process as the common law and constitutional interpretation evolve. The fact that we do not know the ultimate outcome of that process does not force us to tolerate the manifest injustice of denying basic rights to beings for whom we know they are appropriate.[44]

What does it take to make a person? Note that a Rights orientation does not require "rationality," in any usual sense. Retarded persons, after all, are not "rational," and are not extended all the rights of citizenship, like the right to vote. But they still have rights, in fact, they are offered even more protections just because they cannot protect themselves as the rest of us can.

The jury is still out on the question. We should note that the question of animal rights in this sense—the question of whether the higher mammals, especially the great apes, should be accorded the rights of humans—is rarely debated unemotionally. The people who believe that apes should enjoy the rights of humans tend to get irrational in the presence of people who don't. They come on like John Brown pleading for the African Americans, like Lawrence of Arabia pleading for the Arabs, and very much like the "pro-life" faction, the foes of abortion, pleading for the lives of the unborn children. They honestly believe that they are pleading not for some special interest or loony sentimental indulgence, but for the extension in our law of rights to which these creatures are fully entitled. They will not give up, and there is a strong possibility that this may be one of the conflicts that becomes violent in the years to come.

ECOTOURISM AND RESPECT

Suppose we decide that apes are, indeed, sufficiently like ourselves to deserve human rights. What follows? Should we treat them the way we treat human beings with limited mental capacities—lock them in homes or institutions, with staff to make sure they dress in the morning, use the bathroom properly, and eat healthful food until they die? God forbid. The central right for any creature with rights is to live according to its own laws with its own community, and that surely cannot happen if we dragoon the apes into human society. (Whether or not they would survive such "care" is another question, one that need not be answered.) That central right alone entails that the apes be left in the wild and left alone, their habitat protected from infringement, and their communities respected as we would respect any human community. In short, the implications of full rights for apes are the same as the conclusions of the conservationists. We must work to preserve the forests where the apes live, we must end all poaching of bushmeat immediately, and we must structure our encounters with all the apes to reflect the respect owed persons with rights, living according to their own customs and laws.

Meanwhile, such respect will carry out the environmentalist agenda of preservation of an endangered species. For the species is complex. We do not really preserve the species by capturing sufficient numbers of the apes and putting them in safe cages to eat and breed. For the apes, like ourselves, do not exist merely as biological organisms, but as social animals under evolved systems of governance. We don't want the only apes left to be those in captivity. We want them wild, to continue to evolve, to anchor their ecosystems and to show us a unique way to live.

An agenda of leaving the apes in the forest, protecting the forest by law and enforcing that law against poachers, satisfies two criteria for sound public policy: it is environmentally beneficial and it is ethically correct. But for such policies to be truly sustainable, they need to be economically viable too. The best way to set up an industry to sustain the apes is through enabling "ecotourism," entertaining tourists who want to visit the apes in the wild. Tourists have been traveling to Africa and Asia to see the animals for several centuries, after all. In ecotourism, they do not come to shoot, but to enjoy and to learn. When ecotourism is established and running well, the tourist dollars support the local economy. For this reason it is in everyone's interest to make sure that the animals are not harmed or frightened, so that the tourists will enjoy themselves and will come back bringing more dollars. Local officials will also ensure that the habitat is protected for that reason; as above, the presence of the apes is becoming the best protection a forest could have.

There is some interest now in promoting international policies (debt relief is foremost among them) to encourage nations in the developing world to protect the remnants of the forest where apes may live. Even those who promote such policies acknowledge that under the present system of global sovereignty, it would be up to every nation to decide for itself whether development money should be put toward the protection of the forests.[45] Our experience with the governments of developing nations is not encouraging on the matter. But there is some hope.

Local experiments have worked well on occasion. Richard Ruggiero, a wildlife biologist in the Office of International Affairs of the U.S. Fish and Wildlife Service, recounts a tale of a lowland gorilla in a village in the Congo, a tale that contains many of the elements of hope and caution that attend the effort to create ecotourism. Named "Ebobo" (Ay-bobo: gorilla) by the Bon Coin villagers, this solitary male had adopted the custom of frequenting the village, especially on the trail where the children went to school. His apparent motive was curiosity, nothing more. (He was too young to challenge the older males of the area for the right to a territory and a family.) The villagers immediately called for a gun to shoot him; gorillas are regarded as very dangerous wild animals and also as very good to eat, and shooting him seemed the best course of action. Ruggiero, assigned to that village for the purpose of studying the wildlife in a local pond, spent hours—months—talking to various groups of the villagers, trying to keep Ebobo off the menu and out of the gunsights. (The gorilla had survived the first visit only because no one could find a gun.) In the end, the most persuasive protectors were the shamans who pointed out that since Ebobo was not acting like normal gorillas (who avoid human habitation as much as they can), he might well be a returned spirit of the dead, and should be treated with respect. As the villagers got used to him, problems arose of the opposite kind; they started wandering very close to him, teasing him, while the children threw stones at him to see what he would do. At equal length, and with equally patient urgency, Ruggiero had to persuade them that while Ebobo was not dangerous unless provoked, he was an accident waiting to happen if teased, and they should leave him alone. At the writing of the article, the villagers had learned to let Ebobo wander where he would, and he was doing no harm—even making his way through cornfields in a way that did not damage the crop. And the village was becoming someplace special because of the resident gorilla— someplace worth going to. That, it seems, is the minimum precondition for the success of ecotourism; it took a bit of education, but it worked.[46]

Zoologist John Blatchford points out that without the help of the local communities, no protection will work, but thinks the enterprise possible.

> A recent experiment in the Bwindi Impenetrable Forest of Uganda— home to 300 of the 650 mountain gorillas alive in 1995—has already shown how this might work. Local subsistence farmers were given limited access to the forest perimeter and allowed to harvest some sustainable resources. They were also permitted to keep their bees there and use the mineral springs. . . . In the experiment, an estimated $30,000 per year, 10% of the revenue generated by tourists visiting the park, was given to the communities living around the forest. Given that a Ugandan family of six must manage on $526 per year, the extra income to the farming community represented a great sum of money, and gave the community an incentive to protect

the revenue-earning gorillas. *These people were, in effect, being paid by the gorillas for their help in maintaining the park.*[47]

Such efforts should be conjoined, Blatchford argued, with efforts to establish protections for apes based on their rights as persons, as discussed in the last section.

Ecotourism will allow apes to stay in their wild habitats and preserve the ecosystem. It will allow, possibly, selective recruitment of individuals from prospering groups for research and possibly (see concluding questions, below) for exhibit. The respect engendered by wide experience with apes in their native communities will ensure that to the extent that they are removed from those communities, kept for display or used in research, they will be treated well. And their fundamental right—the ability to run their own communities according to their own laws—will be honored.

QUESTIONS FOR REFLECTION

+ As far as we can observe, chimpanzees recruited into traveling shows thoroughly enjoy the experience. Apes regularly associating with humans have no objections to them, and seem to enjoy the attention and company. They don't even mind being dressed up in tutus. May such practices continue?

+ As above, it would be tremendously useful to be able to continue research with chimpanzees. But how can we do this? If we must treat them as humans, they cannot give consent, so we cannot use them. We can treat them as animals, very humanely, no doubt, but they will still be forced to live in cages and suffer blood draws and strange diets and possibly odd surgeries. Is this justifiable?

+ When an infant (now known to the world as Baby Fae) was born with hypoplastic left-heart syndrome some years ago, a baboon (Goobers) was killed so that her heart could be transplanted to the infant. It didn't work, and no one has tried it since. But what if we could make it work? Would it be justifiable to kill an ape to get its heart for a child?

+ Are we under any duty to enhance the lives of the apes? If they find themselves in an environment that is not totally to their liking, what is the extent of our duty to go beyond protection to ensuring the flourishing of the community?

+ The next time the chimpanzees get genocidal, do we have an obligation: (1) to intervene, as we did in Bosnia when humans got genocidal, in order to stop the slaughter, or (2) not to intervene, in order to let chimpanzees live and die by their own laws?

✦ These are all one question, of course: are the apes really human? And how much are we invested in treating them as human? This is a question unlikely to be solved within the lives of the remaining members of Leakey's Angels.

Notes

1. Laura Spinney, "Monkey Business," *New Scientist* (2 May 1998): p. 18.
2. Ibid.
3. Donald G. McNeil Jr., "The Great Ape Massacre," *New York Times Magazine* (9 May 1999): pp. 54–57.
4. Fred Pearce, "Eating Our Relatives," *New Scientist* (29 April 2000).
5. Laura Spinney, "Monkey Business."
6. Ibid.
7. Ibid.
8. Ibid.
9. "Bushmeat: Logging's Deadly 2nd Harvest (Wildlife Harvest in Logged Tropical Forests)," *Science* (23 April 1999).
10. Ibid.
11. Donald G. McNeil, Jr., "The Great Ape Massacre," p. 56.
12. Eugene Linden and Michael Nichols, "A Curious Kinship: Apes and Humans," *National Geographic* (March 1992): pp. 1–45.
13. Ibid.
14. Jane Goodall Institute Press Release, April 1999.
15. Jane Goodall, "At-Risk Primates," *Washington Post* (8 April 2000): p. A17.
16. Patricia Reaney, "Growing Demand for Bushmeat Endangers Wild Animals," *news.excite.com* (10 October 2000).
17. Ibid.
18. Cheryl Knott and Tim Laman, "Orangutans in the Wild," *National Geographic* (August 1998): pp. 30–55.
19. Ibid.
20. Joseph B. Verrengia, "Bushmeat Hunters Push Primates to Extinction," Associated Press (23 July 2000).
21. Eugene Linden and Michael Nichols, "A Curious Kinship," p. 22.
22. Ibid., p. 24.
23. Ibid., pp. 32–33.
24. Boston: Little, Brown and Company, 1995.
25. M. Birute, F. Galdikas, and Nancy Briggs, *Orangutan Odyssey* (New York: Abrams, 1999).
26. See her account of her work, *Jane Goodall: 40 Years At Gombe: A Tribute to Four Decades of Wildlife Research, Education, and Conservation* (Ridgefield, CT: The Jane Goodall Institute/Stewart, Tabori and Chang, 1999).
27. "$5m voted to save apes," *Connecticut Post* (21 October 2000): p. A8.
28. Ron Moreau, "A Shove Toward Extinction," *Newsweek* (8 December 1997): p. 33.
29. Ibid.
30. John Toon, "Gorillas in the Bits: Remote Sensing Technology Boosts Efforts to Protect Endangered Mountain Gorillas and Rebuild Rwanda's Economy," *Research Horizons* (Spring 2000).

31. John Travis, "Human, Mouse, Rat . . .What's Next? Scientists Lobby for a Chimpanzee Genome Project," *Science News* (7 October 2000): p. 236–239.

32. Eugene Linden and Michael Nichols, "A Curious Kinship," pp. 10–45, esp. pp. 33ff.

33. A good account of these studies, and the controversy they caused, may be found in Gregory E. Pence, *Classic Cases in Medical Ethics*, 3rd Ed. (Boston: McGraw-Hill, 2000): pp. 225ff.

34. Roger Fouts, with Stephen Tukel Mills, *Next of Kin: What Chimpanzees Have Taught Me About Who We Are* (New York: William Morrow & Company, 1997).

35. He pointedly ignores the efforts of other research centers, especially the Yerkes Regional Primate Research Center in Atlanta, to improve the treatment of apes in captivity. See Deborah Blum's review of the book, *The New York Times Book Review* (12 October 1997): pp. 11–12. Interestingly, Fouts' career tracks those of Fossey, Galdikas and Goodall, from research scientist to activist on behalf of the apes.

36. Eugene Linden and Michael Nichols, "A Curious Kinship." Emphasis added.

37. John Blatchford, "Apes and Gorillas Are People Too," *New Scientist* (29 November 1997): p. 56.

38. David Pearson, "Justice for Apes," *New Scientist* (3 January 1998): p. 46.

39. Rachel Nowak, "Almost Human," *New Scientist,* (13 February 1999): p. 20.

40. News item, *New Scientist* (29 May 1999).

41. Rachel Nowak, "Almost Human."

42. Ibid.

43. David Wagner, "Should Great Apes Have Some of the Legal Rights of Persons? No: At Stake Is a Valuable Philosophical Consensus on the Uniqueness of Human Beings," *Insight* (1 November 1999): p. 41.

44. Steven M. Wise, "Should Great Apes Have Some of the Legal Rights of Persons? Yes: Chimpanzees Have Mental Abilities Similar to Young Children and Deserve Some of the Same Legal Rights," *Insight* (1 November 1999): p. 40.

45. John Blatchford, "Apes and Gorillas Are People Too."; Tam Dalyell, "Thistle Diary," *New Scientist* (24 January 1998).

46. Richard Ruggiero, "Phantom of the Forest," *Wildlife Conservation* (September/October 2000): pp. 51–55.

47. John Blatchford, "Apes and Gorillas Are People Too."

CHAPTER *5*

A Question of Responsibility
The Legacy of Bhopal

QUESTIONS TO KEEP IN MIND

Why did the factory in Bhopal suffer the explosion of toxic gas?

What did the various players in the drama seek to do about the explosion and its effects? What was their motivation?

How could the explosion have been prevented? What ought we to do to make sure that technical enterprises in developing nations are safe for the people of the nation?

DESPERATELY SEEKING WARREN ANDERSON

Warren M. Anderson, chairman of the Union Carbide Corporation during the 1984 chemical disaster at Bhopal, India, has apparently gone into hiding to avoid a summons to appear in a Manhattan federal court as part of civil proceedings against him and the company, say lawyers who have hired a private investigator to locate Mr. Anderson."[1]

As of March 4, 2000, he was apparently not at his last-known address in Florida; Union Carbide, with corporate headquarters Danbury, Connecticut, has refused to accept a summons on his behalf. (*Sierra* helpfully published a "Wanted" poster of him in their July/August 2000 issue.)[2]

The first time the public met Warren Anderson, then CEO of Union Carbide Corporation, he was on an airplane on the way to India. Two nights before, on December 2, 1984, a pesticide plant in Bhopal, India—built by Union Carbide Corporation, and run at that time by Union Carbide India Limited (UCIL)—had sustained a monstrous explosion. Forty tons of methyl isocyanate (MIC) gas had blown up, releasing into the air surrounding the plant a lethal mixture of MIC, hydrogen cyanide, monomethyl amine, and carbon monoxide, among other chemicals.[3] The figures are still in dispute and will probably remain so, but an estimate in March, 2000 put the dead at 3,000 and the injured at 200,000.[4] Anderson could not have known the figures as his plane approached the airport, but he knew that many had died, many were injured, and he had announced immediately that the company took full moral responsibility for the disaster. The victims would be compensated. He brought with him on this trip authorization from his Board of Directors to commit from $1 million to $5 million in cash immediately to help the victims, and to find out what further was needed to remedy the damage.

It was not to be. Anderson was arrested by the Indian authorities as he stepped off the plane, taken to a company guest house and put under house arrest. He was charged with murder, "culpable homicide." He was not allowed to speak with the victims, nor with his managers from the plant, nor was he allowed to offer help in public. Promised interviews with the governor and the prime minister never materialized; not even the environmental minister would talk to him. In a few days he was put back on a plane, still not allowed to talk to anyone, and sent home.

The next months must have been a nightmare for Union Carbide's management.[5] They addressed the problem as directly as they knew how, placing the resources of half the company on the trail of the explosion, to find out how it happened, how such an explosion could be prevented in the future, and what might be done to remedy the damage done by it. Warren Anderson personally took charge of this investigation. It was very difficult, since they had to reconstruct the route of the reaction through hypothetical scenarios at a distance. It was many months before they were permitted to visit the plant (it had been closed off as a "crime scene" by the Indian equivalent of the FBI) or interview the workers. Not until July were they permitted to go to the wreckage of the exploded tank to take out the core samples of sediment that would show them how the explosion occurred. Not until then could they determine that only a deliberate act of sabotage could have caused it.[6] Incidentally, the UCIL managers on duty the night of the explosion had claimed at the time that the blast was the work of a saboteur. They later retracted that assertion.[7]

What ever happened to Warren Anderson? After the investigation was complete, he saw the resulting litigation, and the negotiations with the Indian government, through to the end. Litigation and negotiations took on a strange significance in the case. The lawyers came from America within days of the explosion to represent the victims in lawsuits that they had every reason to believe would be very profitable. International ambulance-chasers of the stripe of Melvin Belli, John Coale, F. Lee Bailey, and eventually Stanley Chesley claimed only that they wanted to represent the helpless widow and orphan, to make sure that the poverty-stricken victims got what was due them. But their plans to take 30% of each of the awards, or at least as much of that as they could persuade a judge to allot them, were openly mentioned and discussed from the time they laid foot in India. First on their own behalf, going from door-to-door persuading the poor of Bhopal to sign retainers appointing them as attorneys, and then (after the Indian government took over that role) in the efforts to persuade the Indian government to hire them as their representatives in the American courts, the lawyers had mentioned sums beyond anyone's imagination: millions for the victims, billions for the government. They were taken all too literally, and the inflated expectations they imported into the situation made the later negotiations that much more difficult.

But the lawyers had an important role to play. It is certain that if American lawyers had not brought the victims' cause to the fore, no one else would have. No Indian lawyer, or indeed the Indian government, showed real interest in compensation for the victims until the American lawyers arrived.[8] In a telling comment to the press soon after his arrival in India, Melvin Belli explained why he wanted the cases tried in the United States: ". . . in court, you don't appreciate the dignity of a man as much as we do."[9] By "dignity," he meant worth: worth as an autonomous individual, worth as a human life, and worth in court in terms of monetary compensation. (Kant to the contrary notwithstanding, "price" and "dignity" are not incompatible in a court of law.) For this is India, "steeped in poverty, apathy, corruption, and greed, an India that, while laudably dedicated to democratic freedoms, still judged the value of a life by the kind of work a person did."[10] And where tort law is concerned, that judgment is crucial. Tort law is undeveloped in India, for "compensation for injuries" is not a matter of fundamental right in a place where injuries occur so often to so many.[11] "Since there are no civil juries in India, judges determine liability and damages, and they are not overly impressed by calamities that kill thousands and simply punctuate the rough rhythm of survival in India."[12] According to all sources, India is not the place for a tort action on behalf of the poor. The poor are expected to accept their lot. Victim and judge both agree that most injuries are a matter of fate and could not have been avoided, and in any case, the value of what was lost—scraps of property, time, health, limb, life—is so small in the social reckoning that the suit is hardly worth the lawyer's effort. Until the Americans arrived, and talked of infinite money, no one else was talking about the infinite value of a human life. (And why should not the value of an Indian life be just as infinite as the value of an American life?)

Litigation began, initiated by teams of lawyers who wanted to represent the victims in damage suits against Union Carbide before U.S. District Court Judge John Keenan, to whom the multifarious suits had been assigned. Their object was to have the cause tried in the United States, where the money was better. On May 12, 1986, Keenan ruled against them on the grounds of *forum non conveniens* ("this isn't the right place to do this"), and sent the collected lawsuits back to India, on grounds that that was where the accident was, as well as the victims, witnesses, documents, and applicable laws. The decision did not sit well with the lawyers, who appealed all the way up to the Supreme Court before accepting that they would have to deal with India.[13] The decision was a significant advance in the case. First, it put the proceedings back where they belonged. Second, the court ordered that Union Carbide should have access to victims, ex-employees of the closed plant, and to documents in the case (including the plant logs) so that they might prepare their defense. It was in those interviews that Union Carbide eventually pieced together the sequence of events that preceded the explosion. Third, the judge instructed Union Carbide, along with the lawyers, to accept the jurisdiction of the Indian courts until the case should be settled. Most significantly of all, the judge accepted $5 million from the company for relief for the victims. That was the first money actually to leave the United States to go to the victims.

And until the final settlement, on February 14, 1989, that was the last money they would see. During the litigation, the victims received nothing. At no time during those years was Anderson permitted to renew his offer of immediate aid, in the millions of dollars, for the victims. By February 1985, three months after the blast, the Union Carbide Employees' Bhopal Relief Fund had collected over $100,000 for the victims, but had no one to give it to. That April, India again rejected "out of hand" any comprehensive settlement. The efforts continued. Union Carbide built a Vocational Training School at Bhopal to relieve the poverty of the area; when the Indian government found out who built it, they closed it. Arizona State University then built a rehabilitation center for the injured with $2 million of UC money. "The center was built, and operating well, but when the state government found that Carbide money had funded it, bulldozers were sent in to knock the building down."[14] Every nonprofit intermediary was contacted to convey UC money to the victims, including the Red Cross and Mother Teresa; all had more political sense than to get in the middle of the dispute, and turned down the money.

The litigation on behalf of the victims lost much of its steam when it was ordered back to India, and the rest of it when the Indian government invalidated all the cases and took over litigation on behalf of the victim. Finally, three years later, when the Indian government realized that they were not going to extract from Union Carbide the billions and billions promised by the American lawyers in the first flush of chasing the international ambulance, they settled, on Valentine's Day in 1989. Judge R. S. Pathak of India's Supreme Court directed a final settlement of all Bhopal litigation for $470 million (reputedly more than Carbide's last offer, but less than the $500 million they were willing to pay if they had to).[15] The amount had to be paid by March 31, 1989; in fact, it was paid at the end of February.[16] The terms of the settlement included the vacating of all "criminal charges" against Anderson and any other individuals, and release of Union Carbide from any further liability with regard to the accident.[17] By the time of the final settlement, Anderson had already resigned from the Board of Directors and retired. He was not available for comment after the settlement, and everyone thought he had gone to Florida.

THE CORPORATION IN INDIA

Why was Union Carbide in India to begin with? What is methyl isocyanate, and why was it considered worth manufacturing, despite its known tendency to explode and kill people under certain circumstances? And given such a lethal chemical, was it right to maintain the relatively low level of security that permitted the sabotage to take place? Could the incident have been prevented?

Despite its American name, the company whose gas exploded into that lethal cloud was largely Indian-owned, and completely Indian-operated. It had been founded (as a branch of the American corporation) almost 50 years ago to provide pesticides for India's agricultural "green revolution"; the plant at Bhopal dated from 1969.[18] There was nothing exotic or extraordinarily dangerous in the operation of its plants; the most common kind of pesticide produced in them was carbaryl, an ester of carbamic acid, a reliable and relatively safe product, marketed in the United States under the brand name SEVIN.[19]

Yet there is no doubt that the chemicals employed in the process of making the pesticide are dangerous. Phosgene, the deadly gas briefly used in World War I on the battlefield (and also in the gas chambers of the Third Reich) is a precursor of SEVIN. The process used by UCIL for its manufacture uses phosgene ($COCl_2$) and a methyl (CH_3) amine (NH_2) to produce the intermediate compound methylcarbamoyl chloride ($CH_3NHCOCl$). The latter compound breaks down with heat into MIC and hydrochloric acid (HCl). Methyl isocyanate (CH_3NCO) is a variation of the cyanide group $(NCN)^{-2})$ of which the highly poisonous hydrogen cyanide (HCN) is probably the most famous. MIC is extremely unstable and dangerous, and as such is not ordinarily studied in a laboratory situation. Its boiling point is 39° C. (102.4° F) Lighter than water in liquid form, but heavier than air in gaseous form, it hugs the ground when released. Its breakdown products include carbon dioxide and stable amines (organic compounds of carbon, hydrogen and nitrogen), but the process releases a vast quantity of heat (exothermic). It reacts violently with water (producing breakdown products and high temperatures), whether it's water that enters the MIC storage tanks or the water in human tissue. Therefore it is an extremely dangerous human poison—and there is no known antidote.[20] OSHA regulations allow human exposure at 0.02 parts per million (ppm) over an 8 hour period, irritation is felt at 2 ppm, and becomes unbearable at 21 ppm.[21] 5 ppm will kill 50% of an experimental rat population (LD50)[22]. Of course, no one measured the concentration of the escaped gas at Bhopal, but as 50,000 pounds of it escaped,[23] the heart of the cloud must have greatly exceeded those limits.

The MIC is then used as an intermediate in the production of SEVIN, which is considerably less poisonous than its chemical precursors.[24] But why make the pesticide in India, in the middle of a dense colony of people, instead of some remote area in the United States, from which the relatively safe finished product could be exported? Because it made a lot of sense to put pesticide plants in India instead of manufacturing the SEVIN in the United States and exporting it: transportation costs (and dangers) were eliminated, and labor costs were a good deal lower in India, making the whole operation safer and more profitable as far as Union Carbide was concerned. It also provided tax revenues and very good jobs in a chronically depressed economy. Indeed, the Indian governments sought, welcomed, and catered to those American companies that were willing to locate plants in their large and needy country. The land on which the plant in question was built was given to Union Carbide by the Indian government for an annual rent of $40 per acre, as part of the plan to bring industry into the area. (Bhopal is the capital city of Madhya Pradesh, the largest and one of the poorest states in the nation.) At the time of the accident, there were 14 Union Carbide plants in India. Ownership was divided; half of the enterprise was owned by UC, the Indian government held about 25% of the stock, and the rest was held by Indian citizens.[25] The management of the plant was wholly Indian; the last American employee had left the Bhopal plant in 1982.

How had a wholly American plant become half-owned and wholly managed by Indian nationals? Since the plant had been established, popular attitudes toward Western enterprises had changed radically, in India and in much of what was then called the Third World. What economic interest had invited, political nationalism now despised. At the time of the accident, UCIL's Bhopal plant was widely seen as an American intrusion into the Indian economy, an outpost of foreign colonialist capitalist greed in a sovereign state. In practice, the divided ownership and consequent division of responsibility for the safety of the plant—the Americans responsible for the design, the Indians responsible for implementation—fostered an attitude of complacency and unconcern for the details of the safety arrangement, and of mutual suspicion for decision-making authority. Those attitudes predict the inexcusable inattention to safety lapses[26] before the explosion and the tragic chain of events that followed the explosion: recriminations, litigation, continuing political hyperbole, threats of further litigation—and no relief at all to the actual sufferers.

Union Carbide is not the only American multinational corporation to experience a reversal of the welcome mat. What, really, is the obligation of an American corporation in such situations? For purposes of this telling of the story, the major concern is with environmental safety and the possibility of environmentally disastrous industrial accidents, which is the domain of the Health, Safety, and Environment Department of the corporation (other accounts might examine only the profitability of such arrangements, and reach different conclusions). When nationalism insists that the plant must be run by national managers, and Americans can no longer exert the kind of control that may be necessary to ensure safety, are they obligated to withdraw the whole operation?

THE EXPLOSION: ACCOUNTS AND RESPONSIBILITIES

How did the explosion happen? When Anderson touched down, no one knew. There would be no evidence until investigators were allowed to search the scene and analyze the chemical residues on the bottom of the wrecked tank. The investigators found, among other junk in the tank, chloroform ($CHCl_3$). That was a contaminant; it should have been removed by distillation earlier, but could not be, due to a higher than normal temperature in the still (the refrigeration unit was broken).[27] The initial heat of the reaction had come from the simple interaction of water and MIC, an intensely exothermic reaction. But it was the chloroform that provided the chlorine ions that attacked the steel lining of the tank, which in turn released the iron ions that acted as a catalyst for what the chemists call "trimerization," (three molecules of MIC reacting with each other to form a more complex molecule), a reaction that is even more exothermic. MIC, usually held at 20° C (ideally at 4.5° C) finally reached 120° C.[28] By now, of course, the MIC had boiled (vaporized), and the pressure blew the tank, releasing a cloud that covered 40 square kilometers. None of the safety devices had worked, and the emptying of the huge tank—and the resulting devastation—was inevitable.[29]

The simmering hostility that had led to the transfer of control over the plant burst into open warfare after the accident. Why, after all, did it take the Indian authorities so long to get money to the victims? The answer seems to be a combination of politics and calculation. On the political side, much advantage seemed to be flowing from portraying Union Carbide as "murderers," who had knowingly foisted a terribly dangerous operation on an unsuspecting community.[30] The political players were soon competing with each other in hyperboles of condemnation and blame of the company, in scornful rejection of any proposed settlement as a tiny fraction of what was really owed, and in posturing as saviors from the unimaginable dangers of anything the company might ever again do with regard to Bhopal. For instance, in what may have been the supreme act of cynicism in the entire Bhopal affair, Arjun Singh, Governor of Madhya Pradesh, created, from whole cloth, a full-blown panic in Bhopal when UC Vice President Van Mynen led a technical team in on December 18, 1984, to convert the remaining MIC to SEVIN (the safest way to dispose of it). Singh urged residents to evacuate the town if they could, but pledged that he personally would guarantee that these "murderers" would do no harm during this routine operation, by personally ordering the appropriate safeguards—which included shutting down all the schools and colleges, which were in the middle of examinations. He then announced that wet cloths would be draped over all the fences, a tent of wet cloths would be erected over the MIC tank, and continually sprayed with water, and, just to make sure, "Indian Air Force helicopters would hover overhead and periodically spray the plant with water."[31] The conversion operation was perfectly safe; but in the panic, more lives and much more property were lost. In such an atmosphere, who would dare sit down at a negotiating table with Union Carbide, and presume to talk about a "fair" settlement?

On his return from India, Van Mynen led the technical approach of UC's response to Bhopal—the effort to determine just what had happened. By mid-March the scientific team had determined that the reaction had been triggered by a large volume of water, confirmed in July when they were able to obtain core samples from the plant. By August they had determined, as above, that the only way that water could have got into the tank was by a deliberate act. They had no access to human sources of information until the Government of India sued Union Carbide for damages later that year. The court action allowed them to request the records from the factory, which the U. S. District Court (S.D.N.Y.) ordered India to make available to them in November. In December, 1985, they obtained access to the logs of the plant, and immediately noticed a pattern of change and falsification[32]; that pattern was confirmed when they were finally, almost a year and a half after the incident, permitted access to plant employee witnesses.

Three obstacles hindered the fact-finding through interviews. First, after a year and a half, given that the plant was now closed and all employees laid off, simply finding the employees on duty that night, and persuading them to talk to the UC investigators, was a major task. Second, for those only peripherally involved in the incident, memories fade, a sense of what was really relevant dissipates, and accounts must be reconstructed slowly and patiently through the sifting of countless details. But third, those very partial accounts, the accounts given by those only slightly involved in the incident, once reassembled, turned out to be the most reliable sources of information, for the most centrally involved parties had a tendency to lie. Ashok Kalelkar, one of the members of the investigating team, describes the team's experience during the interviews:

> . . . as the interviews with the operators and supervisors directly involved progressed, it became apparent that there were massive contradictions in their stories. For example, operators and employees from other units and another plant downwind of the MIC unit, together with some MIC operators, reported sensing small MIC leaks well before the major release occurred, and they notified their shift supervisors. However, those Bhopal plant supervisors denied hearing any reports about earlier leaks. In addition, the supervisors were unable to plausibly account for their activities during the 45-minute period prior to the release. They placed themselves with people and in locations for reasons that were entirely different from those that had been given by those individuals they were supposedly with.[33]

Why the discrepancies? Apparently, to cover up the fact that several of them, contrary to instructions, had taken their tea break together. The other discords in the logs and in the interviews, too, can be explained all too readily as consistent attempts to place the person giving the account as far away from the scene as possible, or as completely ignorant as possible, as long as possible, of any trouble brewing.[34]

Early in the interview process, they found confirmation for the causal explanation they had deduced from the core samples. An instrument supervisor from the plant, otherwise not involved in the explosion, had surveyed the area of the tank on the morning following the explosion, and found that a pressure gauge had been unscrewed from the tank and was missing. That would explain how water got into the tank. Further, a hose normally used for cleaning was still attached to the faucet not far from the tank, and water was still running out of it. That would explain the source of the water.[35] Apparently further investigation uncovered the name of the employee who had performed this senseless act of sabotage. He had recently been, or was about to be, demoted, and he was angry. He surely had no intention of causing that kind of explosion. His family probably lived nearby. But he knew water would ruin the batch, and that's what he intended to do. Union Carbide investigators quietly turned their information over to the local authorities. In the light of what was occurring around them, they cannot have been surprised that those authorities paid little attention to it.

Meanwhile, a long time had passed, and the journal readers of the world had accepted a totally mistaken theory of the causation of the accident. Unlike UC officials, journalists had full access to anyone they could find to talk to, and they brought their own agendas. Journalists love a story. They want it to be exciting and they want it to be true, and if the two conflict, the exciting at least gets a shot at acceptance. Above all, they want it fast, and they settle on their conclusions quickly, for deadlines await at home. These imperatives of journalism worked against UC and the truth in the complex aftermath of Bhopal. Isolating all UC spokesmen from the Indian press ensured that unlimited speculation would rule the "background" stories. "It is remotely possible," de Grazia pointed out (writing less than a year after the incident), "that the research facility [on the factory grounds] was being used or intended for use to test the chemical warfare potential of MIC or to develop other chemicals that would be hazardous in themselves or when compounded. Indian journalists have raised such issues, and have found a large audience receptive to the theories."[36]

More bothersome than these fantasies was the early acceptance, prior to exhaustive investigation, of the theory that simple worker negligence was the cause of the water entering the tank. For months, the account of the incident faulted a missing "slip blind" for the explosion. (The slip blind, a circular disc inserted in a pipe while it was being washed, was supposed to isolate the piping being washed to keep the water from leaking backwards past the valves into the tanks of chemicals.) The first report issued by UC (March 1985), for that matter, was noncommittal about the source of the water that would have been needed for that reaction to take place, and noted that the slip blind appeared to be missing.

In this period, theories jostled for news-magazine space. The amount of water necessary to trigger that reaction became a serious question, as was the timing of the entry of the water. The Indian investigating team hypothesized that only a small amount of water would be necessary to cause the reaction via a different chemical route (and therefore it could have easily been an accident), while the Union Carbide team hypothesized that 120 to 240 gallons of water must have entered the tank, and that it was a deliberate act.[37] Additional questions arose as to the amount of time necessary for the reaction to produce the temperature necessary to corrode the steel tank and release the catalytic iron ions. If, as one Union Carbide manual had described, it took more than 23 hours, the saboteur would have to have allowed the water to enter the tank the day before (and presumably be found out). Union Carbide stated that if the large amount of water they hypothesized had entered the tank, there would have been a reaction in two hours.[38]

At this point, journalists had every reason to accept the "accident" theory and to suspect the "sabotage" theory. An analyst who followed Union Carbide for 10 years for the First Boston Corporation, Anantha K. S. Raman, when commenting in April, 1985 on Union Carbide's conclusion that the cause of the disaster was sabotage, said it was "a carefully orchestrated attempt to influence the upcoming legal hearings."[39] By August, however, when they had been able to obtain core samples, UC realized (and proved) that the sheer amount of water needed to cause that kind of reaction could not have come from leaks from pipe-washing. (There were many other reasons to reject the slip blind or "water-washing" theory.[40]) But two years later, when access to plant workers for interviews had spotlighted the missing pressure gauge, and made the cause of the accident quite clear, some journalists still defended the slip blind theory. They were apparently (with Raman, above) still under the impression that UC's legal responsibility for the accident would be lessened if it were established that the water had been introduced to the tank deliberately.[41] But even after the legal issues were resolved, the battle continued, suggesting that some quantity more ephemeral, more symbolic, than money was involved. For in the Fall of 1989, after the battle was over and the settlement paid, a seminar at Bentley College, in Waltham, Massachusetts, took up the topic again. Ronald Wishart, Union Carbide's Vice President for Public Relations, asserted in answer to a question that the company would never reveal publicly the name of the employee who had committed the sabotage. The reasons for his refusal were reasonably clear. The Indian government has forgotten, or pretends that it has forgotten, that any police report was made at the time, and will not back up any accusations UC brings now. To mention the ex-employee's name is simply to invite more lawsuits for libel and emotional injury and heaven knows what else from the outraged accused, with his government and a claque of industry detractors to back him up, and nothing but legal expenses and more negotiated awards in the offing. Wishart expressed a firm desire not to reopen the case. Yet the controversy continued, in the seminar and beyond.[42] With the legal case out of the way (despite political rumblings at the time about the new Indian government wanting to set the verdict aside and try for a higher one), the focus of the critics was clearly moral responsibility, not monetary awards.

Let us examine the possibility. Would UC's responsibility for the accident be less if a disgruntled employee tucked a garden hose into the hole left by a removed pressure gauge, than if a careless janitor slopped water back through a pipe missing a slip-blind? There is some part of us that would say that it would: that in the case of the leak from the water-washing (involving faulty valves and the like) "the plant" was to blame primarily, and the careless worker only secondarily; that in the case of sabotage, the perpetrator of the act was to blame, and it was no more than a regrettable shame that no one caught him at it. That part of us tunes easily to the criminal law and the *mens rea* ("guilty mind," or intent to do wrong) that, except in rare instances, is necessary for the existence of a "crime." Responsibility in the criminal law thus rests on the guilty saboteur himself, and on no one else. In cases of ordinary negligence, no one is held to be "guilty" (although the negligent tortfeasor may have to pay the bill for the damages), and it is psychologically easier to blame the surrounding circumstances, in this case the factory, for whatever happened.

But from the perspective of the civil law and Union Carbide, there is no distinction between responsibility in the one case and in the other. In both cases, we have sloppy procedures (careless washing and omission of the slip blind versus no security around a tank full of dangerous chemicals), and bad personnel practices (inadequate training and supervision of the washer versus inept handling of an employee demotion), both of which are culpable deficiencies in the plant management. Besides, UC had been prompt to admit full responsibility for the disaster; it remained only to establish what the actual, real, damages were, and they would be paid in full. So why did the controversy continue?

We seem to have a case here of deflected anger—anger at the rich nations who have the money and do not share it generously with the poor, anger at all Americans who suffered no injury when the accident occurred, and finally anger at the whole system that placed the insecticide plant in Bhopal to begin with. In the next section we will widen the Bhopal inquiry to include a brief examination of the activities of multinational corporations generally in their dealings with environmentally sensitive materials. In the final section we will review what, ultimately, the Chemicals Manufacturing Association (now the American Chemistry Council) decided to do about it.

THE VARIETIES OF MULTINATIONAL CORPORATE ACTIVITY

In the light of the story so far, it is tempting to conclude that as far as India is concerned, the entire affair is no more or less than an opportunity to shame the United States before the world and to extract billions in reparations to be spent as India, not Union Carbide, will choose. That conclusion reduces the whole affair to a spiteful contretemps between the two most self-righteous nations in the world, a vindictive and emotional conflict entertaining to the core. One wants to put up bleachers for the spectators.

But that reduction will not do, and not only because it leaves out the victims. The decisions that went into the planning of the enterprise, the decision to put the plant in India, the whole rational context in which the issues arose, need serious examination. Those questions fall into two categories. The first category is that of management responsibility. What are the complex moral obligations incumbent upon multinational corporations in dealing with other governments, international nongovernmental organizations (NGOs), and their own corporate offspring on foreign soil and operating according to foreign corporate cultural rules? Pursuit of this fascinating question would take us far afield of the environmental objectives of this essay. We are primarily concerned with the second category, of the environmental impact of corporate decisions. The questions raised in this section concern the decision to manufacture large quantities of this sort of pesticide. Ironically, for these purposes, the explosion was a good thing. It brought the question to our attention and required that we address it.

The questions arising from Bhopal have to do with the existence of that plant in the first place, and our alleged reliance on "development strategies that are inherently violent, manipulative, and wasteful."[43] (They may, ultimately, be part of a larger question, on technological civilization generally, on how we can use our most modern and ingenious developments in ways that will not turn upon our fellows and destroy them,[44] but that question is beyond the scope of this chapter.) It is hardly surprising that chemicals formulated to kill other species will also kill our own. Is there no other way to feed ourselves than by slaughtering all species that eat the same food we do? If we must keep insects, and rodents, at bay to ensure an adequate harvest, are there no alternatives to the use of deadly chemicals? On the plausible hypothesis that those chemicals are poisoning the soil in the long run, are they not doing more harm than good? Should we rethink our mass industrial approach to agriculture—the chemical-dependent "factory farm"—and see if we can find more environmentally friendly ways to get our food? All these questions emerge in the wake of Bhopal, calling our attention to the need to reconsider our stewardship of the land.[45]

For Bhopal is not alone. The pesticide industry is global big business, worth billions of dollars per year, all aimed at killing the insects, molds, weeds, and rodents that compete with the crops for sun and water, or compete with us to eat them. Our own large-scale farms have become dependent upon them. In the Third World, pesticides are an essential part of the "green revolution" that was expected to feed the hungry of the world. In Africa alone, pesticide use quintupled between 1976 and 1986.[46] When a major corporation moves into the pesticide trade in the Third World, immediate questions of influence arise: "By 1974, a decade before the Bhopal tragedy, for example, Union Carbide was marketing its products in 125 countries, 75 of which had smaller economies than the corporation."[47] Often the multinationals, of all nationalities (the United States is not alone, either), used or were suspected of using very substantial financial muscle to persuade cabinet-level officials of the developing nations to allow the establishment of chemical plants in rural areas.[48]

And once these plants are established, the scenario for poisoning is inevitable. Weir quotes a United Nations official who did not wish to be identified:

> Even those companies that say they will maintain the same standards as in the developed world find it difficult to resist the temptation to take a shortcut. Even if they have a good design for their plant, however, there's no good infrastructure in the underdeveloped countries. Even if they put it away from population centers, who will check and control that the people don't come in around it?[49]

Jan Huismans, the United Nations Environmental Program (UNEP) official who maintains the IRPTC (International Registry of Potentially Toxic Chemicals), takes it from there:

> In Africa, for example, they start with a little planning and try to locate these plants outside a populated area. But in no time, these cities grow and the industrial areas are engulfed by population settlement, surrounded by shantytowns. Also, there are no adequate waste disposal facilities for these plants. There is a lack of awareness generally about how dangerous pesticides are. There's a lack of skilled regulatory personnel and controls. There is, in sum, a whole syndrome of problems.[50]

It is what we have come to call the Bhopal Syndrome.

SOME QUESTIONS TO THIS POINT

The Bhopal case is informative because this is an ecodisaster of the first magnitude—a tremendous environmental event, clearly caused somehow by human beings, which has caused enormous amounts of environmental damage and human suffering. How do we assign responsibility in such cases? Who is responsible, and how do we judge them? Case writers have assigned blame and responsibility; let us take some key points and sift through our reactions.

First: how do we allot responsibility for operating the Bhopal plant when nationalism insists on local control?

Second: Part of the problem is public perception. Why did Anderson go to India, and why was he arrested?

Third: The victims needed the most aid right away. Who is responsible for the delay in aid getting to the victims?

Fourth: What role was played by the media? To what extent were the media manipulated?

We may never be able to assign responsibility for the Bhopal case. There are so many issues of foreign policy and political posturing involved here that it is very difficult to assign responsibility in any clear way.

THE INDUSTRY'S "NEVER AGAIN"

Bhopal was not the first disaster to strike the chemicals industry. Following the discovery of large quantities of toxic wastes in an abandoned chemicals dump at Love Canal in Niagara Falls, a wave of unfavorable publicity had inspired the U.S. Congress to pass legislation designed to get the dumps cleaned up and make the chemicals industry pay for it (the Comprehensive Environmental Response Compensation and Liability Act [CERCLA], commonly known as "Superfund"). In an unusual move for any trade organization, the Chemicals Manufacturers Association (CMA)[51] decided to face the problem squarely and do something about it. In June, 1983, the outgoing chairman of the CMA, Bill Simeral of DuPont, presented the Association with a challenge:

> In recent years we have witnessed one sensational media story after another in which our products have been depicted as direct threats to the safety of people and the environment: PCB's, saccharine, fluoro-carbons, formaldehyde—the list goes on. The problems of haz-ardous wastes and abandoned dumps have almost become syndicated features in many newspapers.[52]
>
> The result has been a veritable phobia in the public mind—a near universal "fear of chemicals."
>
> Public relations and advertising campaigns have their place, but what the public really wants is concrete action.
>
> What should we do? *To start, we can clean up the dumps.* It doesn't matter whether your company or mine has anything to do with a specific site. We are all being tarred with the same brush . . .
>
> What the public needs to understand—and what we have to continue to remind ourselves—is that the chemical industry represents the major resource of technical capability that the country has for dealing with this problem. . . . I'm convinced that the best way to get the job done is for us, wherever feasible, to organize the cleanup ourselves and execute it ourselves. . . .[53]

In the following year, the CMA took the unusual position of favoring the reauthorization of Superfund, on grounds that the project could better be completed in cooperation with the Congress than in opposition. So through 1984, Simeral's successor, Louis Fernandez of Monsanto, testified in favor of the Superfund, and offered the services of CMA experts on technical matters before the Committee. Just as that debate was winding down, the plant in Bhopal blew up. Edward Holmer, Fernandez's successor as president of CMA, took the position that the crisis was not UC's alone, but affected every one of the CMA's members. So in 1985 he assembled a committee, a special-purpose study group, and embarked on the task of a response to Bhopal. From this work, the initiative now known as Responsible Care eventually emerged.[54]

The most obvious flaw in the safety provisions at Bhopal was the total lack of communication with the community. All the safety provisions, operable or not, stopped at the factory gate. No one had ever tried to make the people in the crowded town around the factory aware of what to do should an accident occur at the plant. As it was, many of the citizens of Bhopal apparently ran *toward* the plant when they heard all the noise—to see what was happening. And when the injured began to turn up at hospitals, no one knew what to do for them. It seemed obvious to the CMA group that injuries could have been prevented by more attention to public warnings. Had the people in the path of the gas known even to put a wet cloth over their noses and mouths, hundreds of lives might have been saved; but no one had thought that that might be a useful thing for them to know. There had been no drills or information. Should there have been? The probability was that there would never be any need at all to know what to do in the case of a massive gas leak, and attempts to "educate" the people might just cause panic. How do you balance, the industry had wondered, the known and certain disadvantages of fearful warnings, with the unknown and unproved disadvantages of chancing a disaster without the warnings? As far as the CMA was concerned, Bhopal landed with the weight of 2,500 corpses on the side of public awareness and education.

How could the industry assure the safety of the towns in which chemical plants were located, in the face of proof that they were terribly dangerous? In 1985, the Chemical Manufacturers Association was given a draft of a set of requirements, for voluntary adoption by the membership. Called the Community Awareness and Emergency Response program (CAER), it required members to communicate with the public outside the plant—not just to answer questions truthfully, but to reach out to the community to begin the dialogue. They had to tell the public what sort of safety provisions the plant had made against various possible accidents, and above all they had to discuss with the local police and fire departments just what sorts of disasters might occur, how to cope with them, and how the chemical company might be of assistance. In a radical development, they were required to work out with local governments some means of conducting a disaster drill once a year. The essence of the program was communication: within each plant (to make sure all emergency procedures were known to all employees), with all local authorities—especially police and fire—and with the public at large, to make sure that the community was aware of the overall plan.[55] The program was well-received.

Then, in mid-1985, as if to answer those who attributed the accident at Bhopal to carelessness unique to such backward places as India ("it could never happen here"), Union Carbide's plant in Institute, West Virginia, also had a malfunction that released MIC into the air. No one was hurt, but the noise of that bell was unmistakable. This was not some foreigners' problem: Union Carbide was a leader of the chemical manufacturing industry; the plant was owned, run, and monitored by Americans in America; and if it happened in Institute, it could happen anywhere. Evidence piled up that the public mistrusted the chemical industry, feared the chemicals and doubted the word of its representatives, and doubted its ability and willingness to keep the citizens safe.

"The public was frightened and angry, because decisions about risk regarding exposure to chemicals were being made for them without their knowledge," observed one of the participants in the industry-to-public dialogue. "They saw decisions being made behind plant fences, in company labs, in skyscrapers. Corporations were saying, 'These are acceptable levels of risk and the public at large wouldn't understand the technical issues anyway.' The industry had found itself awash in a sea of mistrust and misunderstanding."[56]

In this climate CERCLA was reinstituted, this time under the title of the Superfund Amendment and Reauthorization Act (SARA), appropriating $8.5 billion to renew for five years the hazardous-waste cleanup program. The funds were to come from a tax on all manufacturing companies (not just from the chemicals industry); initial estimates had the cost of a total cleanup of just the existing hazardous waste sites at $100 billion.

Included in Title III of SARA were unprecedented legal provisions for public accountability. U. S. plants had to report typical inventories of dangerous chemicals to the local communities, and work with police and fire departments to prepare plans for any spill, explosion, sabotage, or other emergency that could endanger the community's welfare. Most significantly, Title III, which was dubbed "The Community Right-To-Know Act," empowered localities to adopt whatever environmental regulations seemed sensible to them to protect their citizens' health and safety, without waiting for the EPA. To the CMA's delight, the legislators adopted whole sections of CAER for Title III, almost word for word. A few years later, Jon Holtzman of the CMA commented on this development: "It taught us that if we were willing to attack a problem that the public is interested in—where government wants success—government will cherry-pick our program and write it into law. Government will buy into our experience because they don't want to fail either."[57]

In 1986, the Canadian Chemical Producers Association made some significant changes to CAER, generalizing it to encompass all activities of the chemical industry, projecting management codes for research, transportation, distribution, health and safety, manufacturing processes and disposing of hazardous wastes, as well as emergency response to accidents. (This very comprehensive program they called "Responsible Care," the name that survives to the present.) They derived a set of "guiding principles" from these practices, a short list of imperatives that would govern the whole enterprise of manufacturing principles, and made adherence to this plan mandatory for all members of the association. There is no misreading the last sentence of the "Statement of Commitment": "The most senior executive responsible for chemical operations in each member company of CCPA has formally accepted these principles and endorsement is a condition of membership."[58] In 1987, the Executive Committee of the CMA agreed that to change public perceptions, they would have to change their performance—radically, permanently, and visibly[59]—and decided to import Responsible Care in its entirety. By September, the Governing Board's decision was unanimous in favor of adopting Responsible Care as mandatory for all members. Members were required to sign a statement of principles, known as the "Guiding Principles," and they had to agree to implement any requirements, or "Codes of Management Practice," that the organization might develop in the future.[60]

No guarantees were available, save that CAER seemed to work—the CEOs of many companies had bought into the idea—and the knowledge that every firm would have to participate or be forced out of the association.[61]

What they had, in short, was trust. On the strength of the same trust, the entire membership voted to change the CMA bylaws to make Responsible Care a condition of membership. Despite lingering doubts about everything from legal liability to equity for smaller firms, the corporations making up the chemical industry in the United States had handed their trade association a mandate: to write rules to protect safety, health, and the natural environment; foster community involvement; and ensure fairness in allotment of burdens, especially where hazardous wastes were concerned. These were rules that the CEO of each company promised in advance to adopt, publicize, sell to his employees, adhere to, and be judged on—by his company, his peers in the CMA, and the public at large. On the whole, it was an extraordinary commitment for a market system.

Does Responsible Care work? Given that serious implementation could not begin until into the 1990s, it may be too early to tell. But the Responsible Care stands alone as a serious industry-wide attempt to ensure that through design of facilities and processes, provisioning of safety devices and training, monitoring of environmental effects of its operations, and sharing of information with the community, Bhopals will not happen again.

Notes

1. Chris Hedges, "A Key Figure Proves Elusive in a U.S. Suit Over Bhopal," *The New York Times* (5 March 2000): p. 4. The suit was filed by one Kenneth F. McCallion in New York City, against Union Carbide and Mr. Anderson personally, alleging violations of international law and the fundamental human rights of the victims and survivors. The lawsuit further states that the defendants are liable for "fraud and civil contempt for their total failure to comply with the lawful orders of the courts of both the United States and India." The Indian court order referred to is an indictment for "culpable homicide," and pursuant to that indictment it has issued a warrant for Anderson's arrest, and notified Interpol that he is a "fugitive." The U.S. court order referred to was a decision by John Keenan, a U.S. District Court judge in Manhattan, dating from May 12, 1986, holding

that Union Carbide "shall consent to submit to the jurisdiction of the courts of India." The company grants the legitimacy of that order, which in any case did not mention Anderson, and argues that it did exactly what the order said. It ended up paying $470 million as compensation to victims of the disaster in a 1989 settlement of a civil case brought by the Indian government. The Indian government dropped the criminal charges against Anderson at that time. That, the company claims, should take care of them, and Anderson too. "The settlement with the government of India in 1989 of all claims arising from the Bhopal tragedy did not just cover Union Carbide, it covered all directors, officers and employees, including Warren Anderson," said Sean Clancy, spokesman at Union Carbide's corporate headquarters in Danbury, Conn. "Based on that settlement, we see no reason to encourage any disturbance of Mr. Anderson, who retired as chairman 12 years ago."

2. p. 19.

3. Ibid.

4. Ibid. Others have estimated the dead as high as 4000—such as Denise Lavboie, writing for the Associated Press, *Hartford Courant* (5 April 1992): D1, D7 ("Bhopal still haunts former Carbide chief")—and up to 8000, such as Dan Kurzman, *A Killing Wind: Inside Union Carbide and the Bhopal Catastrophe* (New York: McGraw-Hill, 1987): p. 77. Kurzman has to hypothesize that the dead were hastily dumped into the river during the night to explain the lack of corpses the next day. Arthur Sharplin, Professor of Management at McNeese State University in Lake Charles, Louisiana, and author of a case study on Bhopal, estimates that 2,000 died (Center for Business Ethics, Bentley College, Waltham, MA.) The estimate of injuries ranges from 3,000 (Union Carbide: "measurable injuries after the fact," which excludes all emotional injury and damage to property), to 20,000 (Lavoie), to 200,000 (Sharplin), to 300,000 (Kurzman). The claims of injuries later lodged with government authorities or reported to lawyers follow a similar pattern. By most estimates, there were no more that 250,000 people in Bhopal at the time (Sharplin estimates 100,000). At one point in the furor following the explosion, there were 600,000 claims for injuries. (There is no account for the discrepant figures in Sharplin's account, which occur within two pages of each other.)

5. Many of the accounts of events within the company are taken from a talk given at Fairfield University, February 11, 1992, by Joseph Geoghan, corporate counsel for UC.

6. Union Carbide, internal document: "Union Carbide Corporation: Bhopal Chronology."

7. Dan Kurzman, *A Killing Wind*, p. 106.

8. Alfred de Grazia, *A Cloud Over Bhopal* (Bombay, India: Kalos Foundation, 1985): p. 50.

9. Kurzman, *A Killing Wind*, p. 175.

10. Ibid., p. 155.

11. Nor did it develop after the case appeared. See comments by Marc Galanter, sidebar in Wil Lepkowski, "Bhopal: Ten Years Later," *C&EN* [Chemical and Engineering News] (19 December 1994): pp. 8–18.

12. Kurzman, *A Killing Wind*, p. 195.

13. *In re Union Carbide Corp. Gas Plant Disaster*, 634 F. Supp. 842 (S.D.N.Y. 1986), aff'd 809 F.2d 195 (2d Cir.), cert. denied 108 S. Ct. 199 (1987).

14. Warren M. Anderson,"Bhopal: What We Learned," distributed by Union Carbide Corporation (Danbury, Connecticut 06817-0001; UC Document #158).

15. Resa King, "Top of the News," *Business Week* (27 February 1989): p. 40.

16. Union Carbide Corporation, "Bhopal Chronology."

17. That wasn't the last we heard from the lawyers. In June, 1989, F. Lee Bailey, Stanley M. Chesley, and others filed in the same court for an order directing reimbursement of "their legitimate costs and expenses" related to Bhopal litigation, to be paid from the $470 million that India had just been awarded. They were turned down (S.D.N.Y. 1989, U.S. Dist. LEXIS 6613, decided June 14, 1989). They tried again to collect their fees in December 1993, in the same court, asking this time for "an attorney's lien against respondent, the Union Carbide Corporation." They were turned down again (S.D.N.Y. 1993 U.S. Dist. LEXIS 18227, decided December 27, 1993). Meanwhile, also in 1993, Judge Wajahat Ali Shah in Bhopal ordered further criminal proceedings, for "culpable homicide," for several UCIL officials and Warren Anderson. To the best of our knowledge, the decision of this court has not been recognized in the United States. "Trial Ordered for Carbide Officials in Bhopal," *The New York Times* (12 April 1993).

18. Warren M. Anderson,"Bhopal: What We Learned"; Kurzman, *A Killing Wind*, p. 21.

19. Ashok S. Kalelkar, "Investigation of Large-Magnitude Incidents: Bhopal as a Case Study" (presented at The Institution of Chemical Engineers Conference On Preventing Major Chemical Accidents, London, England, May 1988), p. 11.

20. "India's Tragedy A Warning Heard Round the World," *U.S. News and World Report* (17 December 1984): p. 25; Pushpa S. Mehta et al., "Bhopal Tragedy's Health Effects: A Review of Methyl Isocyanate Toxicity," *Journal of the American Medical Association* Vol. 264, No. 21 (5 December 1990): p. 2781.

21. Mehta et al., "Bhopal Tragedy's Health Effects."

22. Kurzman, *A Killing Wind*, p. 50.

23. Union Carbide Corporation, Bhopal Methyl Isocyanate Incident Investigation Team Report, Danbury, CT (March 1985).

24. Ibid.; also see Ehrlichs, et al, *Ecoscience*, (San Francisco: W. H. Freeman & Co., 1977); Kurzman, *A Killing Wind*, p. 22; David Weir, *The Bhopal Syndrome: Pesticides, Environment and Health*, (San Francisco: Sierra Club Books, 1987).

25. Warren M. Anderson,"Bhopal: What We Learned"; Union Carbide, "Union Carbide Corporation: Bhopal Fact Sheet," p. 1.

26. Investigations after the incident revealed a litany of collapsed systems. Weir (pp. 41–42) gives us a partial list:

> Gauges measuring temperature and pressure in the various parts of the unit, including the crucial MIC storage tanks, were so notoriously unreliable that workers ignored early signs of trouble. The refrigeration unit for keeping MIC at low temperatures (and therefore less likely to undergo overheating and expansion should a contaminant enter the tank) had been shut off for some time. The gas scrubber, designed to neutralize any escaping MIC, had been shut off for maintenance. Even had it been operative, post-disaster inquiries revealed, the maximum pressure it could handle was only one-quarter that which was actually reached in the accident. The flare tower, designed to burn off MIC escaping from the scrubber, was also turned off, waiting for

replacement of a corroded piece of pipe. The tower, however, was inade-
quately designed for its task, as it was capable of handling only a quarter of
the volume of gas released. The water curtain [high-pressure spray], designed
to neutralize any remaining gas, was too short to reach the top of the flare
tower, from where the MIC was billowing.

27. John Rennie, "Trojan Horse: Did a Protective Peptide Exacerbate Bhopal
Injuries?", *Scientific American* (March 1992): p. 184.

28. Dan Kurzman, *A Killing Wind*, p. 47.

29. UCIL's tanks were unusually large for such an operation, which (in retrospect) has occasioned criticism. The UCIL tank's capacity was 57,120 liters and
was almost full at the time of the explosion. In Germany, the United States, and
Korea, MIC tanks have a capacity of 17,500 liters and they are filled only to 50%
of capacity as a safety precaution. Pushpa S. Mehta et al, "Bhopal Tragedy's
Health Effects," p. 2781.

30. In a (non-Indian) presentation of this view, Arthur Sharplin describes the
American exit from positions of supervision and control in the plant over the
three years from 1979 to 1982, acknowledges that the departure was demanded
by the Indian government, acknowledges that the Indian management did not
make any safety or other reports to UC, and then concludes: "It is hard to imagine that such an extreme 'hands-off' policy could exist without strategic intent,"
the intent to mount a credible defense of nonresponsibility in the case, say, that
the plant should blow up. His account is not a parody, or at least was not apparently meant to be."

31. Dan Kurzman, *A Killing Wind*, p. 142.

32. Ashok Kalelkar, engineer and senior vice president of Arthur D. Little,
reported that in some plant logs, "the pages relevant to the period in question had
been either completely, or partially, ripped out." Richard Koenig and Laurie
Hays, "Carbide's Contention of Bhopal Sabotage Is Supported by Arthur D.
Little Engineer," *The Wall Street Journal* (11 May 1988): p. 6.

33. Ashok S. Kalelkar, "Investigation of Large-Magnitude Incidents," p. 21.

34. Ibid.

35. Ashok S. Kalelkar, "Investigation of Large-Magnitude Incidents."

36. Alfred de Grazia, *A Cloud Over Bhopal*, p. 34.

37. J. Peterson, "After Bhopal, Tracing Causes and Effects," *Science News*
127 (30 March 1985): p. 196.

38. J. Peterson, "After Bhopal," p. 88.

39. Neal Carlan and Peter McKillop, *Newsweek* (1 April 1985): p. 35.

40. Ashok S. Kalelkar, "Investigation of Large-Magnitude Incidents,"
pp. 14ff.

41. David Weir, *The Bhopal Syndrome*, pp. 48–49.

42. W. Joseph Campbell, "Corporation's Theory About Cause of Disaster Still
Subject of Debate," *Hartford Courant* (11 February 1990): p. 12.

43. Anwar Fazal, foreword to David Weir, *The Bhopal Syndrome*.

44. Alfred de Grazia, *A Cloud Over Bhopal*.

45. David Weir, *The Bhopal Syndrome*.

46. Ibid., p. 24.

47. Ibid. Cited from "Union Carbide: A Study in Corporate Power and the
Case for Union Power," Oil, Chemical and Atomic Workers International Union,
June 1974.

48. Ibid., p. 26.

49. David Weir, *The Bhopal Syndrome*, p. 62.

50. David Weir, *The Bhopal Syndrome*, p. 63.

51. Now the American Chemicals Association (ACA).

52. "Clean Up Old Hazardous Waste Dumps to Allay Public Fear, Simeral Urges," *CMA News* (Summer 1983): pp. 6–8.

53. Ibid. All emphasis in original.

54. Special Report, issued by the CMA, 1985: *Bhopal: The Industry Stands Together, Communicates, Prepares Action Plan*.

55. Christopher Cathcart, "CAER means educating communities," *CMA NEWS* (April 1985).

56. Interview with Bob Kennedy, Chairman and CEO, Union Carbide Corporation, Danbury, Connecticut (3 May 1990). Cited Harvard Business School Case Study, Rayport and Lodge, "Responsible Care," President and Fellows of Harvard College, 1991. Case N9-391-135: 15 January 1991.

57. Interview with Jon Holtzman, Vice President-Communications, Chemical Manufacturers Association, Washington, D.C. (23 May 1990).

58. Canadian Chemical Producers Association (Ottawa), "Responsible Care."

59. Interview with Jonathan Holtzman, cited in "Process Safety: Underscore Safety from Start to Finish: The Chemical Industry Responds with 'CAER' and the 'Responsible Care' initiative," *1992 Safety Manager's Guide*, Bureau of Business Practice, pp. 320–332; Interview with Clyde H. Greenert, Director, Public Issues and Contributions, Union Carbide Corporation (3 May 1990), cited in Rayport and Lodge, "Responsible Care," p. 9.

60. Interview with Holtzman, p. 324.

61. Rayport and Lodge, "Responsible Care," p. 10.

CHAPTER 6

The Silence of the Birds
Rachel Carson and the Pesticides

QUESTIONS TO KEEP IN MIND

What evidence convinced Rachel Carson, and others, that pesticides, especially DDT, were harmful to the birds?

What role do insecticides play in American agriculture? Could they be done without? What are the alternatives? What effect would their prohibition have on the way we grow our food?

What role do pesticides in general play in the American economy? What impact on the economy might be expected if they were generally prohibited?

What new ethical concerns are raised by the practice of exporting pesticides that are banned here but not banned abroad?

THE WAKE-UP BOOK

It was 1962. For fifteen years and more, the United States had been the major—indeed, the only—industrial power in the world, developing new products and new technology with magical skill, doubling and tripling the real standard of living for its people, effortlessly dictating to the world a new measure of achievement in productivity and convenience. We created a new class (the new working-become-middle class, employed in the rapidly growing corporations with the first generation of college degrees, obtained on the GI Bill), as well as a new area of living (never before seen "suburbs"); settled into the new mode of transportation that it required (the automobile, with attendant highways); reformed religion, politics, economics, and the household (with the deep freeze, washing machines, and vacuum cleaners); and showed the world how to live.

Leading the way in the technological parade of miracles was the chemicals industry. It had developed the pharmaceuticals (antibiotics, especially penicillin) that saved the GIs during the war, and sent the infant mortality rate plummeting immediately after it. And it developed the insecticides. DDT, focus (villain?) of the story for this chapter, was first synthesized by a German chemistry student in 1874, but it was only in 1939 that a Swiss chemist, Paul Muller, recognized its use as an insect killer. Its worth in World War II cannot be measured: sprayed liberally by the Allies in all theaters, it killed the mosquitos that carried malaria, filiariasis and yellow fever, the lice that carried typhus, and the fleas that carried—for yet another century—the bubonic plague.[1] This is no small accomplishment. Wars have always been races between the generals and the insects, and the generals have rarely won: "Typhus, with its brothers and sisters—plague, cholera, typhoid, dysentery—has decided more campaigns than Caesar, Hannibal, Napoleon, and all the inspector generals in history."[2]

This huge outpouring of technological progress—in construction, in automobiles and the roads to drive them on, in plastics, fuels, pharmaceuticals, and in all products of chemistry—came on the heels of, and because of, the war that we had fought to protect our nation. Possibly for that reason, there was a widespread impression that opposition to progress—read, further development of goods and services for the health, enjoyment, and convenience of the American consuming public—was downright unpatriotic, insufficiently celebratory of the American victory. Victory was a gift from God; the attendant prosperity, the greatest *relative* prosperity the world has ever known, was part of that gift; one does not look gift horses in the mouth, especially Divine gift horses.

Until 1962, that is, when a noted author and naturalist, Rachel Carson by name, published *Silent Spring*. In it she claimed, and to a large degree demonstrated, that the pesticides that we use to kill insects are really killing the birds, and eventually killing us. Of the first importance is the place of this book in the nationwide celebration of victory: this was the first book (Ralph Nader's *Unsafe at Any Speed* did not come out until 1965) that raised doubts about the quality of our triumph, that dared to wonder if concerns for human and environmental safety had possibly been ignored in the march to bigger and better consumption.

That insecticides kill the birds was not news to much of the scientific community. As early as February, 1945, Gove Hambidge, then Coordinator of the Agricultural Research Administration of the

Department of Agriculture, and author of the article cited above that celebrated victory over the insects, worried simultaneously that DDT "may be a little *too effective* for comfort. For it is capable of blotting out insect life so completely throughout large areas that it may upset the whole balance of nature."[3] He noted that it killed the pollinators of the crops, and might well be poisonous to livestock and human beings. His concerns were backed up by observations from the mid-1950s onward, that suggested that pesticides were killing the birds. In 1957, grebes were dying in California's Clear Lake, and biologists blamed DDD, a DDT relative that had been sprayed on local farms.[4] In 1958, Roy Barker of the Illinois Natural History Survey at Urbana documented the decline of local robins, and showed how the spraying of DDT to control Dutch Elm Disease had fed them a diet of poisoned earthworms.[5] By 1960, the scientists generally recognized that there was something wrong, but it was certainly news to us. Where did this come from? Why was the reaction against it so ferocious? How did we respond to it (and to its successors)? For starters, who was Rachel Carson?

RACHEL CARSON, NATURALIST AND PROPHET

Rachel Louise Carson was born on May 27, 1907 in Springdale, Pennsylvania, to a strong-willed mother and a father who farmed his 65-acre parcel and dabbled in real estate, both with very indifferent success. The area was generally industrialized, but Rachel grew up in a rural setting.

Her interest in writing surfaced early—she published her first story at age ten[6]—as did her interest in nature, encouraged by her mother. (Upon her mother's death she wrote of her, ". . . more than anyone else I know, she embodied Albert Schweitzer's 'reverence for life'"[7]). She was particularly fascinated by the sea, despite her inland upbringing. She was a quiet, good student; a bit of a loner, yet known for friendliness and kindness to her fellow students and her elders.

During her college years at the Pennsylvania College for Women, conflict between the Biology and English departments drove her to change her major to Biology from English, to the intense consternation of the English Department (which had supported her with scholarship funds, in recognition of her ability as a writer). She completed her educational career with a combination of work, financial aid, and loans, earning first her A.B. (summa cum laude) at Pennsylvania College, and then an M.A. in marine zoology at Johns Hopkins, made possible in part by a summer fellowship at Woods Hole, Massachusetts. Her interest in writing never waned, however; she once commented that "Eventually it dawned on me that by becoming a biologist I had given myself something to write about."[8]

After her father and sister died, Rachel took on the responsibility for her mother and her sister's two daughters; she abandoned academe to take a position at the Bureau of Fisheries (later to become the Fish and Wildlife Service), in the employ of which she remained from 1935 to 1952.[9] By then, she was gaining recognition as a fine science writer by both scientists and the literati; and it was during this time that her literary career took off. She believed that there was "no separate literature of science. The aim of science is to discover and illuminate truth. And that, I take it, is the aim of literature."[10] Her first book, *Under the Sea-Wind,* was published in 1941, followed by the immensely popular *The Sea Around Us* in 1951, and *The Edge of the Sea* in 1955.[11] These works and others brought her numerous awards, and literary as well as scientific praise.[12] While her writing was noted for scientific clarity combined with poetic expression, her sense of humor, noted by friends and in her letters, was not reflected in her published works. She evidently felt that if she, as a woman, was to be taken seriously as a writer of science, humor should not interfere. When some readers could not believe that a woman wrote *The Sea Around Us,* she commented, prophetically, given the forthcoming reaction to *Silent Spring,* "Among male readers, there was a reluctance to acknowledge that a woman could have dealt with a scientific subject."[13]

By 1952, she was able to buy a cottage on the Maine coast near her beloved ocean, and devote full time to her writing. It was here that her friendship with Dorothy and Stanley Freeman was formed, which enriched her remaining years;[14] it was along the Maine Coast where parts of *Silent Spring* would be written. She was preoccupied with the need to care for her adopted son, the child of her deceased niece; as well as her mother, who died in 1958, over some of this period.[15] But by that year she had decided that pesticide poisoning would be her next focus.

She had been aware of DDT and its potential for ecological disruption since 1944, and had joined other scientists in unpopular warnings that it might not be the panacea, sought since biblical times, that would finally win the war against the insects. These warnings fell on deaf ears. After all, as above, DDT had saved American GIs lives from a typhus epidemic in Italy during World War II; it had been sorely needed and roundly praised by the sick, undernourished, and flea-infested Dutch after liberation in 1944. DDT stopped the spread of infection, permitting the Allied armies to operate, and saved the first crops after the war, establishing adequate nutrition in Europe.[16] But numerous communications detailing the pesticide's effect on birds and other species, as well as continuing rising concerns among her colleagues, led her to the decision that this issue would be the next she addressed.[17]

"The time had come," she reflected later, "when it must be written. We have already gone very far in the abuse of this planet . . . the ideas had to be crystallized, the facts had to be brought together in one place . . .

knowing the facts as I did, I could not rest until I had brought them to public attention."[18]

This book would be a departure from her earlier paeans to the sea, ". . . no longer the delights of . . . Maine rocks at low tide . . . the exploration of coral reefs. . . ."[19] This book would be a declaration of war. Rachel Carson was fully aware that the book would be controversial and that the response from the chemical industry and a number of policy makers would be intense. To make the response more manageable, she tried to keep the work under wraps until publication. She had been warned that upon its publication she would be subjected to ridicule. Typically, therefore, she proceeded with meticulous, time consuming research, which included correspondence with experts worldwide. Her interest in exploring the links between pesticides and cancer was perhaps more than academic; she had been diagnosed with breast cancer in 1957, and was in poor health for much of the writing of *Silent Spring.*[20]

THE REACTION TO THE BOOK

Robert Downs, reflecting on Rachel Carson's work in the year of the first Earth Day, commented that "*Silent Spring* was comparable in its impact on public consciousness, and demand for instant action, to Tom Paine's *Common Sense,* Harriet Beecher Stowe's *Uncle Tom's Cabin,* and Upton Sinclair's *The Jungle.*"[21] Prior to publication of the hardcover edition, the public had had a chance to learn its major themes. In June, 1962, *The New Yorker* started a three issue condensation of *Silent Spring,* and responses poured in. Excerpts were read into *The Congressional Record,* and President Kennedy was questioned about pesticides at a news conference. The official publication occurred on September 27, 1962, to excellent reviews: Loren Eiseley, a well-known naturalist from the University of Pennsylvania called it ". . . a devastating, heavily documented, relentless attack upon human carelessness, greed, and irresponsibility;" Supreme Court Justice William O. Douglas called it "the most important chronicle of this century for the human race."

But even before official publication of the book, in July, the *New York Times* headlined a controversy: "Silent Spring is now Noisy Summer; Pesticides Industry Up in Arms Over a New Book. Rachel Carson Stirs Conflict—Producers Are Crying Foul." The article went on to describe the distress in the industry: "Some agricultural and chemical concerns have set their scientists to analyzing Miss Carson's work line by line. Other companies are preparing briefs defending their products. Meetings are being held in Washington and New York. Statements are being drafted and counterattacks planned. . . ."[22]

Reactions came from far and wide. The Toledo, Ohio, Library ordered gallons of ladybugs as a biological control for aphids. Friends wrote that

Silent Spring was the prime topic of conversation in their communities. By way of contrast (and typically!), the Bethlehem (Pennsylvania) *Globe-Times* surveyed local county farm offices and found that "No one in either . . . office who was talked to today had read the book, but all disapproved of it heartily."[23]

Even some in the scientific community reacted cautiously. Typical of Carson's thorough research was her consultation with experts in each field about which she wrote, asking them to review appropriate chapters. Not all of them were prepared for war. A. W. A. Brown, a zoologist from the University of Western Ontario, had been consulted, and had in fact made some helpful comments prepublication. Once the book became controversial, he complained publicly that his suggestions had not been taken and that, by using his name, Carson "had put him in a bad light with his colleagues."[24] Carson searched her notes, discovered that all she had used of his was already published, pointed out icily that he had surely been free to complain when he reviewed her manuscript before it was in print, and requested that he represent the facts accurately in future. She expressed regret that he was unhappy with the result, but did not back down one inch.[25]

Typically, critics patronized Carson as a sentimental woman lacking in scientific objectivity. *Time* magazine reported that "Many scientists sympathize with Miss Carson's love of wildlife, and even with her mystical attachment to the balance of nature. But they fear that her emotional and inaccurate outburst in *Silent Spring* may do harm by alarming the nontechnical public, while doing no good for the things that she loves."[26]

But it was the chemical companies and other agricultural interests that launched the most vigorous attacks. The Velsicol Chemical Corporation, sole manufacturers of the pesticides chlordane and heptachlor about which Carson was highly critical, responded rapidly and fiercely. Having been alerted by the *New Yorker* articles, they wrote Carson's publishers, urging them not to publish a book so full of "inaccurate and disparaging" statements that was designed to sabotage Western capitalism. A portion of what has become a notorious letter reads:

> ". . . members of the chemical industry in this country and in western Europe must deal with sinister influences, whose attacks on the chemical industry have a dual purpose: (1) to create the false impression that all business is grasping and immoral and (2) to reduce the use of agricultural chemicals in this country and in the countries of western Europe, so that our supply of food will be reduced to east-curtain parity. Many innocent groups are financed and led into attacks on the chemical industry by these sinister parties."[27]

Other comments from those threatened by the book were less formal, but equally revealing. Some dismissed Carson as an unimportant member of some fringe group. The director of the New Jersey Department of Agriculture spoke for many: "In any large scale pest control program we are immediately confronted with the objection of a vociferous, misinformed, group of nature-balancing, organic-gardening, bird-loving, unreasonable citizenry that has not been convinced of the important place of agricultural chemicals in our economy."[28] Others leveled personal attacks such as that from a member of the Federal Pest Control Review Board, quoted as saying, "I thought she was a spinster. What's she so worried about genetics for?"[29]

Many of the Chemical and Agricultural interests treated the publication of *Silent Spring* as a public relations problem. The Nutrition Foundation put together a "fact kit" that contained defenses of pesticides, negative reviews of the book, and a letter written by the Foundation president claiming that the Carson's supporters and advocates included "food faddists, health quacks, special interest groups, [that are] promoting her book as if it were scientifically irreproachable and written by a scientist."[30] These "kits" were distributed among universities, agricultural organizations, public health officials, women's organizations, state, county and local officials, and libraries.[31] Another approach used the National Audubon Society's annual Christmas Bird Census to point out that, contrary to Carson's warning, birds are abundant. (The Audubon Society tends to discount the accuracy of this annual event.)[32] As Paul Brooks, her editor, said in his book about her work, *The House of Life,* "Perhaps not since the classic controversy over Charles Darwin's *The Origin of the Species* just over a century earlier had a single book been more bitterly attacked by those who felt their interests threatened."[33]

Nevertheless, by the end of 1962, *Silent Spring* had had a tremendous impact on the ordinary public. There had been 40 bills introduced to various state legislatures to regulate pesticides, and on the public side, "CBS Reports" scheduled "The Silent Spring of Rachel Carson" for April 3, 1963. (Some of the sponsors of that program, predictably, opted out, including Standard Brands and Ralston Purina.) By May 15, 1963, President John F. Kennedy's Science Advisory Committee echoed the criticism Carson had initiated against chemical pesticides. In a report on that date, it strongly agreed with her evaluation of the danger inherent in the insect eradication program—the danger posed by pesticides that are persistent, and the apparent lack of concern in dealing with the application of synthetic chemical pesticides. This report was headlined in *The Christian Science Monitor* as "Rachel Carson Stands Vindicated."[34]

By the summer of 1963, she knew she was dying, but nevertheless, before her last trip to Maine, she detoured to testify before a Congressional committee at which she urged regulation, research, education, and registration for pesticides.

The chemical offense was not yet stilled. A consultant to Shell Chemical Company testified that "Miss Carson is talking about health effects that will take years to answer. In the meantime we'd have to cut off food for people around the world. These peddlers of fear are going to feast on the famine of the world—literally." During a recess, one of the agricultural "experts" commented, "You're never going to satisfy organic farmers or emotional women in garden clubs."[35]

Rachel Carson died on April 14, 1964. Her funeral in the National Cathedral in Washington, D.C. was attended by many dignitaries, among whom was Senator Ribicoff (CT), before whose committee she had testified, and who eulogized her as "this gentle lady who aroused people everywhere to be concerned with one of the most significant problems of mid-twentieth century life—man's contamination of his environment."[36]

THE TROUBLE WITH DDT

Rachel Carson, now dead for more than thirty-five years, is a national institution—almost a national icon. But let us backtrack. *Why* is she so justly celebrated on this issue? How do pesticides work, that makes them at once so apparently valuable and so apparently deadly to the birds?

The trouble with DDT is that it kills things, and that it persists in the environment. That's what's good about it, and that's what's bad about it. Insecticides are designed to kill the insects that enjoy the same types of food that we do, and that try to get to it before we do. If they were not toxic, they could not do their job. And they stay around. They do not dissolve and disappear in the next rainstorm; otherwise their effectiveness would be very limited. But that is also the root of their harmfulness.

DDT is an organochlorine, a synthetic insecticide of the chlorinate hydrocarbon group. These substances are "persistent"; that is, they do not break down in the environment. Instead, they accumulate through the food chain (from plant to worm to bird, for instance). Soluble in fat or oil rather than water, they concentrate in the fatty tissues of the animals at the top of the food chain. And they are deadly. In ways that are not completely known, these organochlorines destroy living cells, affecting the nervous system in particular, and end the life of the organism that ingests them.[37]

They are distinguishable by the range of their toxicity, their solubility, their persistence, and the breadth of their killing spectrum. If one wanted to kill every insect in sight (and many other creatures along the way), one would use a broad spectrum, highly toxic, fat-soluble, and very persistent insecticide, such as DDT. Historically, that has been the approach taken, and its drawbacks soon became apparent. The broad spectrum insecticides resulted in the death of nontarget insects, including the insect pest predators that lived on the target insects and the pollinators essential to the growth of flowering crops. A fat-soluble pesticide is not soluble in water, and therefore impossible to flush out of an organic system;

it cannot be cleared from animal bodies by the kidneys and washed out in the urine. The persistence meant that the poison did not begin to break down into other chemicals for years, but accumulated and concentrated in the food chains. That is, each organism higher in the food chain will have a higher concentration of a poison than their prey. For in order to survive, consumers must, eventually, eat more than their own weight in the plants or animals they eat. So, to use the rule of thumb, 0.1 part per million (ppm) concentration of an insecticide in algae becomes 1.0 ppm in zooplankton that eat algae, 10 ppm in minnows that eat zooplankton, 100 ppm in small fish that eat minnows, and 1000 ppm in large predator fish.

Rachel Carson recognized this problem: "One of the most sinister features of DDT and related chemicals is the way they are passed . . . through all the links of the food chains . . . hay containing residues of 7 to 8 parts per million may be fed to cows. The DDT will turn up in the milk in the amount of about 3 parts per million, but in the butter made from this milk the concentration may run to 65 parts per million."[38]

Meanwhile, the undiscriminating toxicity of DDT threatened with extinction numerous unintended species, especially the birds of prey (the raptors) that ate the owls (that had eaten the snakes that had eaten the mice that had eaten the acres of insecticide treated plants). *Silent Spring*, written in 1962, contains myriad descriptions of senseless unintended poisonings. The next thought of course is: what is the effect on humans, who are high on the food chain? The effect is terrible. That is why the eating of fish caught in contaminated waterways is banned, and why some poisons exist in human milk in higher concentrations than allowed in cow's milk.

All this devastation, and the effectiveness of the insecticides is really very limited. There are more than one million insect species. That's *species*—not individuals; and only those that are known to us now. If we talk *individuals,* there are about four billion insects found per square mile. Carson put it this way: ". . . 70 to 80 per cent of the earth's creatures are insects. The vast majority of these insects are held in check by natural forces. . . . If this were not so, it is doubtful that any conceivable volume of chemicals . . . could possibly keep down their population."[39] Given these numbers, it is reasonable to expect that among an insecticide target species, there would be a number that were genetically immune to the poison (just as some humans are immune to poison ivy). Now, if the insecticide is an effective one, it will kill all those that are not immune. Left behind are those unaffected by the poison, who reproduce like crazy, passing the trait along to a population that is presented with a feast, such as a corn field, with *no competition* from either their own species or predator species (also dead from the insecticide). We now have an insecticide resistant strain of an insect species. The next step for the farmer is usually to try a different, generally more expensive, insecticide, and the process starts all over again. This is often referred to as "the pesticide treadmill."

Carson documented a large number of observations of insecticide resistance worldwide, and mused that "Darwin himself could scarcely have found a better example of the operation of natural selection than is provided by the way the mechanism of resistance operates." She explained that ". . . it is the 'tough' insects that survive chemical attack. Spraying kills off the weaklings. The survivors are . . . the parents of the new generation, which, by simple inheritance, possesses all the qualities of 'toughness' inherent in its forebears. Inevitably, it follows that intensive spraying with powerful chemicals only make worse the problem it is designed to solve. After a few generations . . . there results a population consisting entirely of tough, resistant strains."[40]

In 1938 there were seven insect species that exhibited pesticide resistance. In 1984 there were 447. Today about the same percentage of our crops—fifteen percent—are lost to insects and weeds as were before the development of synthetic pesticides.

Rachel Carson's comment made in 1962 is as relevant today as it was then: "To have risked so much in our efforts to mold nature to our satisfaction and yet to have failed in achieving our goal would indeed be the final irony. Yet this, it seems, is our situation."[41]

NATIONAL RESPONSE: REGULATION

As soon as the book came out, as above, there were cries for regulation of the use of pesticides in general and DDT in particular. DDT was generally banned for all use and sale in the United States in the federal Insecticide, Fungicide, and Rodenticide Act (FIFRA). That was the first comprehensive approach to the problem. The Act has been amended a number of times, most recently in 1988. It provides that all pesticides used in the United States must be approved by the Environmental Protection Agency (EPA). The pesticide manufacturer submits data to EPA regarding their product, and the EPA then, using that data, determines an acceptable daily intake of the poison as a residue on food. EPA's approval does not constitute an approbation for the chemical, merely a judgment that if used as directed, its benefits are greater than its risks. No pesticide can be advertised as safe.

Enforcement of the Act has always been a problem. The EPA does not have the manpower or resources to evaluate the 450 active ingredients and 1,820 "inert" ingredients used in pesticides today. Although EPA can ban a chemical any time, it must compensate the manufacturer for stored supplies and the like, which would bankrupt EPA if no other way can be found to sell the pesticides legally. The upshot is that many chemicals on the market have not been fully and reliably tested by an objective organization.[42]

THE UPDATE ON PESTICIDES

Unbelievably, the pesticide problems and controversies continue. DDT is showing up in albatrosses at Midway Island in the middle of the Pacific Ocean. A World Resources Institute report indicates that many pesticides seem to affect the immune system. The Institute reviewed a large number of studies on pesticides and immunity, including laboratory animal tests, tests on animals in the wild such as Baltic seals, and Soviet studies on changes in human immunity. In the Soviet Studies, the scientists reported high levels of infections in areas containing pesticide residues beyond "accepted standards." In addition, a Canadian study of Inuit children, whose mother's milk contained high levels of organochlorides, found that their immune response was so low that they couldn't be vaccinated, given their lack of antibodies.[43]

Where are these Canadian, Arctic, and Pacific residues coming from? Pesticides in use in the United States, and presumably other industrialized countries, are pretty well accounted for, but the United States (and again, other countries) exports tons of pesticides to less-developed countries, especially in Africa and South America. Protecting the safety of workers and populations where these substances are in use is subject to difficulties familiar to the nongovernmental organizations that monitor international health. Often, those who use the imported substances cannot read the labels, are unused to sterilization and safe spraying practices, and cannot take remote dangers into account. Agencies of their governments that are supposed to monitor imported chemicals are understaffed, inefficient, often corrupt. The pesticides in use are often banned or restricted for use at home, so antidotes and special precautions are never developed. Between 1992 and 1994, the U.S. exported 4,950 tons of unapproved pesticides, 11,000 tons of "severely restricted" pesticides, and 100,000 tons of pesticides with some U.S. restrictions. In 1992 alone, the United States exported 1,950 tons of pesticides that are either banned, suspended, or discontinued at home. The farmer tends to believe that if the product comes from the United States, it's safe—the label, if there is one and it's understandable, doesn't tell him it's banned in the United States.

It is estimated that the U.S. exports 250,000 tons of *recorded* pesticides per year, but the export data is scarce and not reliable, and that from the EPA spotty, given that the EPA doesn't track unregistered pesticides-and the staff is overwhelmed anyway, due to budget restrictions. Many are volatile and sprayed indiscriminately, causing numerous poisonings locally, and resulting in airborne chemicals that are deposited all over the world. Atmospheric scientists are just now beginning to think of monitoring pesticide "emissions" as they do other air pollutants. Dr. John Giesy, a toxicologist from Michigan State University who was a member of the team studying Midway Island, opined that ". . . our research demonstrates that global controls on the distribution of persistant, bioaccumulative, toxic compounds need to be considered. The problem can't be approached on a country-by-country basis."[44]

Consider that insecticides are only the most visible of the pesticides, a billion-dollar industry. This in turn is dwarfed by all the other petrochemical operations—plastics, synthetic fibers, and thousands of other chemicals. There are 100,000 synthetic chemicals being used worldwide, with about 1,000 new ones being put on the market each year, "most of them without adequate testing."[45] There is a movement afoot to eliminate all synthetic chlorinated hydrocarbons (including the pesticides like DDT that have that chemical make-up) in some U. S. quarters. Recently, all chlorinated hydrocarbons, such as PCBs, dioxins, and pesticides, have come under attack on account of these effects. In a study done by the World Wildlife Fund, it was found that of 42 chemicals that affect the reproductive system, 55% contained chlorine. A senior economist with Environment Canada posits that "no other class of industrial—or natural —chemicals is known that exhibits so many detrimental properties at the same time."[46] Greenpeace, the environmental activist association that started the attack, has adopted the position that "no further organochlorine pollution should be permitted,"[47] entailing the complete cessation of the use of chlorine in manufacturing. The chemicals industry is pursuing substitutes for chlorine, but tend to view the proposed chlorine ban as "an extremist position," and generally ridiculous. "[W]e're not well served by blanket solutions to complicated problems."[48]

ALTERNATIVES TO PESTICIDES

What can we do? Alternatives to chemical warfare against the insects are under study, some of them on the horizon. For starters, not all pesticides have to be chlorinated hydrocarbons; a number are organophosphates, which do not persist in the ground as long as the organochlorines. Some have less dangerous chemical formulas, such as carbamates. Some very interesting research is being done in the area of IPM—Integrated Pest Management—using carefully measured minimal doses of pesticide, along with biological and mechanical controls on insect pests. The cultivation of insect predators is already under way; perhaps we should look into the capacity of plants to defend themselves, quite without our help. "Besieged by armies of voracious creatures but unable to run away, plants over the eons have evolved cunning defenses that include deadly poisons, oozings of toxic glue and hidden drugs that give leaf-eaters serious indigestion. . . . Many plants . . . wait until a predator actually starts munching before they unleash their most noxious washes of chemicals."[49] The obvious suggestion is to learn how they do that, and figure out how to teach, or modify, our agricultural staples to do the same. Then we would not have to use chemical pesticides at all. That would be good for the farmers, good for the land, and a fitting tribute to the foresight and to the memory of Rachel Carson.

CONCLUSION

It seems fitting to let Rachel Carson have the last say. She finished *Silent Spring* with the following castigation:

> "The 'control of nature' is a phrase conceived in arrogance, born of the Neanderthal age of biology and philosophy, when it was supposed that nature exists for the convenience of man. The concepts and practices of applied entomology . . . date from that Stone Age of science. It is our alarming misfortune that so primitive a science has armed itself with the most modern and terrible weapons, and that in turning them against the insects it has also turned them against the earth."[50]

QUESTIONS FOR REFLECTION

Where should we place responsibility, or accountability, for the deleterious effects of pesticides? On the chemical companies? On the farmers? Why not on the consumers and their demands for perfect appearance in their fruits and vegetables?

What is the difference between the way we ascribe blameworthiness to individuals and to corporations? Can you blame a whole country for taking a wrong turn? Can American consumerism and reliance on technological fixes be regarded as morally blameworthy?

What course should the chemical companies follow to ensure that their products are safe? What would follow from the Responsible Care initiative described in Chapter 5?

Can pesticides be made completely safe for use around humans and on products consumed by humans? If not, why not? If so, how?

Notes

1. Gove Hambidge, "The New Insect-Killers," *Harper's Magazine* (February 1945): p. 264.

2. Ibid., citing Hans Zinsser.

3. Ibid., p. 265.

4. Frank Graham, Jr., *Since Silent Spring* (Boston: Houghton Mifflin, 1970): p. 16.

5. Ibid.

6. Phillip Sterling, *Sea and Earth, The Life of Rachel Carson* (New York: Thomas Y. Crowell, 1970): p. 2.

7. Carol B. Gartner. *Rachel Carson* (New York: Frederick Ungar Publishing, 1983): p. 7.

8. Frank Graham, Jr., *Since Silent Spring,* p. 5.

9. Mary A. McKay, *Rachel Carson* (New York: Twayne Publishers, 1993): p. 13.

10. Ibid., p. 2.

11. Carol B. Gartner, *Rachel Carson*; see Chronology.

12. Ibid.

13. Ibid., p. 17.

14. Mary A. McKay, *Rachel Carson,* p. 19; Martha Freeman (ed.), *Always, Rachel The Letters of Rachel Carson and Dorothy Freeman* (Boston: Beacon Press, 1995).

15. Carol B. Gartner, *Rachel Carson,* p. 21.

16. Mary McKay, *Rachel Carson,* p. 63.

17. Ibid., p. 63ff.

18. Paul Brooks, *The House of Life: Rachel Carson at Work* (Boston: Houghton Mifflin, 1972): p. 228.

19. Ibid.

20. Mary A. McKay, *Rachel Carson,* pp. 69, 80; Carol B. Gartner, *Rachel Carson,* p. 21ff.

21. Robert B. Downs, *Upsetting the Balance of Nature,* London: Macmillan, 1970); quoted in Mary McKay, *Rachel Carson.*

22. Phillip Sterling, *Sea and Earth, The Life of Rachel Carson,* p. 172.

23. Frank Graham, Jr., *Since Silent Spring,* p. 48.

24. Ibid.

25. Ibid., p. 60.

26. Paul Brooks, *The House of Life: Rachel Carson at Work,* p. 293.

27. Frank Graham, Jr., *Since Silent Spring,* p. 49; Marty Jezer, *Rachel Carson* (New York: Chelsea House, 1988): p. 95.

28. Frank Graham, Jr., *Since Silent Spring,* p. 56.

29. Ibid., p. 50.

30. Ibid., p. 60.

31. Ibid., p. 59.

32. Ibid., p. 60.

33. Paul Brooks, *The House of Life: Rachel Carson at Work,* p. 293.

34. Ibid., pp. 72–79.

35. Ibid., p. 86–88.

36. Frank Graham, Jr., *Since Silent Spring,* p. 89.

37. Ibid., p. 15 (note).

38. Rachel Carson, *Silent Spring* (Greeenwich, CT: Fawcett Publications, 1962).

39. Ibid., p. 220.

40. Ibid., p. 240.

41. Ibid., p. 217.

42. G. Tyler Miller, Jr., *Living in the Environment,* 9th Ed., (Belmont, CA: Wadsworth Publishing, 1996): p. 598.

43. Janet Raloff, "Pesticides May Challenge Human Immunity," *Science News* Vol. 149 (9 March 1996): p. 149.

44. Janet Raloff, "The Pesticide Shuffle," *Science News* Vol. 149 (16 March 1996): p. 174; Les Line, "Old Nemesis, DDT, Reaches Remote Midway Albatrosses," *New York Times* (12 March 1996): p. B1.

45. "Hormonal Sabotage," *Natural History* (March 1996): p. 46.

46. Ibid.

47. Joe Thornton, "Chlorine, Human Health, and the Environment," *Greenpeace* (October 1993), quoted in J. A. Raloff, "The Role of Chlorine—and Its Future," *Science News* (22 January 1994): p. 59.

48. Joe Thornton, "Chlorine, Human Health, and the Environment."

49. Carol Kaesuk Yoon, "Nibbled Plants Don't Just Sit There: They Launch Active Attacks," *The New York Times* (23 June 1992): p. C1.

50. Rachel Carson, *Silent Spring*, p. 261.

CHAPTER 7

The Loss of an Ally

The Emergence
of Antibiotic Resistance

QUESTIONS TO KEEP IN MIND

How do antibiotics work?

What is "mutation"? What causes mutation?

What agricultural practices lead to antibiotic resistance?

THINKING LIKE AN ECOSYSTEM

How does an ecosystem think? Tyler Miller defines an ecosystem as "a community of different species interacting with one another and with their nonliving environment of matter and energy."[1] (He goes on to point out that the choice of what counts as "an ecosystem" for purposes of study is essentially arbitrary. An ecosystem can be as small as a child's aquarium or as large as the Earth. The ecosystem that we will be studying in this chapter is the human body.) Each organism feeds on other organisms, and is food to yet others. In their interaction, the species of a mature ecosystem are kept in balance by limiting factors in the system. Each species, we may assume with Thomas Malthus, will reproduce as often as it can, and will overrun the earth unless it is kept in check by predation (other species eating it) or the natural limits of the food supply. (The food supply, plant, or animal, reproducing as fast as it can, is limited in turn by the amount of water available. And so forth.) Within each species, there is fierce competition among individuals to reproduce. The biggest, prettiest, most sexually attractive members succeed in mating and having babies, while the less attractive ones often do not.

Imagine an ecosystem composed of open grassland dotted with deep swamps and thickets. Herds of wild deer roam the grasslands, preyed on by a few packs of small wolves. Deep in the thickets lives a species of small pigs, feasting on wild cabbage. There are no predators in the thickets, so periodically, if the cabbage has a really good year, the pigs become too numerous for the thickets, wander into the grasslands, and are promptly eaten by the wolves. The system is in balance.

But there are periodic crises. Every once in awhile the pigs mutate into a huge species, led by nasty tusked boars. They rapidly outstrip the food supply in the thickets, and charge on to the grassland. Sometimes the wolves can kill enough of them to save the grassland, and sometimes they are just overwhelmed. When that happens, the wild pigs can crowd out and destroy all the other organisms of the ecosystem, and the ecosystem collapses.

Now introduce a park ranger and a few prides of lions to the ecosystem. When the ranger sees that the great big pigs are overwhelming the wolves, he turns loose about three dozen lions, who gobble up the pigs on the grassland and in most of the thickets too, and then go back to their cages. The wolves recover, and the system is again in balance.

Add a twist to the mix: the lions (although not the wolves) have a distinct color preference in their food. They like dark-colored prey. They won't eat light food. That works well for the ranger, for almost all the pigs, large or small, are dark, almost black; it seems that the dark pigs are much more sexually attractive to pigs of the opposite sex, and experience proportionately more reproductive success. Some pigs are white; the lions won't eat those. But after the lions have finished with the dark-colored ones, the recovered wolves can easily polish off the few white ones that are left.

The intelligent park ranger will not send out the lions unless there is one of those crises, just because the system generally works so well by itself. But now suppose some bureaucrat in the National Park System decides that it would be better to be proactive about protecting the ecosystem. He orders that a pride of lions should be deployed anytime a pig is seen anywhere near the grassland, or anytime that wolves seem to be nervous about pigs *possibly* entering the grassland. Or, he wants a pride of lions permanently living in the system, to grab outbreaks of pigs before they start. For whatever reasons, anyway, we begin to have lions living full time in the ecosystem. The lions, recall, differ from the wolves on two accounts: they are just as much at home in the thickets as in the grasslands, and they don't eat white pigs.

What's going to happen to the pig population? The lions will contentedly munch on the thicket-based native population of pigs, and on minor outbreaks of pigs that the wolves probably could have handled, but very selectively—they will eat only the dark-colored ones, which up to now have been the vast majority of the pig population. With the pig population down, the cabbage flourishes, and pigs that would not ordinarily be able to find mates and reproduce suddenly discover that they too can have families. White pigs begin to be seen in the thickets with far more frequency. After many generations of this, we have a new majority—most of the pigs are light.

What will happen the next time the pigs mutate into the large tusked variety and charge in enormous numbers into the grasslands? Prides of new lions will come out to the grasslands to aid the wolves, but will leave most of the raging pigs alone, for by now, most are the color they won't eat. The ecosystem has depended, for its defense, on the wolves and the lions together; now the overwhelmed wolves and the finicky lions are simply unable to mount a defense, and the ecosystem is doomed.

Suppose we could interview the ecosystem on its preferences for its own survival. What would its priorities be? First of all, no offense intended, it would like to be left alone. It doesn't need lions to munch on the pigs in the thickets. The pigs were fine there, and kept the cabbage from getting out of hand. It doesn't need ranchers to shoot the wolves, gardeners to spruce up the grassland, or the introduction of cats, dogs, rabbits, zebra mussels, swans, or kudzu, for any reason whatsoever. There is no telling what an exotic thing is going to do in an ecosystem, and the fewer of them the better. Second, we should note that the major defense against those wretched pig outbreaks is the health of the wolf packs and the system generally. If we want to protect it, we should watch its general health, not just its pigs. And third, just to reinforce that, please note that the introduction of lions to eat the pigs on a regular basis has made it impossible to handle those foreseeable periodic outbreaks, and that makes each outbreak life-threatening. Have we any ideas for how to restore the natural balance?

The human body is an ecosystem, which lives ordinarily (in good times) in natural balance that we know as "health," a condition that is not incompatible with several less-than-optimal conditions. That is, a person can be "healthy" (for purposes of this chapter) while severely physically or mentally handicapped, missing limbs, brain-damaged, even in a condition approaching a persistent vegetative state. We are focusing only on the internal landscape of the body, and the balance of its organisms. Among those organisms are colonies of microorganisms—bacteria, protozoa, fungus—that are doing no particular harm to the body and may be doing some good. (Years ago we found out that colonies of bacteria were essential to digesting our food.) These colonies are the pigs in the thickets. Roaming through our body are the many cytophages and other cells that make up the "immune system," routinely eliminating the germs that we inhale with every breath and mobilizing to attack infectious outbreaks of alien microorganisms (the mutant pigs). (That's why we don't die every time we cut a finger or catch a cold.) These are our wolves. They are our first line of defense, and until the middle of the twentieth century, they were really our only line of defense. Before the introduction of the "antibiotics"—species of fungus, usually, that like to eat bacteria—any outbreak of infection, even to scraped knees and sore throats, could easily be fatal to the whole ecosystem.

The antibiotics are our lions. They attack germs anywhere in the body, as long as the germs are the kind they can eat. There are always a few germs of all kinds that are "resistant" to the antibiotics, germs that they just cannot get rid of. But the wolves are still around, and as long as they are not permanently put out of action by some other enemy, they can rally to destroy the germs that are left after the antibiotic has killed all it can kill.

The problem we address in this chapter is the steady and alarming increase in "antibiotic resistance," a condition in which our old reliable lions are no longer eliminating the pigs, and we are dying of infections that we thought we had licked. We need to ask, first, what practices are contributing to this very alarming turn of events, and second, are those practices justified on balance by the advantages they were instituted to secure? We will address them in that order.

THE SLOW DESTRUCTION OF AN ECOSYSTEM

The lions were spectacularly successful when they were introduced, shortly after World War II. Penicillin, discovered in 1928 as a pollutant in imperfectly monitored bacterium cultures, had found its first major use in World War II, knocking out infections in wounds and venereal disease with the same lethal thoroughness. After the war, it came into widespread use and rapidly developed a well-deserved reputation for magical effectiveness against diseases that had often been fatal. Every family has a penicillin story dating from those times, often several. My husband's father, for instance, almost died of kidney disease in 1943, but because he was in the military, he received penicillin and lived. An older sister, however, died in the late 1930s of a skinned knee she suffered while roller skating—the infection got into the bone and killed her. I almost died in 1946 of a raging fever (probably due to a bacterial infection secondary to bronchitis), but since the hospital to which I was taken was an old Army Air Corps facility, they had a supply of penicillin, so I got well. And so forth. There was nothing those lions couldn't do.

But beneath the surface of the "magic bullet" antibiotics, there was a selective process at work. Antibiotics, like the lions in the hypothesized ecosystem, don't kill all the germs. They only kill the ones that are susceptible to their attack. Some germs (because they have thicker cell walls, or because they can expel the antibiotic through their waste disposal system, for instance) are not.[2] The wolves, the immune system, should get the rest of them and bring the outbreak to a close. There may be problems with the assumption that they can. First, if there's something really wrong with the wolves—if the immune system is badly compromised (see "AIDS," below)—even a few of the white pigs, the resistant germs, may be too much for the weakened immune system to handle, and the disease will simply continue. At that point the resistant germs will multiply without opposition, and infect many more people, it may be, before they finally kill the patient. "Through natural selection, a single mutant can pass such traits on to most of its offspring, which can amount to 16,777,216 in only 24 hours! Each time this strain of bacterium is exposed to penicillin or some other antibiotic, a larger proportion of its offspring are genetically resistant to the drug."[3]

Second, if the lions are called off too soon—if the patient is "noncompliant," and does not take the entire dose of the antibiotic as prescribed—too many pigs of all kinds may be left on the grassland, and the wolves may be unable to get rid of them. In that case, of course, the proportion of white to dark pigs will be higher than it was before the lions first attacked. When the wolves, the immune system, can't handle the problem, the symptoms of the disease will reappear, and the patient may begin to receive an antibiotic again. That amounts to letting loose a few more lions. They will happily eat dark pigs, but by now the white ones may have multiplied to the point where they alone can overwhelm the wolves. At some point in this process of inadequate medication, the tipping point will come, and there will simply be more germs, antibiotic resistant germs, than the body can handle, and the disease will become fatal.

Why are antibiotics a problem now? They were entirely too successful. We now have magic bullets to conquer the diseases that used to take our lives. Wonderful! If they can do that, I'm sure they can cure my cold, my child's cold, and earache, and sore throat. To an unexpectedly large extent, it became, throughout the 1960s and 1970s, standard medical practice (especially pediatric practice) to treat hundreds of self-limited conditions with antibiotics. Parents insisted on it.

There are two major consequences from the practice of prescribing antibiotics liberally for self-limited medical conditions. First, we now have many more antibiotics in the ecosystem of the human community than we had before; all those who have taken antibiotics become little sources of antibiotic-resistant microbes. Second, antibiotic noncompliance becomes epidemic, without anyone noticing it. It is normal human behavior, after all, to take a medicine when you are feeling sick, and to stop taking the medicine when you are feeling better. If, in the scenario suggested above, the medical condition for which the antibiotic was prescribed is in fact a potentially lethal infection, then a decision to halt antibiotic treatment before the prescription is finished will be noticed quickly, as the disease will return. But if the antibiotic was prescribed for a cold (a viral condition), or any other self-limited medical condition, the condition will disappear on its own, and the patient can stop the antibiotic at any time without noticing new symptoms. Noncompliance, the patient will conclude, does no harm, saves money (the pills not taken can be sold, or saved for another sickness), and might as well become a habit.

"Overprescribing," noncompliance, and the existence of diseases that impair or destroy the immune system's ability to mop up the resistant germs left over from antibiotic attack, are factors that lead to the spread of antibiotic-resistant germs. To understand the full extent of the threat, however, we're going to have to leave the lions and pigs behind, for bacteria operate in strange and alarming ways. When a resistant and nonresistant bacterium come in contact with each other (in our bodies, for instance), they can pass resistance from one to the other. They can also pick up resistance from viruses that have invaded and expropriated DNA from resistant bacteria. "Indeed, the exchange of genes among different bacterial cells is so pervasive that the entire bacterial world can be thought of as a single huge multicellular organism."[4] An organism that feasts on human flesh. It is not a comforting thought.

Less comforting yet is the fact that the places where we would ordinarily seek treatment for disease can be the most fertile sites for bacterial proliferation.

In 1998, officials at the Centers for Disease Control and Prevention estimated that about 2 million patients (most with a weakened immunity system) develop a hospital-acquired infection in the United States each year and about 90,000 of these patients die. In at least 70% of these hospital-acquired infections, the organism is resistant to at least one antibiotic. In 30–40% of infections, the organism is resistant to the best drug available for treatment. Currently, the risk of contracting an infection during a stay in a U.S. hospital is 1 in 15, and the rate of such infections increased by 36% between 1975 and 1995.[5]

Hospitals are not the only culprits. Any location that brings large numbers of human beings into close enough contact, under unsterile conditions, for them to exchange germs, can be a similarly fertile focal point for the transfer of resistance to more strains of disease-causing organisms. The crowded urban areas of the developing world, without access to adequate supplies of pure water or the means to boil it, are perfect for the task. At the other end of the economic spectrum, the jet-setting world travelers carry strains of bacteria out of their home areas (where the organisms on which they feed may have built up, by the same mechanisms, some degree of resistance to them) into new parts of the world where they may flourish unhindered. If the traveler brings antibiotic resistance in his bacteria, that resistance can be transferred to bacteria at the ends of the earth, that have never been exposed to any antibiotics at all.

How on earth can they do this? The mechanisms of resistance transfer are complex. Bacteria genes do not stay demurely on the chromosome, as they do in more civilized species. Segments of genetic material called "transposons" can jump from the chromosome to free-floating loops of DNA called "plasmids," or from plasmid to chromosome. This jumping ability makes it possible for an exchange of genes that happens, in mammals, only among members of the same species, and only at mating—in the fertilization of egg by sperm—to happen in bacteria through "conjugation," the transfer of a plasmid from one bacterium to any other with which it is in contact. The bacteria do not have to be of the same species. The recipient of the plasmid encodes its contents and can then pass on the genetic traits, including antibiotic resistance, to all its offspring (numbering in the millions overnight). "It is a process akin to a computer software program being copied from the hard drive of one computer onto a floppy disk, then passed on to other computers."[6] Gram-negative bacteria, responsible for many common infections of urinary tract and lung, often carry the genes for antibiotic resistance in their plasmids. (The mechanisms of "resistance" are themselves complex, and vary from strain to strain of bacteria: some eat the antibiotic, some evade it by hiding the features by which the antibiotic recognizes it, some deceive it by making it bond to a site where it can do the bacterium no harm.)[7]

The implications of this ability are multitudinous and frightening. For instance, some strains of a bacteria called *Enterococcus* are resistant to the antibiotic vancomycin by virtue of a transposon that changes the composition of the cell wall so the vancomycin can't grab it and disable it. The number one cause of infections in the United States is the family of *Staphylococcus* bacteria, which can be brought under control only with vancomycin—all other antibiotics are ineffective against it. Now, what happens when an *Enterococcus* meets a *Staphylococcus* and shares a plasmid with the resistance transposon on it? It's happened in the laboratory, and in 1998, three real cases of vancomycin-resistant staphylococcus infection turned up.[8] By now there may be many more.

The major hope for retaining the usefulness of the antibiotics is to persuade the bacteria to abandon their resistance. This may not be as difficult a task as it sounds. Antibiotic resistance is expensive for a cell to maintain, requiring mechanisms, triggers, and other materials that have to be fed, just as it is expensive, for instance, for an oil company to maintain the capability to contain and remedy an oil spill at sea. In a world without oil spills, the company that maintains, at its own expense, the capacity to contain a spill will be at a market disadvantage to those who do not maintain such a capacity. That's why many years without an oil spill can tempt a company, very strongly, to dismantle its spill-containment capability.[9] Given an environment free from antibiotics, bacteria will tend to release their resistance-carrying plasmids, or lose out in the evolutionary competition to those who do (or who never had them).[10] Then why is resistance so prevalent, and increasing at such a terrifying rate? Because sloppy practices maintain an antibiotic-rich environment in which resistance continues to pay off. Several factors have already been suggested: physicians overprescribe because their patients demand antibiotics, hospitals fail to maintain a sterile environment, crowded urban settings proliferate in the developing world, increased transportation carries the genes for resistance over the entire world. Nor are these conditions likely to get better by themselves; on the contrary, they are intensifying. The U.S. health care system's trends encourage antibiotic use and therefore antibiotic resistance. With the advent of "managed care," physicians find themselves with less time to talk to each patient in the office and therefore more motivation to prescribe something that will satisfy the patient and send him away happy. With less time to spend with each patient in the hospital, they have less time to carry out the time-consuming sterilization procedures (washing, changing gloves) between patients. With limited reimbursement for time and tests, they are less likely to order the careful cultures that identify the specific germ and permit the narrow-spectrum antibiotic, and more likely to order the broad-spectrum antibiotic that most contributes to resistance.[11]

Conditions fostering antibiotic resistance across the world are getting worse, not better. With the advent of agribusiness and the consequent dispersal of peasants from their ancestral villages in rural areas of the developing world, more varied bacterial populations are crowding together in the urban slums. With the globalization of all economic activity, resistance carrying plasmids hitchhiking on world travelers are more likely to show up in the remote areas of the world now favored for manufacturing.

It would be very difficult to clear the vast "multicellular organism" (the bacteria of the world) of the antibiotic resistance acquired from our health care system, and it is unlikely to happen. But there is another source of antibiotic resistance, one that may be just as recalcitrant to change its ways.

DOWN ON THE PHARM

The other is the use of antibiotics in agriculture, especially in the raising of livestock, hogs, and cattle. This use of the miracle drugs stemmed from a chance discovery. There was an American Cyanamid plant on the Pearl River, just north of New York City, in 1949. It made tetracycline, a powerful antibiotic. Downstream from the plant, the fish were bigger than you'd expect. Curious, chemist Thomas Jukes found out that Cyanamid extracted the drug from mold grown on a grain mash in enormous vats, then discarded the rest of the mash—into the river, of course. Jukes tried feeding some of the mash to lab animals, and found they grew 10 to 20% faster than average. Delighted, Cyanamid promptly started marketing the leftover mash as a feed booster. Eventually, Jukes discovered that it was the drug, all by itself, that was doing the boosting. Animals fed low doses of antibiotics grow faster, larger, with less feed, probably because their bodies are not constantly fighting bacterial infections. That, according to Shannon Brownlee, "helped America become the agricultural powerhouse it is today. But," she continues, "there is no free hamburger, . . . and Jukes's discovery has turned out to have a potentially deadly downside: the more we use antibiotics, the more bacteria evolve into forms that resist them."[12] The concerns are not new. Twenty-five years ago, Lester Crawford, a scientist who worked with Jukes on the super-growing feed, recognized the danger, and was among the first to try to get the FDA to end the use of antibiotics. They lost that battle in 1980. Maybe it's time to try again.

With enough time, bacteria will grow resistant to any drug. We've already established that. But for that very reason, all who use drugs for any reason want the newest drug. In 1986, for instance, a new class of antibiotics, the fluoroquinolones, was approved for human use, because the old drugs were not working. "Only nine years later, in 1995, the FDA gave the go-ahead for veterinarians to begin dosing sick chickens with fluoroquinolones for the same reason: The old drugs no longer worked."[13]

The percentage of antibiotics used just to promote growth is not large—about 6.1% of the drugs sold for animal use. The rest of the farm drugs are used to treat sick animals or, significantly, to keep animals crammed into pens for long periods of time from getting sick from each other. Still, the number of animals affected is enormous. "That is because growers give antibiotics, in low but daily doses, to entire herds or flocks. . . .75 percent of the 92 million pigs in this country routinely chow down on feed laced with antibiotics. So do about 6 percent of cattle, 25 percent of chickens and half the turkeys."[14] Low doses of antibiotics in animals have exactly the effect predicted from noncompliance and overprescribing; slowly but very effectively, the susceptible bacteria are overcome by the resistant bacteria, until that is the only kind left.[15]

What kind of clinical evidence have we that the overuse of antibiotics in animals can cause human disease? It is very difficult to prove that any particular case of bacterial infection came from animals, let alone any particular case of antibiotic resistant infection. But in 1999, *The New England Journal of Medicine* published a case that demonstrated the connection. *Campylobacter jejuni* is a microbe that lives readily in livestock, but causes acute gastroenteritis in people—affecting somewhere between two and eight million people a year in the United States. Tracking only the "invasive" cases, when the germs escape from the intestines and enter the bloodstream, and only in Minnesota, a farming state that kept particularly good records, the *Journal* investigators found a pattern of increase in antibiotic resistance that could only have come from the local chicken farms.

In 1992 . . . . only 1.3% of the Minnesota cases were caused by strains of Campylobacter that were resistant to fluoroquinolones. By 1998, the number had risen to 10.2%. That's a pretty steep rise, and the researchers determined it was almost certainly because of antibiotic use on farms. Only a small fraction of the patients had ever taken fluoroquinolones themselves; and the genetic strain of resistant bacteria found in a significant number of the samples matched the genetic strain found on a variety of chicken products purchased at local grocery stores. Out of 91 chicken products, 80 were contaminated with Campylobacter. Twenty percent of those bacteria were resistant to ciprofloxacin, a fluoroquinolone that is needed to treat invasive gastroenteritis in humans.[16]

The National Chicken Council insists that "properly handled and cooked chicken product would be free of *Campylobacter*," and no doubt, in an ideal world, it would be. But that leaves us with the world that is, where there are each year 78 million cases of food-borne illness, 5,000 of which are fatal.[17] *Salmonella* bacteria, which have been around even longer, have developed a new strain, DT104, that is resistant to most common antibiotics; a recent victim contracted the bug almost certainly from working around antibiotic-laced animals. Another source of infection is the local water supply, recipient of antibiotic and bacteria rich runoff from the enormous factory farms on which we grow hogs, chickens, and beef cattle. Bacteria can travel freely from the farm to the supermarket to the home and hospital, and exchange resistance genes at every step of the way.[18]

We started using antibiotics on livestock to help them reach market size quicker, healthier, and with less food, all adding up to a better product less costly to produce. The free market surely justifies the practice of dosing the animals with antibiotics. But the consequence of the practice is that we are running out of medicines that work on us when we are very sick. "It's time," Shannon Brownlee concludes, "to stop squandering drugs as precious as antibiotics to reduce the price of meat by a few cents a pound," and she calls on the Food and Drug Administration to do something to restrict their use.[19]

The first time any international body voted to do anything about antibiotics was on December 14, 1998, when the European Union's agriculture ministers met in Brussels. Despite apparently intense lobbying by the drug manufacturers, 12 of the EU's 15 farm ministers voted to prohibit the use of virginiamycin, spiramycin, tysolin phosphate, and bacitracin zinc as growth promoters for livestock.[20] All these drugs are also used, or have close relatives that are used, to treat human diseases. The debate leading up to the meeting was vigorous. Against the ban, farmers feared for their income,[21] and the antibiotic manufacturers claimed that the digestion-enhancing antibiotics reduced waste products and feed use, and therefore helped the environment. Meanwhile, the Soil Association (an organic farming association) claimed that antibiotic use was out of control and threatened human health.[22] Both sides claimed that "the safety of the food supply" depended on adoption of its view. Three of the ministers abstained. The immediate consequence of the vote was the announcement by the affected drug manufacturers—Pfizer, Rhone-Poulenc, Elanco and Alpharma—that they would sue the European Commission for either withdrawal of the ban or monetary damages. (The damages could be serious; sales of the four antibiotics, much of that for farm use, was estimated to be about 211 million pounds sterling, or about $150 million.)[23]

Six months later, in April 1999, just before the bans were to go into effect, a plan to monitor antibiotic use in farm animals—to find out if resistance genes were resulting from the practice—was recommended by a pan-European scientific conference meeting in Paris.[24] Thereafter, and through the summer, the discussion on the use of antibiotics continued in the agricultural literature. The topics covered are much the same as those that came up before the ban was voted, and in some of the exchanges, the same trading of accusations reappears: the Soil Association accuses farmers of overusing antibiotics, and the National Office of Animal Health (an animal-raising industry association) accuses the Soil Association of scaremongering.[25] But in others the tone is different. The articles now emphasize that farmers are very well aware of the dangers of breeding antibiotic-resistant germs, but strongly oppose the withdrawal of all antibiotic use, on grounds that it would raise the price of meat in the market and might endanger public safety. (It also might badly compromise their ability to make a living.) They agree that monitoring for resistance is a good idea, and are particularly emphatic that the same rules should apply to all. In any free-market setting, antibiotic-dosed meat, by their calculations, will be able to undersell antibiotic-free meat, and they would be very resentful if their adherence to healthful rules should render them noncompetitive with other growers who do not obey such rules. One segment of the industry, the Grampian Country Food Group, which produces a third of all U.K.-reared chickens, claimed that the antibiotic growth promoters were not necessary in raising chickens "if high quality management systems and the right environment are in place."[26]

What are the alternatives to massive use of antibiotics in agriculture? The Grampian group talks of very careful sterile procedures, which they can be sure of because they raise all their own eggs and chicks. Occasionally in the literature, certain current "factory farm" practices, which require a very high density of animals to make their operations profitable, have come under direct attack. Many farmers, for many reasons, would like to see their livestock spread over more space, with room to move around and less chance to spread germs. These "free range" practices are a few steps away from what the Soil Association and its equivalents in the United States favor, which is a strict interpretation of "organic farming." Already the organic farmers have come down firmly on the side of simple ban of all antibiotics. To be "Certified Organic" by the U.S. Department of Agriculture, food must not have been produced using sewage sludge, pesticides, hormones, or antibiotics; irradiation and genetic modification are prohibited; and livestock must be given organic feed. Is "organic" a viable alternative to the usual sorts of farming? The market for certified organic food is significant, and still rising; but it has never been large, and we do not know if it could feed the world or any significant part of it.[27]

Plants, too, can contain antibiotics. In 1993, John Seabrook, writing in *The New Yorker*, introduced Calgene's controversial tomato, Flavr Savr, designed to resist pests and not get all squishy on the way to market. (You might review Chapter 1 at this point.) Despite investor enthusiasm (or because of it), environmental activists led by Jeremy Rifkin, president of the Foundation on Economic Trends and an antitechnology activist of long standing, had already organized a boycott against it. One of the problems of the Flavr Savr, besides just being a genetically modified organism (GMO) generally, was that it contained an antibiotic to cut down on bacterial attack. Rifkin and his followers fully understood the dangers of antibiotic resistance, and saw the Flavr Savr and its genre as very dangerous to human health[28] Six years after the tomato's appearance, Marie Woolf documented the arrival in Britain of a type of GM corn that seemed to threaten the usefulness of antibiotics.[29]

What is the place of antibiotics in agriculture? First, antibiotics are used to treat sick animals, just as they are used to treat sick humans. No one seems to oppose this practice. Second, they are used as routine prophylactics for animals crowded into pens for fattening, or raised in huge mobs for economy of land and manpower. There is strong sentiment, especially among the organic farmers, that those economies are too dearly bought. For the moment we cannot do anything about them and have the farmers stay in business, but an agriculture of the future will not need antibiotics for such purposes. Third, they are used lifelong, in low doses, as growth promoters. This is the use that seems to be most under attack; it is likely that the current EU ban will be extended to other antibiotics and the whole practice phased out.

PLAGUE YEARS: AIDS, TUBERCULOSIS, AND THE FUTURE OF DISEASE

Where else can antibiotic resistance come from? Let us begin with an account of AIDS in South Africa.

By now, everyone knows what AIDS is. It is a syndrome, not a disease in itself. It is caused by the human immunodeficiency virus (HIV), which may have several forms, which attacks and destroys the immune system of the victim. As the immune system collapses, the sufferer falls victim to one "opportunistic infection" after another, bacterial or fungal attacks that would be dispatched immediately by any healthy immune system, but which the compromised immune system of the AIDS patient cannot handle. Increasing amounts of antibiotics are required to fight the increasingly frequent infections. Eventually they all fail, and the victim is simply eaten alive by the incurable infestations. When AIDS first showed up in the United States—in the gay community of San Francisco and the intravenous (IV) drug subculture in New York, and other large cities— no one knew how it was transmitted. (We used to have ethics classes on the obligation to give routine medical and nursing care for AIDS patients, for doctors and nurses who were terrified of catching it.) What we found out was that the conditions of transfer are very demanding. There must be direct, blood-to-blood contact of bodily fluids. The virus is carried in blood (and on the needle withdrawn from the vein after IV drug injection), in semen, and in mother's milk. It can be transmitted from sexual partner to partner in sexual relations unless blocked by a condom, it can be transmitted from one drug user to another in sharing needles during IV drug use, and it can be transmitted from mother to child in childbirth and in breastfeeding a baby. Before we knew to screen the blood supply, some people got HIV from blood transfusions; it can also (rarely) be transmitted by accidental needlesticks in hospitals, or by getting the blood from an HIV-positive patient in any open cut or sore.

We cannot cure AIDS, or remove HIV from the blood. But the infection is not, in the developed nations, the death sentence it once was. There are "cocktails," or combinations, of retroviral drugs that have shown a great deal of promise in slowing the destruction of the immune system once HIV is found. It is possible that a seropositive patient of the future will be able to live for a long time on these drugs, without developing full-blown AIDS. They are not easy to manage. They must be taken at precise times in precise order, and the drugs themselves have nasty side effects. Life with HIV will not be easy for anyone. (Worse, glowing reports of the effectiveness of these cocktails seems to have diminished caution among certain susceptible communities. The gay community of San Francisco had seen HIV infection rates plummet with the adoption of safe sex; it is now again on the rise.)[30] Retroviral drugs or no, the best course will always be prevention.

By now, everyone knows how to prevent the transmission of HIV. Use a condom in any and all sexual relations; use only clean needles while injecting IV drugs; use Universal Precautions (fresh gloves, face masks, repeatedly sterilized tools and surfaces) in all dealings with patients in hospitals. And by now, everyone knows why these measures are so difficult to implement. There are strong cultural resistances to the use of condoms (using a condom is like "wearing a raincoat when you take a

shower," or "eating a candy bar with the wrapper on"), and the influence of such institutions as the Roman Catholic Church has made them
more difficult to obtain. The free distribution of bleach kits for needles,
or a needle exchange to provide sterile needles for unsterile, meets up
with vigorous resistance from those who see these measures as condon-
ing illegal drug use by taking away one of the natural penalties. Universal
precautions take a lot of time, and when hospital staff are overworked,
they may be easily forgotten. There is no such resistance in dealing with
the transmission of HIV from a seropositive mother to newborn child,
which occurs during the process of childbirth itself. To prevent mother-
child transmission, successful trials (many in Africa) have shown that
short-course administration of antiviral drugs like ziduvidine (AZT) or
nevirapine, given to a mother shortly before she gives birth, will reduce
dramatically the rate of transmission of HIV during childbirth.
Unfortunately, if the mother then goes on to breastfeed the child, the
advantage is lost. Of course, if the mother acknowledges that she is HIV-
positive and asks for infant formula to feed her child, that result could
be avoided. But at that point we run most squarely into the cultural
peculiarities of Africa.

South Africa is in some ways a microcosm of sub-Saharan Africa generally, with a large underemployed native population, poverty and disease rampant, and the cultural inheritance of centuries of tribal life. But
in some ways it is not. It bears the imprint of several centuries of British
rule, with a working bureaucracy, earnest attempts to keep good records,
and access to journalists. Part of the Dark Continent, it is yet one on
which we can shine a flashlight.

And what we see is not reassuring. South Africa offered to host the 13th
International AIDS Conference in Durban, in part because the delegates
would be meeting in "the most-infected province of the most-infected
country on the most-infected continent," and would have no trouble relat-
ing to the terrible reality of the epidemic.[31] In that setting, South African
President Thabo Mbeki outraged the delegates in his opening speech, in
which he suggested that the link between HIV and AIDS was not as clear
as had been thought, and that the major cause of AIDS was poverty.[32] The
delegates were aware that Mbeki had been pursuing "dissident" opinions
in the AIDS debate, including those of Berkeley professor Peter Duesberg,
as alternatives to the orthodox scientific view that HIV causes AIDS. (The
dissidents, characterized by Helen Epstein in *The New York Review* as "a
murky group of California scientists and activists," believe that AIDS is
caused by "a vague collection of factors, including malnutrition, chemical
pollution, recreational drugs, and by the very pharmaceutical drugs that
are used to treat the disease." They think the HIV-AIDS link to be "part
of a vast conspiracy cooked up by the pharmaceutical industry to justify
the market in anti-AIDS drugs, such as AZT, worth billions of dollars a
year.")[33] Why did Mbeki, a well-educated and dedicated public servant,

elect to go this kooky route? From other remarks he has made, there is a strong feeling that he rejects "western-imposed" science, and wishes to find a pure African explanation of this disease—and an African remedy. He had intervened, to a degree very unusual for any politician, in the AIDS research in his country, openly supporting (for instance) trials of "virodene," a substance developed at the University of Pretoria, whose developers claimed that it would cure AIDS. The nature of the stuff (which includes dry-cleaning fluid) suggested that it would do AIDS sufferers much more harm than good, and Mbeki was severely criticized by the South African medical establishment for his open support of it. The controversy lasted for months; it became clear that the drug's supporters saw the matter as a conflict of Africa versus the West, even as it became even clearer that the politicians' involvement with virodene was financial as well as intellectual. (A court battle brought to the surface documents that showed that the African National Congress [ANC] was to share in the profits of its company.)[34]

It is easy to see Mbeki's speech as symptomatic of the worst ills of the AIDS fight in South Africa. The major battle concerning AIDS in Africa has always been the battle for honesty. We were able to make the progress that we did in the United States—the isolation of the virus, the discovery of ways to prevent transmission, eventually the retroviral drug cocktails that can keep people alive—because the first U.S. citizens who suffered from it, the gay communities on both coasts, insisted that the nation must face the disease squarely and deal with it. Even so, as soon as apparently reassuring news came from the drug companies, the AIDS infection rate started rising again in the United States. Although some hopeful advances have been made in Uganda and Zimbabwe in particular, sub-Saharan Africans in general cannot yet acknowledge the problem, face it in their own bodies and their own families, and set out to prevent its transmission by all the unpleasant ways that are required.[35] Death certificates are falsified to conceal the death from AIDS, women are beaten senseless if they tell their husbands that they are HIV-positive (the men refuse to be tested, so the assumption is that the woman must have got it from someone else), and a decision not to breastfeed a child is taken as an admission, by the woman, that she is HIV-positive. That is why the short-course doses of antiviral drugs to prevent mother-child transmission are ultimately not very useful.

Meanwhile, the traditional position of women in southern African society makes it very difficult to control the spread of the disease by teaching women to refuse unwanted or unsafe sex. Even the right of the woman to refuse gang rape, or to report it, is not yet established in South Africa.[36] Teaching "safe sex" to males has not proved effective:

> . . . these and other efforts . . . have so far proved no match for custom, cultural confusion and peer pressure. "They say, 'We are

going to die anyway, so what's the use of using a condom,'" says Sheila Mathemba, 20, of the Viros, a township rap group. "They say, 'Unless it's flesh on flesh, it's not real sex.' They don't want to take responsibility."[37]

The result of this culturally compelled inattention to the spread of AIDS has had predictable results. About 4.2 million South Africans have AIDS. The HIV-infection rate is now almost 20%, up from 13% two years ago. The most vulnerable class of southern Africans are young women. The percentage of 15- to 25-year-old women with HIV (whether or not AIDS has yet developed) tops 15% in Namibia, Zambia, Malawi, and Mozambique; it tops 25% in Zimbabwe, South Africa and Lesotho; and it hits an incredible 34% in Botswana.[38] And in most of that area, there are too many cultural barriers to discussing AIDS to make any significant progress. The situation can only get worse. The United Nations estimates that about half of all 15-year-olds in these countries will die of AIDS.

That, of course, is why the Durban conference was called "Break the Silence." The delegates arrived in Durban expecting a clarion call for action from the President of South Africa. Instead they got one more evasion, one more attempt to blame AIDS on absolutely anything except the behavior of South Africans. No wonder they were furious.[39] In retrospect, analysts have at least sympathized with his position—AIDS drugs are terribly expensive for a poor country, accepting free drugs from generous drug companies only increases the nation's dependency, since the victims must be supported for the rest of their lives, and all the expensive drugs in the world won't attack the underlying problems of southern African ill-health—the extreme poverty of the area.[40] In an ominous appraisal of the condition of AIDS-infested Africa, Lawrence Goldyn focused on the role of "pharmaceutical-based" medicine in South Africa. It is not just that, at an average allotment of $40 per person for health care in the country, the $10,000 to $15,000 per AIDS patient for the retroviral cocktails is beyond their means. It is also that they simply have not the infrastructure to support drug treatment.

Their battle with tuberculosis is instructive. They have cheap, easy-to-take drugs, but infection rates continue up, because the TB patients known to the state are not taking them. TB drugs are widely sold on the black market, to those who have reason not to come in contact with the health care system or any public system, largely obtained from patients enrolled in treatment plans concealing their drugs instead of taking them. Prices for TB drugs are high, higher for "dry" (untouched) pills than for "wet" pills (concealed under the tongue while the public health worker watches the patient swallow the water, spat out later for sale.) Imagine, Goldyn suggests, the black market price that could be commanded for HIV drugs, virtually unobtainable elsewhere in sub-Saharan Africa.[41]

What role is played by South Africa in cultivating antibiotic resistance across the globe? It may just be the ultimate incubator. As antibiotics overused in inadequate doses in my body may make me more susceptible to resistant germs, as antibiotics overused in inadequate doses in the livestock may expose an entire population to antibiotic-resistant bacteria, so antibiotic-resistant germs grown with the help of Western medicine in the AIDS regions of Africa may attack the entire globe. Consider what a fine incubator of antibiotic resistant bacteria is an AIDS population. All sufferers from AIDS are repeatedly attacked by opportunistic infections, like *pneumocystis carinii,* a nasty lung infection that leaves alone those of us with intact immune systems. We fight it with antibiotics (bring on the lions). South Africa has access to all antibiotics. But often the patient is noncompliant, and keeps back some of the antibiotics for later sale (the lions are called off too soon), or by now the patient's immune system is so weakened that it cannot deal with the bacteria left over after the course of antibiotics (the wolves are gone). In either case, the patient is now one huge petri dish for the cultivation of antibiotic-resistant disease.

The important point is that the diseases so cultivated are not confined to Africa. There is no way they could possibly be confined to Africa, given the huge traffic across the oceans occasioned by the globalization of all business, especially agribusiness. And once the disease gets a passport, we are all equally at risk. Antibiotic-resistant tuberculosis will kill us, any of us wealthy middle class with all access to good medicine, with the same inevitability that it killed off our great-grandfathers, before there were antibiotics at all. It is certain that much of the tuberculosis that the underdeveloped public health system of South Africa is unable to treat is by now resistant to the usual antibiotics. As AIDS spreads, it is certain that any disease treated with standard antibiotics will rapidly mutate into one that is resistant, since the antibiotics do not have a working immune system to back it up. We are, as the *New York Times* put it, "Losing Ground Against Microbes," and we may soon be back at the battle lines of the early twentieth century.[42]

THE SEARCH FOR BEARS

Where do we go from here? The best bet is that all existing antibiotics will be useless for most serious diseases within the next few decades, as the African-born disease organisms join those emerging independently in the overfed and overprescribed West. What other approaches to bacterial disease control can we use?

As the first word in alternative energy development must always be conservation, so the first word in the treatment of bacterial disease is prevention. We know how to prevent the spread of bacteria, through scrupulous attention to washing (hands, tools, foods and surfaces), through the use of disinfectants in any context at risk of carrying bacteria, through thorough cooking of all food, and through avoidance of situations involving close contact with strangers. All of this is true, and in hospitals and other major sources of microbial infection, preventive scrubbing is the most important first line of defense. But the standard little list of cautions just doesn't seem to match up with the situation of the urban worker on the subway eating his fast-food lunch with one hand, while he sorts through his calendar for the next appointment with the other. Punctilious sterilization of everything, everywhere, is not in the cards.

There is some stop-gap help in the addition of a few more lions. A new drug, for instance, Synercid, developed by Rhone-Poulenc, showed promise of success where others have failed. But its days too are numbered: virginiamycin, one of the four antibiotics banned by the EU in 1999, is very similar in structure to Synercid, and has been around since 1974 in cattle feed. Germs that are immune to virginamycin seem to be immune to Synercid too.[43]

Are there other ways to make our food safer? One suggestion is to lower the incidence of harmful bacteria through systematic irradiation of the food supply. Food irradiation is done by passing food through an irradiator, a closed chamber, in which it is exposed to an ionizing energy source. In the United States, the source of the gamma rays tends to be cobalt-60, contained in stainless steel rods. That kind of radiation does not break down other atoms (no chance of "chain reaction" or meltdown), and makes nothing radioactive. But it does kill germs. Irradiation has been carried on for more than forty years in small applications. There seems to be no downside to the process. There were initial claims that vitamins or other nutrients might be destroyed, or that the food would contain new "radiolytic" (radiation-produced) substances that would be harmful. After exhaustive research on the point, it seems that at the worst, the inactivation of vitamins caused by radiation is 1.5% of nutrient lost (of B and C vitamins only, and only in some foods). That loss is less than that occasioned by cooking. The radiolytic substances produced in meats also turn out to be those that are produced in cooking anyway. After examining the issue at some length, the American Dietetic Association endorsed the use of food irradiation as "an important approach in protecting the safety and quality of the food supply."[44] John Henkel, writing for the Food and Drug Administration, presented an extended defense of the effectiveness and safety of the procedure in the *FDA Consumer* in the Spring of 1998.

> . . . as long as radiation is applied to foods in approved doses, it's safe, says FDA's Pauli [Dr. George Pauli, FDA food irradiation safety coordinator]. Similar to sending luggage through an airport

scanner, the process passes food quickly through a radiation field—typically gamma rays produced from radioactive cobalt-60. That amount of energy is not strong enough to add any radioactive material to the food. The same irradiation process is used to sterilize medical products such as bandages, contact lens solutions, and hospital supplies such as gloves, sutures and gowns. Many spices sold in this country also are irradiated, which eliminates the need for chemical fumigation to control pests. American astronauts have eaten irradiated foods since 1972.[45]

There is general agreement with the FDA and the ADA's position, especially in the light of recent bacterial infections: the DT104 *Salmonella,* and especially the lethal *E. coli* O157:H7, both recent mutated arrivals on the infectious scene, both presenting problems of diagnosis and treatment. Irradiation of food prior to sale, especially of food (like hamburger) that may be served only partially cooked, will prevent these infections. It should also eliminate *Campylobacter* from the chicken supply. More speeches to food handlers about sterile precautions, and more inspections, may help, but ultimately, Minnesota Health Department's chief epidemiologist argued, the only way to ensure that food is free from infectious microorganisms is to irradiate it.[46] The World Health Organization, the American Medical Association, and most trade groups in food handling also agree that the process is safe and effective. In a recent note, the *Tufts University Health & Nutrition Letter* announced that the larger food processors (Cargill, Tyson Foods, IBP Incorporated) planned to use a new kind of irradiation that dispenses with radioactive compounds and uses electricity as the energy source instead (electron beams rather than gamma rays). The note adds that irradiation is already in use in nursing homes, for patients with compromised immune systems.[47]

As in other recent developments in food merchandising (see Chapter 1, again), the proposal to irradiate the food supply has drawn fire from some groups. The Washington, D.C.-based Nuclear Information and Resource Service (NIRS) warns "that zapping food with the same radioactive materials used at Chernobyl and Three Mile Island is inviting disaster—particularly because these substances are being used in industrial buildings that do not use the same precautions that nuclear reactors do. 'The opportunity for unplanned exposure of workers and nearby businesses or residences is quite real,' NIRS executive director Michael Mariotte says."[48] Greenpeace also is opposed to radiation. In a secondary campaign, some groups have asked for "labels" to identify irradiated food—essentially, the three-segment "radiation danger" sign from the days of the fallout shelters.[49] (Unsurprisingly, the food packaging industry is opposed to conspicuous labeling of that sort.) It is difficult to find any factual basis for the anti-irradiation campaign.[50] That difficulty does not seem to be slowing it down. (Incidentally, the *Tufts*

H & N letter mentioned above takes on the three most common fears about irradiated foods—that the food is radioactive, that the irradiation creates radiolytic compounds that can cause cancer, and that irradiated food is of diminished nutritional quality—and undertakes to answer them.)[51]

Irradiation may help kill off some of the worst of the microbes in some of the more dangerous places they live. But you can't irradiate the whole world. In the end, we will continue to get bacterial infections, just as we always have. If our lions are no good anymore, are there bears to keep the raging pigs under control? The surprising answer is that yes, there may very well be, and the source of the bears is the Soviet Bear itself: a decrepit laboratory in Tbilisi, Georgia, of the former USSR For 70 years, the bacteriologists of the Eliava Institute in Tbilisi have been perfecting Felix d'Herelle's work with "bacteriophages," tiny viruses that eat germs for lunch.[52]

> Viral predators only one-fortieth the size of the average bacteria cell, they swarm unseen around us, busily searching and destroying their favorite food: germs. . . . They are so tiny that a single drop of tap water may contain a billion of them.[53]

Like all viruses, they kill by attaching to a microbe, inserting their own genetic material into the cell, and proceeding, over the next hours, to commandeer the entire cell to the production of new versions of the phage. Then all the little new phages go hunting. They work very well.

Why don't we use them? Thereon hangs a political tale. When d'Herelle discovered them in Paris in 1917, he was convinced they would revolutionize the treatment of disease. But the laboratory science of the time was nowhere near exact enough to isolate and store the phages. There are hundreds of types of phages, and each one kills only one type of bacteria. "Predator and prey must be perfectly matched, a daunting process."[54] Nor were the researchers of the time able to purify the solution of phages. So although Eli Lilly actually manufactured phage-based medicines in the 1930s, they were not perfected by the time penicillin came along and drove everything else from the field. D'Herelle took his work to the Soviet Union in 1934, and with Stalin's support, helped George Eliava develop precisely targeted phages for the Red Army during World War II. Eventually the Eliava Institute had over 300 clones of known bacteriophages in their library.

Why didn't we hear about this? First, because we had antibiotics, and needed no more. Second, because, well, what of good could come out of the Soviet Union? Bacteriophage research was widely ignored all over the West. While Stalin lived, the Institute was protected, mostly (Eliava himself was shot by Lavrenti Beria, Stalin's chief of secret police—not over science, but over a woman). While the Soviet Union prospered, the Institute prospered. But now, Georgia is in poverty. The people cannot afford to buy the medicines, or any medicines. There is no support for the Institute, and its laboratories are crumbling. When the electricity fails, any number of clones in the library can be lost, for they require refrigeration to live. The Institute is in deep trouble, and the skills and knowledge built up here may die unless help arrives soon.

Help may or may not be on the way. There is Western interest in bacteriophages now, largely because of bacterial resistance to antibiotics, and Western notions of "venture capitalists" and "start-up companies" have entered the traditional Marxist idea-system of Georgia. But what will the new Westerners do with the knowledge that has been shared? In 1996, a "partnership," between a Seattle facility and one in Tbilisi, to be known jointly as Phage Therapeutics, collapsed as soon as it started. The Americans insisted that no Western market would accept any product from the former Soviet Union, so they closed the Tbilisi facility. But they kept the research, and the knowledge, and are now readying products for the American market. "We gave the Americans access to all this background research," said Nina Chanishvili, senior researcher at the Institute, "and they simply walked away with it. They told us we were stupid at business. Well, that at least was true."[55]

There is a long way to go with phages. Right now work is being done by Carl Merril of the National Institutes of Health (NIH) to use techniques of genetic engineering to give phages a longer lifespan, to make them more effective against disease. Then come purification techniques and years of animal testing. Ironically, the testing on humans has been done, in unconsented field trials on the construction crews of the Baikal-Amur railroad in Siberia in the 1970s, but the results are not acceptable for FDA approval. Phages are still in regular use in Russia and Georgia, primarily to treat burn wounds and postsurgical infections. Phages are the only thing they have against staphylococcus aureus infections. Increasingly, when that and similar staphylococcus infections run riot in the West, the Institute is called for help.

Does this show, as claimed, that "phages are ready to be used in the West"?[56] Will they replace vancomycin, and all the other exhausted legions of miracle drugs? We are surely at the end of a 50-year run of Magic Bullets from the mold-based antibiotics. Maybe phages will be the Magic Assassin's Knives of the future. If the epidemic of resistant diseases, now brewing all over the world with its epicenter in Africa, proceeds the way it seems it will, we will need all the Knives we can get.

QUESTIONS FOR REFLECTION

+ Did we rely too much on antibiotics? How?
+ What's wrong with our medical practices, that antibiotic resistance results? How might we do this better?

✦ What's wrong with our agricultural practices, that antibiotic resistance results? How might we restructure those practices?

Notes

1. G. Tyler Miller, *Living in the Environment,* 11th Ed. (Pacific Grove, CA: Brooks/Cole, 2000).
2. Ibid., p. 452.
3. Ibid.
4. Ibid.
5. Ibid.
6. Paul F. Kamitsuka, "The Current Peril of Antibiotic Resistance," in G. Tyler Miller, *Living in the Environment,* pp. 466–467.
7. Ibid.
8. Ibid.
9. Lisa Newton and Catherine Dillingham, "Oil And Water: The Case of the Exxon Valdez," in *Watersheds II* (Wadsworth, 1997).
10. Ibid.
11. Ibid.
12. Shannon Brownlee, "Antibiotics in the Food Chain: Farmers Who Give Animals Drugs to Make Them Grow to Market Weight Faster Unwittingly Contribute to Antibiotic-Resistant Diseases in Humans," *The Washington Post* (21 May 2000): B3.
13. Ibid.
14. Ibid.
15. Ibid. As Lester Crawford put it, "Low doses don't kill off bacteria —they just make them mad." We all know that's not what's happening, but isn't it a cute way of putting it?
16. Ibid., citing Kirk Smith, J. M. Besser, C. W. Hedberg, F. T. Leano, J. B. Bender, J. H. Wicklund, B. P. Johnson, K. A. Moore, and M. T. Osterholm, "Quinolone-resistant *Campylobacter jejuni* Infections in Minnesota, 1992–1998," *The New England Journal of Medicine* 340(20) (1999): 1525. See also report by Amanda Spake, "Do Livestock Breed Drug-resistant Bugs?", *U.S. News and World Report* (31 May 1999): p. 65, commenting on the same *NEJM* article.
17. Nicols Fox, *Spoiled: The Dangerous Truth About a Food Chain Gone Haywire* (New York: Basic Books, 1997): pp. 13–14. Nicols Fox asserts that "Official estimates are that the cases in the United States run as high as 81 million cases a year, but recently the CDC's Dr. Morris Potter pushed that number up even higher," even as high as 266 million cases a year.
18. Ibid.
19. Ibid.
20. Katherine Butler, "European Ministers Ban Four Antibiotics from Animal Feed," *The Independent* (15 December 1998): p. 4; Michael Smith, "Brussels Bans Antibiotics in Animal Feed: Food Safety Legal Action Threatened," *Financial Times* (15 December 1998): p. 3.
21. Michael Hornsby, "Farmers Fear £160m Cost of Antibiotic Ban," *The Times* (4 December 1998).

22. Charles Arthur, "Ban Antibiotics in All Farming," *The Independent* (7 December 1998); Cathy Comerford, "Soaring Use of Farm Antibiotics Presents Threat to Humans," *The Independent* (8 December 1998).

23. Susie Whalley, "Bacteria Threat of Mass-Farmed Meat," *Supermarketing* (11 December 1998): p. 12; Jonathan Riley, "Antibiotic Restrictions Are Urged," *Farmers Weekly* (11 December 1998): p. 6; "Organic Farming Campaigner Calls for Ban on Animal Antibiotics," *Chemist and Druggist* (12 December 1998): p. 28; Charles Arthur and Cathy Comerford, "Europe Set to Curb Farm Antibiotics," *The Independent* (14 December 1998): p. 6.

24. "Closer Watch on Resistance Signs,"*Farmers Guardian* (9 April 1999): p. 7.

25. Patricia Lieberman, "Antibiotic Resistance High-priority Cattle Issue," *USA Today* (25 June 1999): p. 14A; Charles Arthur, "Farmers 'Failing' to Limit Drug Use," *The Independent* (29 June 1999): p. 9; Robin Young, "Health Risk as Farms Overuse Antibiotics," *The Times* (19 August 1999): Home News; "Industry Rubbishes Threat of Drug-resistant Disease," *Farming News* (20 August 1999): p. 2; "Antibiotics Claims Alarmist, Say NOAH," *Farmers Guardian* (27 August 1999).

26. Alistair Driver, "Antibiotics 'No Advantage' in Boosting Poultry Growth," *Farmers Guardian* (10 September 1999): p. 17.

27. Deborah L. Shelton, "Going Organic," *Essence* (July 2000): p. 81. Anita Manning, "'Certified Organic' to Reflect Consumer Demands," *USA Today* (8 March 2000): 6D.

28. John Seabrook, "Tremors in the Hothouse: The Battle Lines Are Being Drawn for the Soul of the American Consumer as Agribusiness Launches the First Genetically Altered Supermarket Tomato," The New Yorker (19 July 1993): pp. 38-39.

29. Marie Woolf, "Modified Corn on Sale in UK 'Kills' Life-Saving Antibiotics," *The Independent* (6 June 1999): p. 13. Granted, the article is passing strange, alleging that the corn itself has an "antibiotic resistance gene," deliberately inserted apparently to protect the corn from antibiotics, that could render useless any antibiotic being taken by someone eating the corn-that can "degrade an antibiotic in the human gut in 30 minutes." I don't think that's true. I think I know what the original problem was, and I don't think that's it.

30. Scott Gottlieb, "The Limits of the AIDS Miracle," *The New York Times* (9 July 2000): Op Ed.

31. Lawrence K. Altman, "Africa's AIDS Crisis: Finding Common Ground," *The New York Times* (16 July 2000): p. 6.

32. David Brown and Jon Jeter, "Hundreds Walk Out On Mbeki; S. African's Speech on AIDS Protested," *The Washington Post* (10 July 2000): p. A1.

33. Helen Epstein, "The Mystery of AIDS in South Africa," *The New York Review* (20 July 2000): p. 50.

34. Ibid., pp. 53–54. Epstein cites, in support of her statements on virodene, S. J. Klebanoff et al., "Activation of the HIV Type 1 Long Terminal Repeat and Viral Replication by Dimethylsulfoxide and Related Solvents," *AIDS Research and Human Retroviruses* 13 (20 September 1997): 1221–1227; "Virodene Is Still Being Sold: SAPS," *The Citizen* (6 March 1998); and many letters to the *South African Medical Journal* by physicians in South Africa. She suggests, without

quite saying so, that some clinical trials that were supposed to be of AZT and nevirapine were actually using virodene, making the patients very sick or killing them.

35. Helen Epstein, "The Mystery of AIDS in South Africa," also Tom Masland, "Breaking the Silence," *Newsweek* (17 July 2000): pp. 30–32.

36. Tom Masland, "Breaking the Silence."

37. Ibid.

38. Ibid. (see table).

39. "AIDS in South Africa," *The New York Times*(12 July 2000): Editorial; David Brown and Jon Jeter, "Hundreds Walk Out On Mbeki."

40. Rachel L. Swarns, "Dissent on AIDS by South Africa's President, Thoughtfulness or Folly?", *The New York Times* (8 July 2000): p. 5; Brown and Jeter, "Hundreds Walk Out On Mbeki"; Rachel Swarns, "South Africa Faults Critics of Its President on AIDS Stance," The New York Times (11 July 2000): p. 3.

41. Lawrence Goldyn, "Africa Can't Just Take a Pill For AIDS," *The New York Times*(6 July 2000): Op Ed.

42. "Losing Ground Against Microbes," *The New York Times* (18 June 2000): Editorial.

43. Shannon Brownlee, "Antibiotics in the Food Chain"; Amanda Spake, "Do Livestock Breed Drug-resistant Bugs?"

44. American Dietetic Association, "Position of the American Dietetic Association: Food Irradiation," *Journal of the American Dietetic Association* 96(1) (January 1996): 69–73. See extensive references attached to this article for a history of research on irradiated food. See also "Red Meat Irradiation Approved," *FDA Consumer* (March–April 1998): p. 2.

45. John Henkel, "Irradiation: a Safe Measure for Safer Food," *FDA Consumer* (May–June 1998): p. 12.

46. Michael T. Osterholm, "No Magic Bullet: More Inspectors is Fine and Dandy, but Don't Kid Yourself: Government Can't 'Solve' the Problem of Food Safety," *Newsweek* (1 September 1997): p. 33.

47. "Irradiation Back on the Front Burner," *Tufts University Health & Nutrition Letter* (March 2000): p. 4.

48. Cristin Marandino, "Is Zapping Food the Answer?" *Vegetarian Times* (December 1997): p. 12.

49. Katherine Gallia, "Food Irradiators 1, Public 0," *Natural Health* (January 1999): p. 23.

50. The website for the Public Citizen (http://www.citizen.org) has a bibliography on the "unwholesomeness of irradiated food." It cites 23 articles in reasonably prestigious journals, all considering the effects of radiation damage on foods. The articles generally date from the mid-1960s through the early 1980s; there are none later than 1986.

51. "Irradiation Back on the Front Burner," p. 47.

52. Lawrence Osborne, "A Stalinist Antibiotic Alternative," *The New York Times Magazine* (6 February 2000): pp. 50–55.

53. Ibid., pp. 51–52.

54. Ibid.

55. Ibid., p. 54. The issue was underscored on the evening following the conversation here recorded, when Osborne visited the head of the Institute and found him watching an American documentary on his cable TV. The documentary was on bacteriophages, and used images that had simply been lifted, without compensation, from the uncopyrighted files of the Institute. The head of the Institute was not happy.

56. Ibid., p. 55.

CHAPTER 8

Skunked

Crisis in the New England Fisheries

QUESTIONS TO KEEP IN MIND

How do we catch fish these days? How did we used to? What difference does this change make in employment, technology, and the social structure of fishing towns?

What has happened to the total catch of fish since World War II? Why?

What measures seem likely to ensure plentiful fish into the future? Or are there any?

TOO MANY BOATS CHASING TOO FEW FISH

In 1973, the Northwest Atlantic fisheries yielded 4.4 million tons of fish; in 1992, only 2.6 million tons, a decline of 42%.[1] The take of Atlantic cod, crucial to the New England economy, had peaked in 1968 at 3.9 million tons; by 1992, it was down to 1.2 million tons—a decline of a horrifying 69%.[2] There were further declines in 1993.[3] Worldwide, the marine catch had been stagnant since 1989, despite an increase in the number and capacity of all boats. From the New England fisherman's point of view, the monetary loss has been staggering, especially in the most recent years: the Northeast catch of the most popular commercial species was worth over $150 million in 1991, not quite $130 million in 1992, and less than $116 million in 1993. The value of the annual catch of Atlantic cod fell from almost $75 million in 1991 to $45 million in 1993, down 40%.[4] In this situation, unprecedented in the human experience, the United Nations Food and Agriculture Organization (FAO) was led to suggest that the only way to increase the supply of fish was "by reducing or temporarily eliminating fishing in many fisheries."[5]

What went wrong? In *Net Loss*, a 1994 Worldwatch Paper, Peter Weber puts the problem very simply: there are too many fishers chasing too few fish:

> Today, world fisheries have on the order of twice the capacity necessary to fish the oceans. Between 1970 and 1990, FAO [United Nations Food and Agriculture Organization] recorded a doubling in the world fishing fleet, from 585,000 to 1.2 million large boats, and from 13.5 million to 25.5 million gross registered tons.[6]

Size alone creates difficulties: each of those boats represents a hefty investment for its owner, who can only pay off the loans by bringing in ever more fish. Since at least until very recently the sorts of boundaries that can limit human predation on land do not apply on the sea,[7] management options are limited to constricting the permissible time for catching fish:

> . . . open access allows fishers to enter a fishery at will. If regulators limit the total catch, they must calculate the potential take of the fishers and adjust the length of the open season accordingly. Fishers then race each other to get the most fish possible. As the number of fishers or their capacity increases, the season gets shorter . . .[8]

This brings about a tendency towards zero as a limit. Under these conditions, of course, the owner who fields the most or the largest boats brings in the greatest share of the prize; the incentive is to increase the capacity to catch and store fish, and the speed to get to the fishing grounds. Therefore, building to overcapacity is structured into the system.[9] The only limit on entry comes when the latest entrant, no matter how efficient, cannot meet his marginal costs. Then the catch may stabilize—but at too low a level to sustain the fishery.[10] The situation is made bad by the free market system, which abhors limits on individual exploitation of the natural world, and then made worse by the tendency of developed nations to vote for government subsidies for the financially distressed but politically popular fisherman, thus keeping boats active in the water that pure market forces would scuttle.

Clearly something has to be done. But it is not in the nature of the fishing industry, carried on by thousands of entrepreneurs who own their own boats, to cooperate in making and enforcing rules to limit the catch, even though such rules are necessary to keep the fishery going for the long run. For fishing, like farming, is not so much a business as a way of life—inherited, valued, and tied up with all other institutions in the regions that have been supported by it. The fishermen keep on doing what they have been doing all their lives, even as it destroys the resource from which they draw. One observer commented: "Indeed what is fascinating—and also tragic—about the fishing industry is that it so actively participates in its own annihilation."[11] Any remedial action, then, must begin outside the industry. Once begun, and accepted as reasonable, it has a chance of obtaining the support of the fishermen; it cannot succeed without their cooperation.

Before trying to crack the political nuts at the center of this natural disaster, let us review some of the history of this craft, profession, and way of life. The analysis and conclusions of this chapter—diagnosis, prognosis, and prescription—will hold good for any fishery anywhere in the world. But each fishery has its own history, customs, and economic and social support systems, without which the environmental problem (and the difficulties with the solutions) cannot be comprehended. Since we cannot cover them all, we will start with the one nearest to us, the one made famous by Rudyard Kipling's novel *Captains Courageous*—the Georges Bank fishery, home of the Gloucestermen. The rest of the Northwest Atlantic fisheries will follow the same pattern.

THE CAPTAINS COURAGEOUS: FISHING IN NEW ENGLAND

The Natural History of Georges

The curious features of the water on the massive shoal known as Georges Bank ("St. Georges' Shoal," on the earliest maps) account for the tremendous concentration of fish. The currents on Georges Bank are strong and complex. William Macleish, who wrote an account (*Oil and Water*) of the Georges as background for the 1980s dispute over the placement of oil rigs on it, includes a short account of these currents. Citing Brad Butman, a physical oceanographer associated with the U.S. Geological Survey, he reports that the current

> . . . has three components. The tidal one is by far the strongest, about a knot and a half up by the shoals. Superimposed on that is the mean flow around the Bank, the clockwise gyre Bigelow [a turn-of-the-century pioneer in oceanography] found and others at Woods Hole have studied for years. That moves usually at about a tenth of a knot. The third component, only recently the subject of systematic measurement, is storm driven. Those currents have been clocked at near one knot at the bottom along the southern flank of Georges and are probably much stronger near the surface.[12]

And then there are internal currents and eddies. The tidal currents are complex, since the water moves much faster over the shallow areas than the deep.

> Out of this swirl come hints, some of them quite strong, of what makes Georges Bank so productive. First, its waters are rich in nutrients like phosphorus and silicates, supplied in part by the cold oceanic water welling up from the depths onto the Bank and in part by planktonic organisms, whose excretions contain some of the nutrients they have ingested. Second, over much of the Bank, waters are sufficiently shallow so that sunlight—essential to the growth of phytoplankton, the tiny plants at the base of the food chain—penetrates all the way to the bottom. Third, tides and winds mix the shallows so that the surface waters, which otherwise would tend to lose their richness to grazing organisms, are constantly being replaced by richer waters from below. Fourth, the clockwise gyre, which appears at times to be a closed circuit, may act to keep nutrients and plankton—including fish eggs and larvae—captive in a productive environment far longer than is normally the case.[13]

The fish who thrive in this rich soup were first cataloged and described by Henry Bryant Bigelow, mentioned above, an early enthusiast of the Western Atlantic. He was the founder and first Director of Woods Hole Oceanographic Institute, and in that capacity did research for the U.S. Fish Commission (predecessor of the National Marine Fisheries Service) on their schooner, the *Grampus*. He studied the Gulf of Maine, out into Georges Bank, from 1912 to 1929, and the work that came from that study, *Fishes of the Gulf of Maine*, written with William Schroeder, is still the best starting place for understanding Georges Bank.[14]

Bigelow started with the haddock, then described all the other fish he found the yellowtail flounder, hake, whiting, pollock, and above all the cod. The cod, as MacLeish describes it, "is the eponym of the gadoids, the family that includes the haddock, the dark handsome pollock, the whiting, and other hakes. It is the largest gadoid. One that must have gone 180 pounds live came in on fishing schooner back in 1838, and another six feet long and 200 pounds was taken on a line off Massachusetts in 1895."[15] The days of the giants are gone, he points out, "and that's an indication of a stock under pressure. Thirty pounds is a fine fish these days."[16] The sad part of it is that there really is no good reason for a well-managed stock of cod to be under pressure; cod will eat anything, survive almost anything, and are enormously prolific. The mindless greed of the fisherman is overwhelming a potentially infinite natural resource.

The importance of the industry for the northeastern section of the continent cannot be overestimated. Harold A. Innis, in *The Cod Fisheries* (1978) argued that despite possibilities for the coastal population to branch out into other industry, both the United States and above all Canada remained dependent on it. It is one of the stablest, most long-lasting industries in the Western Hemisphere.[17] There was, as far as anyone knew at the beginning, fish in overabundance: John Smith (the soldier and adventurer who brought Pocahontas back to England for a visit) urged England to embrace the industry as a source of unending prosperity. And indeed, the ready availability of inexpensive fish contributed enormously to Europe's prosperity before the Revolution. Cod could be shipped directly to Europe, pickled in brine, but was generally salted and dried on frames on the beaches. "Men killed and governments threatened war over which stretch of beach would be used by what ships."[18] By the same token, the newly constituted United States could not afford to lose the fish. Parceling out the fishing rights on Georges Bank between the United States and (British) Canada was an essential, and hotly contested, point in the Treaty of Paris in 1783 ending the American Revolution. (The same dispute surfaced again in the 1980s, leading to the drawing of the "Hague Line," separating U.S. and Canadian fishing rights.)

The Gloucester Fishing Industry

In *Down to the Sea: The Fishing Schooners of Gloucester,* Joseph Garland gives us an exciting history of the Gloucester enterprise, illustrated with an incredible wealth of contemporary photographs. His account is essentially a celebration, with qualifications, of the fishing way of life.

> Three pinkies first tried fishing for cod on the tricky shoals of Georges Bank, 125 miles to the southeast of Gloucester, in 1821. They anchored and were so whipped around by the rip tides that nine years passed before Captain John Fletcher Wonson of East Gloucester and his crew screwed up the courage to tackle the Georges again. They found the great bank teeming with gigantic halibut, discovered they could anchor and fish without being dragged under by the current after all, and thus opened up the richest fishery in the North Atlantic.[19]
>
> By 1859 [Gloucester's] fleet stood at 301 schooners crewed by 3568 men and boys, augmented by another fleet of smaller craft. Together they brought in, that year alone, 60,000 barrels of mackerel, 11,400,000 pounds of codfish and 4,590,000 pounds of halibut, and a few million more of haddock, hake, pollock, herring, sole and other species, lobsters and clams, tongues, sounds and oil.[20]

The first codfishing on Georges, as Garland describes it, was "handlining," over the rails along the side of an anchored boat. The "Georges gear," sinkered tarred line with several hooks, was let down to just off the bottom. The lines of the fishermen were kept apart by "sojers," wooden pins every four feet or so on the fishing rails. When cod got on the lines, the fisherman hauled back, maybe taking half an hour to wrestle a pair of big ones to the surface and gaff them aboard.

The codfish were worked off the hooks, their tongues cut out for keeping tally, and the gangings replaced with a pair baited in the meanwhile, and back over with the lead. This way, a high-line fisherman (the best or luckiest fisherman—the one with the highest catch) on his best day might boat nearly two hundred fish, and a lucky crew as much as thirty thousand pounds in the round, eviscerated. If he chanced upon a halibut, each man cut his own distinctive mark in it for counting in his favor.

By 1879, new fish products were bringing prosperity to Gloucester and the surrounding region. In that year Gloucester packed off 14 million pounds of its widely advertised "boneless fish"—salt cod packed in boxes. By that time also the "fish cake" was enormously popular. Potatoes would be brought down from Aroostook County, Maine, by the carload, with a stove (and stovetender) in the boxcar to keep them from freezing. They'd be shredded, mixed with chopped salt cod, and the mixture tinned, ready to be scooped out, fried, and served up with ketchup.[21] As may be expected, the factory owners got most of that prosperity, with the fisherman still scrabbling for a living.

> The average Gloucester fisherman in 1879 made $175, although the Goode study estimated that if he worked like the devil for twelve months, including winter, he stood to earn as much as $300 to $500, the skipper usually double that. [22]

By 1900 the town and the entire region depended on that catch for their livelihood.

Garland's celebration of fishing and its role in New England is sobered by his grim reminders of the cost.

> The fish were there all right, but what a deadly game! The best fishing was in the worst place, naturally, the east and southeast rim of the shoals in two to twelve fathoms, where the waves broke in rough weather. This was one hell of a lee in an easterly storm . . .[23]

Brave souls but damn fools, observers at the time agreed. They would not raise—or more realistically, cut loose—the anchor, in a storm, for fear of losing fish, for fear of losing face with their rivals, and for (a very Yankee) fear of expense: their anchor cables, first to go in any rough weather, were not insurable.

Many lives were lost. Garland documents the loss and danger associated with that way of life, and the callousness, even then, of the capitalist system that underlay this example of American industry.

> . . . in the twenty-five years between 1866 and 1890 Gloucester lost 382 schooners and 2454 fishermen. All of those men didn't go down with their ships, nor did every ship let down its men. Dories capsized or went adrift. Men were washed overboard, fell out of the

rigging, or were struck by booms. Schooners were lost through negligence or in storms and under conditions that no vessel could be
expected to survive. All the same, as Chapelle has been quoted on
an earlier generation of schooners, ". . . the men lost cost the
shipowner nothing, and insurance could take care of the loss of vessel property."[24]

. . . No one knows how many men and boys—fishing vessels usually carried one or two youngsters as apprentices—were lost from
the town. One estimate, which seems high, puts the figure at 30,000
since the beginning 350 years ago. Ten thousand seems more like it,
and still appalling. A good many went down tumbling in the wildness of Georges Bank.[25]

There was, for instance, the storm of February 23, 1862, when a hundred
or so boats, most of them from Gloucester, were fishing the Bank.
Thirteen went down in collisions, all hands lost, while two more were
abandoned. About 138 people drowned in 24 hours.[26] And on the night
of February 20, 1879, a gale wiped out 13 Gloucester fishing boats, at a
cost of 143 men. "Before the year 1879 was out, the count would be
twenty-nine Gloucester schooners and 249 men, by far the most of them
gone down with their vessels."[27]

How long could such an industry have continued? There is no sign
that the Gloucestermen were willing to give up their fishing because of
the danger. And had they continued in their old wooden schooners, as
Garland points out, their simple ways of fishing could have gone on
indefinitely: there was a nice balance between human need and technology and the natural supply of fish.[28] We need only compare the proud
yield of 5.7 *thousand* tons of cod brought in by the huge fleet in 1859
with the 3.9 *million* tons brought in 1968. When the technology changed,
starting with the diesel engines and ending with the huge factory trawler,
the balance was destroyed.

The Russians Are Coming! And the Germans, Poles, and Spanish. . .

The disaster began in the mid-1950s, when a new kind of fishing vessel
began to sail the Atlantic waters. It was huge (the earliest were over 300
feet, and they ranged higher), it fished from the stern instead of over the
side, and it swiftly processed and froze everything it caught. It was called
a "factory-equipped freezer stern trawler," or factory trawler, for short,
and it spelled doom to any fishery it visited.[29] For the most part, the factory trawlers were foreign.[30]

The Soviets showed up with their giants at the beginning of the six-
ties, and then the Germans and the Poles and the Spaniards. . . . The

new technology moved in floating cities, and it broke the back of the fisheries from Labrador to Georges and on southwest.[31]

At first the fleets fished for squid and red hake and the like, species not customarily marketed in New England ports. But they were fishers of opportunity, and then, in the mid-1960s:

> There occurred one of those periodic blooms of haddock, or, more precisely, haddock surviving to a catchable size.

The trawlers took most of them and came back for more.

> There were more Russians on Georges by then than there were Americans. The foreigners swept the bottoms and the midwaters. To them, Georges was just one of many shoalings in the high seas, places with names like Whale Deep and Flemish Cap off Atlantic Canada, No Name Bank off Greenland, Bill Bailey's Bank off Iceland, Viking Bank and Tiddly off Scandinavia, Skolpen and Parson's Nose off the Soviet Union. Processors and trawlers moved along the chain pulse-fishing, setting their nets for one species until the catch became too small to bother with, and then moving on or setting their nets for another. The system worked so well that shortly it failed.[32]

It is not clear whether it was concern for the preservation of the fishery or concern for national sovereignty that prompted the U.S. Congress to move, but move it did. For the intolerable had happened: the Russians were now the highliners.

> In 1960, just before the foreigners arrived on Georges, American boats were taking 90 percent of the harvest there, and most of the remainder went to the Canadians. Twelve years later the Yankees were taking 10 percent and the foreigners the rest. It wasn't just the long-distance fleets. New England's total catch had been dropping, with some surges here and there, ever since 1950. But you couldn't tell that to the captains. From Rhode Island to Maine, they sat in their small, wood-hulled, fifteen-year-old boats and roared.
>
> The response from Washington was the Fisheries Conservation and Management Act of 1976, known as the Magnuson Act. . . .[which] extended United States fishery jurisdiction out to two hundred miles. [33]

Other countries claimed 200 mile limits too, of course; the "Exclusive Economic Zones (EEZs)" of 122 coastal states totaled 10% of the ocean's surface in 1992. (That area included all the good fishing.)[34] Ten percent of the total EEZs belonged to the United States. Even after the World Court required the United States to shave off the eastern corner of the Georges Banks for Canada, the fishermen thought that now there'd be plenty of fish for all of them, and no limits.

In 1980, fishermen caught about 294 million pounds of fish and shellfish from Georges Bank, worth a little under $200 million dockside and considerably more when processing and marketing are thrown in. The Americans, fishing all over the Bank, took three quarters of that poundage and two-thirds of the value. The Canadians, restricted by joint agreement to the eastern third, took almost all the rest, mostly scallops.[35]

But the fishery continued to decline. The fishermen were wrong: by this time our own fishing capacity was sufficient to overwhelm the capacity of the Georges. The act gave the government power to set quotas to conserve threatened species, and shortly these became necessary.[36] For the fishery did not recover; New England had "replaced overfishing by foreign fleets with overfishing by their own," and the catch continued to decline.[37] By 1993, cod and yellowtail flounder were at record lows off New England; after the haddock catch plunged 63% in one year, the federal government shut down part of the Georges Bank completely.[38]

The days of mass-production fishing are essentially over. According to William Warner (in *Distant Water: The Fate of the North Atlantic Fisherman*) the factory trawlers were on their way out by the late 1970s. There were no more of the "floating cities—the massive concentrations of one hundred or more distant water vessels once so common on prime grounds."[39] They didn't seem like the wave of the future, but rather dinosaurs of the past; with a daily operating cost of about $13,000 each, and operations scaled to a very high catch of single species at one time, they could not possibly make a living on the quotas they had been assigned by coastal states. The 200-mile limit had made the difference.

By 1980, when the last German ships were recalled from New Zealand, the industry had about folded in Germany. England had perhaps a dozen distant water ships in 1982; the Hull Fishing Vessel Owners Association (the port authority that ran the fishing docks in that city) went bankrupt in 1980, and Hull itself took on the aspect of a maritime ghost town. The Spanish boats continued to fish; less controlled by government or central agencies than the others, they simply went on doing what they knew how to do, catching fewer fish each trip.[40] Spanish and Portuguese fishing boats, flying flags of convenience to evade international treaties to which their nations are signatory, have been seized by Canada as recently as 1994 for predatory overfishing, with equipment that has been banned and in grounds where, according to the Canadians, they have no right to be. [41] We are looking at the tail end of an industry; the Grand Banks, like the Georges, are overfished, and large-scale fishing can no longer survive there. The question now, is whether any fishing can survive.

A Short History of a Short Controversy:
Oil Versus Fish

In the late 1970s and early 1980s, when oil prices were high, several American oil companies undertook to extend their offshore drilling operations from the friendly shores of the Gulf of Mexico to the decidedly less congenial shores of rocky New England. This controversy is treated at length in a highly readable account by William MacLeish (*Oil And Water: The Struggle for Georges Bank*), published in 1985. In a sense, the controversy is of only historical interest, since not enough oil was discovered in the drillings that were made to make the enterprise commercially worth while. But at the time, there was strong interest in drilling, and controversy over sale of the leases for drilling gave the nation an opportunity to weigh the value of the fishery over against the value of a new source of petroleum. For the first time, the nation came to grips in the public forums of Congress and courtroom with the importance of the Georges Bank fishery.

One of the first legal actions, for example, came about over the sale of Lease Sale Forty-Two—roughly translated, the government's sale to an oil company of the right to lease a particular patch of ocean for the purpose of drilling for oil. It was in January 1978, that the Commonwealth of Massachusetts brought suit to delay that sale, and Judge W. Arthur Garrity—the same who ordered the busing to integrate Boston's schools—granted a preliminary injunction against it. He stated:

> This is no ordinary fishing ground. It is as important a resource as the people of this state will ever have to rely upon. . . . The plaintiffs are looking for a delay of a relatively few months to preserve a resource that has taken millions of years to accrue, and which will be with us, for better or for worse, for untold centuries to come. . . .The opposing considerations here are use for a period of about twenty years as a source for gas and oil, as against the preservation of the natural resource . . . for the indefinite future. . . . If there ever was a public interest case, this is it.[42]

The U. S. Government and the oil companies promptly sued to stay the injunction, in the United States Court of Appeals for the First Circuit (Boston). Judge Levin H. Campbell said absolutely not; the decision of the "judge below" was quite correct:

> There may be issues more serious than ones involving the future of the oceans of our planet and the life within them, but surely they are few.[43]

Five years later, for another example, in March, 1983, a part of the controversy came to a head in a suit by the Conservation Law Foundation and several other environmental organizations (including Greenpeace and the Massachusetts branch of the Audubon Society) to obtain an injunction against another of the lease sales. In granting the injunction, Federal Judge A. David Mazzone emphasized the importance of preserving the fishery. He wrote:

> . . . Georges Bank represents a renewable, self-sustaining resource for the entire nation. . . . in light of the significance of the Georges Bank fishery resource that may be jeopardized by that sale, I find that the plaintiffs have adequately demonstrated that they will suffer irreparable harm if this injunction does not issue.[44]

We will never know what would have happened, in the event that oil had been found in abundance beneath the Georges. At the least, the dialogue on its value—after two centuries!—had begun, and a foundation laid for a discussion of what we lose when we thoughtlessly destroy a major national resource.

PRESENT AND FUTURE

Taking Stock

Where are the North Atlantic fisheries at this point? Peter Weber, in *Net Loss,* points out that overfishing has long-term environmental consequences. The chief cause

> . . . of the decline of the Atlantic cod and haddock fisheries off North America . . . appears to be long-term overfishing, which has reduced the average size of the cod and haddock, as well as their overall numbers. By removing such a large number of these predators, fishers may have also caused a long-term transformation of the North Atlantic ecosystem. Populations of dogfish and skate— types of shark—have boomed and are now filling the niche left by the cod and haddock. Because dogfish and skate prey on young cod and haddock as well, they are reinforcing this ecological shift. Although the ecosystem is still producing fish, the fishers lose out because there is little demand in North America for dogfish and skate, which do not store well.[45]

If fish become scarce, how may we reduce pressure on the fisheries? Weber points out that the first reaction of fishing nations tends to be to adopt programs (consolidation, licensing, quotas, etc.) that put fewer fishing boats on the water. These surviving boats tend to be the most "efficient," in terms of operating cost per-unit of fish processed; these, of course, turn out to be the biggest, the newest, and those that employ the least crew. Weber, who is at least as concerned for worldwide employment as he is for the fish, finds that solution perverse: what we need is a proliferation of small local fishers, who tend to employ many more persons in the process of taking many fewer fish, and whose simple fishing methods can never damage a large fishery.

The employment issue on the Georges is addressed directly in documents prepared for the East Coast Fisheries Federation, by its executive director, James O'Malley. He cites the estimate by the New England Fishery Management Council that "50% effort reduction"—cutting back the amount of fishing by one half—will be needed to replenish the stock of fish on the Georges.[46] The fishing fleet in the Northeast will shrink. How will it do this? Scenarios include the contraction of the fleet through bankruptcy, attrition by age, the commercial consolidation of fishing power into fewer hands, or through a buyout of existing vessels. All of those scenarios are costly. The loss of independence of the fishers undermines the social structure of the towns. Widespread bankruptcy is socially unacceptable. Furthermore, the economic failure of any vessel does not mean that its fishing power is removed from the fleet; only that it will be resurrected at a lower price by the next purchaser, leaving the same level of fishing pressure on the resource.

Shades of the arrival of the Spanish and the Portuguese! There is no sign that attrition will have any significant effects soon; consolidation may mean fewer boats, but working at higher efficiency to bring in more fish per boat. As long as the marginal costs of the low-end producer are met, the fishing will continue; the market, unaided by government, does not hold a solution for the Georges.

The major obstacle to any rational plan is the entrenched opposition of fishermen to any restrictions *at all*; this industry has never had them. For the families who are invested in the industry, as Michael Parfit has observed, all such measures are anathema:

> . . . as I learned one evening in New England at a hearing on bluefin fisheries. All it took was a speaker to gingerly suggest limiting numbers of fishermen. A gray-haired man leaped to his feet, furious.
>
> "Don't go to limited access!" he shouted across the room. "I don't want to be limited! That's not American!"

Is It Possible to Strike a Balance?

From a variety of sources, a pattern emerges of suggested solutions in order of priority:

1. First of all, we need immediately to reduce the fishing, and allow the fishery to recover. That means taking boats off the water—temporarily or permanently. The Grand Banks has already been temporarily closed to fishing, to allow time for the fish to breed and grow. But we will need programs to help the transition. Weber identifies

> . . . a $30 million package for New England fishers and their com-
> munities. Twelve million dollars of this is earmarked to help indi-
> vidual fishers move into other fisheries and other industries.[47]

The solution, a typical "bail out" designed to keep present fishers in business somehow, is admittedly less than ideal; there are no more unex-
ploited fisheries in this world, and it makes little sense to take pressure
off one fishery only to destroy another. And what "other industries" did
we have in mind? New England would like to know.

2. Second, we surely need international agreements to prevent the kind
of flag-of-convenience raiding that the Spanish boats were caught at by
the outraged Canadians. On August 8, 1995, the *New York Times*
applauded the first international agreement that might do some good:

> The United Nations Food and Agriculture Organization, once an
> ardent booster of highly mechanized fleets that sweep up fish by the
> ton, now says that virtually every commercial fish species is either
> declining or at serious risk. . . Last Friday, after two years of pro-
> tracted and bitter negotiations, delegates from 100 countries meet-
> ing under the auspices of the United Nations approved the first
> international treaty to regulate fishing on the high seas.[48]

The agreement only regulates "straddling" fish, that migrate from coastal
waters to high seas. Still, the *Times* believes, it will reduce appalling
waste of "bycatch," undesirable fish caught in indiscriminate nets,
rejected and dumped dead back into the sea. The agreement at least regulates the nets, prohibiting the kind that catch everything, and provides
for some international inspection. It is also time, the editorial concludes,
that we stop "bailing out" the fishing fleets through subsidies that allow
inefficient fishermen to continue in business.

Third, we need to establish "individually transferable quotas"
(ITQs), which assign quotas of certain numbers of certain fish to present fishermen; no one is then allowed to take fish at all without owning
such a quota. The fishermen may use, give, bequeath, assign, sell, or
otherwise treat that quota as personal property—thus, "individually
transferable." For those presently in business, the ITQ is pure bonus,
unbought value, a windfall. For the purchaser, it is a barrier to entry
into the industry, which is the point.[49] As the ITQs can be regulated—
their number increased or decreased as the fishery waxes or wanes—
there is a theoretical possibility of controlling the amount of fishing effort.
But then, of course, there is the problem of enforcement—someone has
to inspect every boat coming in off those foggy and storm-tossed waters.
Such quotas have not been tried.

Fourth, a frank buyout might be a more adequate solution. A buyout
would require that fishers turn in their licenses once and for all and scrap
their boats, in return for some federally funded retirement or retraining

package. Such plans have worked in the United Kingdom, and are currently proposed for New England.[50]

Fifth, that buyout might work better if put in combination with severe limits on the hunting seasons; the less efficient boats would have the hardest time making a living in a short season, and would have an incentive to retire.

Sixth, there is the possibility of limiting the technology. Theoretically, limits on boats and methods should work—the Gloucestermen could have fished indefinitely. But such measures are very difficult to implement. Recall the cry of Parfit's fisherman—limits are not American!—and sailing boats insult the machismo of the machine-oriented American male. Besides, American ingenuity would sabotage the effect.

Finally, for long term supply of fish for the world, we must encourage fish farming. It could be argued that the technological level of the fish industry is at this time about where the technological level of the beef cattle industry was at the time of Buffalo Bill—we find the wild species in their largest concentrations, then use our best technology to slaughter them. No wonder the fisheries are crashing. What could be accomplished if we put our technology to work breeding fish, experimenting with new breeds of fish, studying their diseases and finding what combinations of food would produce the best flesh for the table?

There are disadvantages to fish farming, or aquaculture, as it is now practiced. First, only fish for the rich man's table, the most expensive species, are raised; they bring in the highest profit. More importantly, we are currently dependent on coastline locations for the farms, since we dare not try to raise marine fish without their native waters. But the coastline is the most valuable land we have, in demand for industrial, recreational, and residential purposes. Worse, the coastal salt marshes, what are left of them, are the essential nurseries for the life of the sea; if we convert them to fish farms, we condemn all wild life in the ocean to death.

The objections can be answered: let the state farms sponsor experimentation—in feeding materials, diseases, and environment—in aquaculture, as they do in animal husbandry; let new nutrient broths be discovered and tried. There is no reason why aquaculture could not take place in the middle of the country, or any place where real estate is more available than on the coasts.

The Sadness Of It All

We have spoken, in the course of this chapter, of the attitudes of the fishermen and their families in this crisis. They are concerned; they are intelligent; they understand precisely the nature of the problem, the catastrophe that attends inaction, and the probable direction of any effective action. Yet they resist it to the core: they are against limits; against collectivization and consolidation; against being regulated, reformed, and brought in line with the common good for the long run. They view themselves as the last livers of an heroic life; the last independents in a corporate country; the last real entrepreneurs; mustering intelligence, tradition, and courage to wrest a living from the merciless sea. All of this will be lost. Whether we do nothing, and allow the fish, fisheries, fishermen, fishing towns and regions to perish together; or whether we do what has to be done to save the resource by, essentially, telling fishers where, when, and for what they may fish—their way of life will be gone. The collapse of the New England fisheries has been compared to the Dust Bowl in the Midwest; as went the family farm, so goes the Gloucesterman. In the course of a community celebration of the fishing way of life in St. John's, Newfoundland, after the closing of the Grand Banks, Michael Parfit found himself meditating on that comparison:

> The Grand Banks disaster has been called the Dust Bowl of fishing. The Dust Bowl did not kill American agriculture, just changed it. It became big industry: highly regulated, tidy. Thus it may be with fishing. Fish farming, the only piece of world fisheries to show a real gain in recent years, will continue to grow. So will regulation of the sea itself. We will still have fish but not the fishermen we knew. In that auditorium in St. John's, the old life was turning from reality to myth before my eyes.

Finally, the frontier is closed, and the government will have to come in and regulate. The old fisherman's protest against being "limited" hits home—in its genuinely American character and in its futility. As Parfit comments,

> His words struck me as a cry of loss, and I imagined them rolling out across this world of inevitable limits, to the very edge of the sea.[51]

QUESTIONS FOR REFLECTION

+ What persuades us of the value of preserving the New England fisheries?
  + Ecosystem preservation?
  + The future of the food supply?
  + The way of life of the New England fishermen?
  + Nothing; let it die and resort to fish farming.

  What do you say?

+ How does it happen that it is in no one's interest to preserve the fishery, but it is at the same time in everyone's interest to preserve the fishery?

Notes

1. Peter Weber, *Net Loss: Fish, Jobs, and the Marine Environment* Worldwatch Paper 120 (New York: Norton, July 1994): 14.

2. Ibid., p. 15.

3. Northeast Fisheries Science Center, *Status of the Fishery Resources Off the Northeastern United States for 1994* (Woods Hole, MA: NOAA Technical Memorandum NMFS-NE-108, 1995).

4. James D. O'Malley, "Preliminary Findings," in *Draft Statement on Buyout Design* (Narragansett, RI: East Coast Fisheries Federation, 1994): p. 8.

5. Ibid., p. 16, citing Food and Agriculture Organization of the United Nations (FAO), *Marine Fisheries and the Law of the Sea: A Decade of Change* FAO Fisheries Circular No. 853 (Rome, Italy: 1993).

6. Peter Weber, *Net Loss*, p. 28.

7. In theory, the use of Global Positioning Systems should make it possible to put up electronic "fences" all along the 200 mile limits of the fishing nations, and patrol them by remote control. No one has yet suggested this.

8. Peter Weber, *Net Loss*, p. 28.

9. Ibid.

10. Ibid., p. 29.

11. James R. McGoodwin, *Crisis in the World's Fisheries* (Stanford, CA: Stanford University Press, 1990): Note 14.

12. William H. MacLeish, *Oil And Water: The Struggle for Georges Bank* (Boston: Atlantic Monthly Press, 1985): pp. 163–164.

13. Ibid., p. 164.

14. Ibid., p. 14.

15. Ibid., p. 17.

16. Ibid.

17. Harold A. Innis, *The Cod Fisheries: The History of an International Economy* (Toronto: University of Toronto Press, 1978). Cited William H. MacLeish, *Oil And Water*, p. 19.

18. William H. MacLeish, *Oil And Water*, p. 21.

19. Joseph E. Garland, *Down to the Sea: The Fishing Schooners of Gloucester*, introduction by Sterling Hayden (Boston, MA: David R. Godine, 1983): p. 9.

20. Ibid., p. 15.

21. Ibid., p. 143.

22. Ibid.

23. Ibid., p. 101.

24. Ibid., p. 17.

25. Ibid., p. 25.

26. Ibid., p. 26.

27. Ibid., p. 104.

28. Ibid., p. 18.

29. William W. Warner, *Distant Water: The Fate of the North Atlantic Fisherman* (Boston: Atlantic Monthly Press/Little, Brown and Company, 1977): p. vii.

30. The United States has some of them, of course, but not for the New England fishery. An excellent diagram of such a ship, with all its activities, is

found on p. 14 of Michael Parfit's "Diminishing Returns," an article on the state of fisheries worldwide, in *National Geographic* (November 1995).

31. William H. MacLeish, *Oil And Water,* p. 201.

32. Ibid., pp. 201–202.

33. Ibid., p. 203.

34. Peter Weber, *Net Loss,* p. 47.

35. William H. MacLeish, *Oil And Water,* pp. 28–29.

36. Ibid., p. 203.

37. Peter Weber, *Net Loss,* p. 53.

38. Frank Graham, Jr., "Defender of the Fishes," *Audubon Magazine* (September–October 1994): pp. 96–99.

39. William W. Warner, *Distant Water,* p. 309.

40. Ibid., pp. 311–315.

41. Peter Weber, *Net Loss,* p. 5. See also Clyde H. Farnsworth, "Canada Acts to Cut Fishing by Foreigners: Will Seize Boats Outside Its Waters," *The New York Times* (22 May 1994); Colin Nickerson, "Pirates Plunder Fisheries," *Boston Sunday Globe* (17 April 1994).

42. William H. MacLeish, *Oil And Water,* pp. 72–73.

43. Ibid., p. 74.

44. Ibid., p. 245.

45. Peter Weber, *Net Loss,* p. 19. He cites as his authority on this change *Massachusetts Offshore Groundfish Task Force, New England Groundfish in Crisis—Again* (Boston: Executive Office of Environmental Affairs, 1990).

46. James D. O'Malley, "Draft Statement: Buyout Design," dated September 1994; available from East Coast Fisheries Federation, Inc., PO Box 649, Narragansett, RI 02882, (401) 782-3440.

47. Peter Weber, *Net Loss,* p. 5.

48. "A Modest Step to Save the Fish," *The New York Times* (8 August 1995).

49. Peter Weber, *Net Loss,* p. 35.

50. James D. O'Malley, "Draft Statement: Buyout Design."

51. Michael Parfit, "Diminishing Returns," p. 29.

CHAPTER 9

To Reclaim a Legacy
The Tallest Trees in America

QUESTIONS TO KEEP IN MIND

What are we trying to save in the forests of the Pacific Northwest coast? Is it the northern spotted owl, a diminutive raptor, which is uniquely adapted to life the ancient forests of the region, and found nowhere else? Is it the forest itself with its millennial trees, likened by all who see it to the great cathedrals of our religious traditions? People have been cutting down trees since there were people and trees; why do these evergreen forests (especially the old groves of northern California redwoods) have a special claim on us? Is it something more abstract, like Nature or Biodiversity—or possibly a vision of a country worthy of being called America the Beautiful, that protects its natural beauty as part of its national gift and identity?

What are the lumber companies trying to gain in their timber operations on the Pacific Northwest Coast? Must they take into account stakeholders other than their shareholders? Do the imperatives of maximizing shareholder wealth justify shutting down lumber mills and exporting raw logs (resulting in extensive unemployment)? Can we use the tale of Pacific Lumber to illustrate the strengths and weaknesses of the present system?

The media has characterized the struggle between the loggers and the environmentalists as essentially a class conflict: the working-class lumbermen against the elite professional class that typifies the environmental movement. How can we sort out the stakeholders and their real interests in these conflicts? How can a balance be found among the interests, real and perceived, in such complex issues?

For the sake of clarity we will consider the issues in the following order:

1. The owl and his trees. The northern spotted owl is found only in the ancient forests of the Northwest; it is ecologically an indicator species, and politically a stand-in, for the forests themselves. It is estimated that there are 2,000 breeding pairs left in the world.[1] It is threatened with extinction by the logging operations of the Northwest Forest. The owl is protected, to some extent, by the Endangered Species Act, but the issues go beyond the law. Why might we have a moral obligation to save endangered species? Why should we care about insignificant far-away birds, anyway? What good is "biodiversity," and what should we be willing to pay to maintain it?

Meanwhile, the owl is not the central character. Ted Gup describes the owl as "a fine bird, yes, but . . . never really the root cause of this great conflict."[2] The trees themselves—great groves of sequoia and other cone-bearing trees, some of them more than 2,000 years old—really fire the imagination. Do we have an obligation to preserve them, just as we would for a singular treasure for the whole world?

2. The business. Meanwhile, we live in a free enterprise system, and generally it serves us well. Do we have an obligation to protect businesses that operate in environmentally sensitive ways, or require that all businesses do so? The case of Pacific Lumber Company pits a company that preserved environmental values against hostile financial initiatives that were good for the shareholders' purses, but bad for the trees. Does the fiduciary duty of the company extend to the environment? Should the trees have a vote at the annual meeting? Is there an obligation to protect the workers (the loggers) in their peculiarly specialized way of life?

3. The government. Consider the alphabet soup of government agencies that deal with environmental issues, as well as the FBI for times when the confrontations get unpredictable. What is the role of the (federal or state) government in protecting: (1) owls, (2) trees, (3) business, and (4) us? What do we want it to be? What should the government be empowered to do, and at what cost?

All the questions turn on one indisputable fact: the Pacific Northwest rainforests, an ecosystem unlike any others in the world, have been logged for a century, to the point of the threatened extinction; not only of the species housed there, but of the forests themselves. They are managed and regulated by an incredible mix of national bureaucracies, the actions of which affect the livelihoods of millions of people and the economies of three states. The loggers and lumber companies are in conflict with the environmentalists; both parties are in conflict with the regulators; the politicians are on all sides of the conflicts, depending on their constituencies; and finally, everything ends up in court. But to this point, nothing has been finally decided.[3]

THE OWL AND HIS TREES

For six months of the year, it rains every day in the Pacific Northwest rainforest. The currents of the Pacific Ocean, providing warmth and abundant moisture to coastal northwest United States during millions of years of evolution, ultimately brought forth the ancient evergreen forests, or "old growth forests," which are at the heart of the controversy. The forests probably appeared in their present form about 6,000 years ago; at present, they have stands of trees up to one thousand years old, trees that are 300 feet tall with 10 foot diameters, and at least twice as massive as those found in tropical rain forests. Each tree, to put this in perspective, contains enough lumber to build two houses. These forests extend from the Alaskan panhandle (Sitka Spruce) south through Washington and Oregon (Douglas fir, western hemlock), to northern California (several varieties of redwoods, ponderosa pine). Despite the poor volcanic, basaltic soil, these forests contain the largest examples of the 25 species of conifers found there. The dead trees (snags) may stand for up to two hundred years, as it takes two to five hundred years for them to decay; nevertheless, the forest floor and streams are littered with decomposing trees that provide nutrients for the living ones, and habitat for thousands of animal species (1,500 invertebrate species were once counted on a single tree).

One of the vertebrate species has become, at least for legal and political purposes, the focus of this controversy. The northern spotted owl is a subspecies of spotted owl; the species as a whole is now officially listed as "threatened" under the Endangered Species Act. It weighs less than two pounds, has a wingspan of two feet, and must eat its weight each day to survive. Estimates of numbers surviving vary. A 1990 source states that a count of the northern spotted owl, and its fellow subspecies, the California spotted owl, netted 2,900 pairs;[4] a later estimate suggests 2,000 pairs for the northern cousin alone.[5] For reasons not well understood, the owl breeds late (after three years old) and dies young, both factors militating against survival. Without the loggers, though, it has held its own; the major cause of its threatened extinction, as in most cases, is loss of habitat.

The owl is one of those species that requires unique stable conditions to survive: it appears to be totally dependent upon old growth forest, and hunts there exclusively. To house the owl, the trees must be dense, and some proportion of them must be over 200 years old. Thus, the future of the northern spotted owl and the old growth forest are linked, and therefore the owl is considered an *indicator* species; that is, a species whose condition will indicate the health of the entire ecosystem (on the order of the canary in the coal mine). Not only does the owl require old growth, it requires a lot of it. Studies show that each pair in northern California ranged among 1,900 acres of old growth, that six pairs in Oregon averaged 2,264 acres as their range, and that six pairs studied in Washington averaged a range of 3,800 acres.[6]

Why the spotted owl requires old growth, and so much of it, is not fully understood, but it is well-documented. (At great pain to the documenters; one researcher commented, "Critics who ceaselessly argue that more research is needed before any management decisions are made should spend a year or two tracking these nocturnal birds across the rugged terrain of the northwest.")[7] Evidently, the owl requires such old growth characteristics as broken branches that provide platforms, debris, and protective thermal cover, characteristics not found in new growth. Additionally, the owls' prey—squirrels, voles, rats—share the old growth habitat and feed upon the fungi that form on the decaying trees.

Furthermore, the competition with other species may be forcing the spotted owl back into the old growth. The younger stands provide habitat for the great horned owls, which feed upon young spotted owls; the great horned owls also do well in clearings and edges of the old growth. So the spotted owl loses its predator protection when it is forced from the density of the old growth, or flies across clear cuts from one old growth stand to another. Further, if the spotted owl survives predation in the clear cuts and second growth, it has to contend with competition for food from the more aggressive barred owl that makes its home there. Finally, the owl's habitat is especially threatened by natural disasters— 25,000 acres of habitat were lost with the eruption of Mount St. Helens —because the owl requires such a large area, and so much of that area is already gone.

The northern spotted owl, then, is clearly endangered. To save it, we must save the oldest trees in large numbers. Given that 90% of that forest has been cut already, that means that virtually all the old growth left, whether in private or public hands, must be preserved. For the sake of the owl, should we do that?

What is our obligation to preserve endangered species? For starters, what does "preservation" mean when species are in question? If the genetic material is all that is in question, we can "preserve" the spotted owl by capturing a sufficient number of breeding pairs (say, 20), putting them in a climate-controlled zoo, and allowing them to produce little owls to their hearts' content—without gumming up the logging operations. (If no zoos have room right now, we could freeze owl eggs indefinitely, and regenerate the species any time it was convenient to do so.)

Or does "preservation" of a wild species always mean preservation in the wild, living as it has evolved to live, naturally? If the latter, then what cost are we to be expected to absorb to preserve the habitat? Granted that the owl is worth something—we would not wish it extinguished, other things being equal—but what is it worth when other things include jobs, regional economies, and the evolved lifestyles of the North Coast loggers?

The preservation of a species contributes to the "biodiversity" of the area—literally, the number and variety of the species that are living there. Why is biodiversity "good," good enough to sacrifice jobs for?

The first answer to that question is that while we may not be able to predict future usefulness for any given species, we are aware that odd species may suddenly become dramatically useful, and therefore species ought to be preserved—not just cuddly species like spotted owls, but lowly fungus and insect species as well. Every unique grouping of chemicals found in a rare species may have contributed to that species' survival, and may turn out to have its purpose in contributing to our own—as the obscure rosy periwinkle of Madagascar turned out to yield chemicals that fight childhood leukemia. We have no way of predicting just which of the vanishing species of the Pacific Northwest will suddenly appear as a cure for cancer.

That possibility used to be argued, where old growth forests were concerned, but only hypothetically, until the discovery of taxol, a drug that has shown better than expected results in treating ovarian and breast cancer, and which originates in the bark (and maybe needles) of the Pacific Yew, indigenous to the old growth. The Forest Service used to consider the Yew a "weed" to be removed from a clear-cut and burned; now we know how valuable it is. Would we ever have found out about this if the old groves were gone? Simple prudence, then, argues for the protection of any species, no matter how humble, no matter what measures are required to preserve the conditions it needs to live. (Ironically, this very discovery poses a new threat to the Yew's survival: there is pressure from many fronts to harvest as many trees as can be found to manufacture more of the drug.)

Second, we know that in any ancient ecosystem, the species have evolved in symbiosis; the destruction of one species, leaving its niche open and its role unfilled, will impact the others unfavorably. Homeowners around the dwindling Eastern forests can testify to the effect of the removal of predators from an ecosystem: it allowed the white-tailed deer population to explode, and now they wander our yards, munching bushes in the summer, and dying of starvation in the winter. What would be the effect of the extinction of the spotted owl? Probably not much, but who knows?

A third argument makes no such appeals to consequences. It holds, very simply, that a species *is*, is a unique grouping, whether specially created by God or uniquely evolved, and that we have no right to abolish it for all time from the possibilities of existence on this earth. Extinction is forever; it means that no member of the group could ever, even in theory, live on the earth again. Setting aside all considerations of consequences for our own future generations—who might, after all, want to see animals of this species—we have no right in principle to destroy forever that which we could never create.

THE TERMS OF THE ACT

Persuaded by such considerations, Congress passed the Endangered Species Act in 1973. According to the Act, the National Marine Fishery Service (Department of Commerce) and the Fish and Wildlife Service (Department of the Interior) are empowered to list marine and land species, respectively, as either threatened or endangered—after which they cannot be hunted, collected, injured, or killed. The bill also prohibits any federal agency from carrying out or funding any activity that could threaten or endanger said species, or their habitats. (It is this latter provision that has caused the most controversy, not only with regard to logging in the old growth forests, but with other projects such as dams, highways, and any other development receiving federal funding.) Therefore, both the Bureau of Land Management (Interior) and the Forest Service (Agriculture), must consult with the Fish and Wildlife Service (Interior) before undertaking any action that might threaten the owl.

The Act is typical of environmental legislation on several counts:

1. Informed by the best science available, it is enlightened, far-reaching, and probably the world's most stringent species-protection legislation. To be in noncompliance with the ESA is a criminal act; both civil and criminal penalties are provided, including imprisonment.

2. It is also among those most pitifully funded. The yearly funding for the Act has averaged $39 million a year—a pittance, given the work that must be done to implement it.[8]

3. Three cabinet-level departments must be working harmoniously together if the Act is to be implemented.

Implementation presents its own problems. According to the 1982 amendment of the Act, economic implications of the protection of a species *may not* be considered in determining its status, whether or not it is endangered; that decision must be based "solely on the basis of the best scientific and commercial data."[9] Economic considerations *may* be considered after the listing, during the required preparation of a recovery plan for the listed species. (In practice, because of the complexities involved, few plans have been prepared.) The act also calls for a determination of the species's "critical habitat," but allows a year to take place after the listing before the determination, and acknowledges that because of complications, it may be indeterminable.[10] But in determining the critical habitat, the FWS *must* include economic considerations. On two occasions, court-ordered reconsiderations on the basis of economic impact have impelled the FWS to reduce the acreage required to preserve the owl. The bureaucratic hurdles to actual protection of the owl are daunting to the most hardened of Washington veterans; nevertheless, it *is* legal protection, and as such the strongest statement that we as a nation can make about the value of the most threatened of our creatures.

THE OLDEST TREES

The owl is not really the central character of the drama of the Pacific Northwest. Central to it all are the cathedral groves of redwood trees, especially in northern California. The redwood trees come in two species, *Sequoia gigantica*, and *Sequoia sempivirens*. What's left of *gigantica*, largest of trees, is almost completely within the boundaries of state and national parks. At issue for this chapter is Sempervirens, the coastal redwood, to the best of our knowledge the tallest trees that have ever lived.[11] These giants, on the misty Pacific coast of northern California, are the focus of increasingly bitter disputes among environmentalists, the timber industry, loggers, and local communities.

Climatically unique conditions have produced these trees[12] in this breathtaking biomass. Coniferous evergreen trees (gymnosperms) dominated the planet before the evolution of flowering, deciduous trees (angiosperms). Angiosperms are generally more successful than gymnosperms, because the reproductive strategy of a flower becoming a seed-bearing fruit is much more effective (likely to result in a new tree) than a cone bearing a "naked" seed. Extended areas of coniferous trees are now found only in those latitudes and altitudes where conditions discourage deciduous plants. In the Pacific Northwest, peculiar climatic conditions— winter cold, despite ample water; and summer drought, despite ample warmth and light—hinder photosynthesis in deciduous trees, and allow the more adaptable conifers to take over. Once established, this forest has proved almost immune from change by natural forces. Most ecosystems are characterized by change and succession: its species change with time, from pioneer species, through more stable species, to the most stable (climax) species, only to change again when some violent event upsets its balance (the eruption of Mount St. Helens is a good example). No such event has disrupted the redwood forests for millennia; the forest has remained, grown, and reproduced itself, resulting in some individual trees as old or older than Christendom. To quote an admirer of old growth, Sallie Tisdale, "There is little on this earth so close to immortal."[13]

BUSINESS AND THE TEMPTATION
TO OVERHARVEST

Unfortunately for those who hope for their survival, these trees are the most commercially valuable in the United States. The extent of the original forest and the acreage that remains is very debatable, and probably depends on one's definition of "old growth," which is generally described as the largest old trees, living and dead, standing and fallen, within a multi-layered canopy. Estimates of the extent of the original forest range from 20 to 70 million acres, depending on the threshold for calling a tree "large," some 70% to 95% of which has been logged over the last century. The rate of logging has increased dramatically over the last decades. Estimates are complicated by the fragmentation of the forest by clear cutting, that leaves some stands isolated islands in a barren landscape.

Clearly, this harvest is strictly limited. Once those old-growth trees are logged, there will be no more: the trees are gone forever. The second growth does not have the characteristics of the old growth in its resistance to insects, disease, fire, and decay (we may suppose that the 20th century remainder of a 2,000-year-old forest is composed of the best survivors of all attacks: the less resistant succumbed centuries ago); nor, of course, is it as massive. The old growth is then an irreplaceable asset, more valuable every year into the indefinite future, demanding careful husbanding and conservative forestry practices. Wise management would require very sparing cuts of the old growth, along with encouragement of plantations of new trees to satisfy demands for no-more-than-ordinary lumber.

It is worth pointing out that the failure to manage such lumber harvest wisely has effects beyond the loss of the wood. Besides the imprudent depletion of a valuable resource, rapid harvesting has serious environmental effects on the region and perhaps on the world. The fish and wildlife of the area may suffer severely from the same destruction of habitat that disrupts the owl. Once the trees go, the erosion of the denuded hillsides in the ceaseless rain carries topsoil into the streams. Once the topsoil is gone from the hills, where it formed only a thin layer, the land is useless for growing trees, even if a lumber company conscientiously replants; once layered into the streams, the topsoil smothers salmon fry that must hatch in the clean pebbles of the bottom of a stream.

One very serious environmental effect of overharvesting, presently unmeasurable, is the contribution to global warming. The old growth is a veritable storehouse of carbon, and carbon dioxide is the most important of the "greenhouse gases" credited with causing the projected global warming. While alive, the trees absorb huge amounts of that gas from the atmosphere in the photosynthetic process. Nature's recycling laws of course require that the same amount of the gas be returned to the atmosphere, as it is through the trees' respiration and eventual decay, but that happens, as noted above, over a period of hundreds of years. When the trees are felled, the photosynthetic carbon dioxide absorption stops. Compounding that effect, when the "debris" is burned, the stored carbon is abruptly added to the atmosphere as more carbon dioxide. (The timber industry has claimed that by cutting old growth and planting young trees that have a faster photosynthetic rate, they actually ameliorate the global warming threat. This claim ignores the relative size of the area of photosynthetic activity. To be sure, a rapidly growing tree absorbs more carbon dioxide than a mature tree of the same size; but a small seedling does not approach the chemical activity of the enormous trees of the Northwest forest, trees that are many times as massive as those found anywhere else in the world.)

But from the corporate viewpoint, rapid logging is just good business sense. "The woods," as the popular show has it, "are just trees, the trees are just wood." Timber appropriate for lumber—for houses, boats, fences, furniture—has always been cut and processed by humans, since the beginning of humans. And the redwoods are eminently suitable for such a harvest. The lumber from the redwoods is durable, light, strong, has good nail-holding capacity, is insect and fire resistant, and is beautiful. Each tree yields about 12 or 13 thousand board feet, on the average —as above, enough to build two houses.[14] It is very profitable now, and has been since it began.[15]

What is "wise management," when a publicly owned company is in question? The theory of business enterprise has it that investors put their money into a company for the sole purpose of making money for themselves, from which it follows that (in the immortal words of Milton Friedman) "the social responsibility of business is to increase its profit."[16] Money now, as every first-year economics student knows, is more money than money later. Business managers fulfill their fiduciary obligation to the shareholders when, and only when, they put profit in the shareholders' pockets as quickly as possible. No other considerations may intrude upon their efforts to that objective. Since cut timber brings financial returns, while uncut timber does nothing but sit there as a tax burden, it would follow that the quickest and most cost-effective (least expensive) harvest of all the trees available for cutting would be the best approach to old-growth forests. In contrast to the conservative forestry practices which are demanded by the long-run best interests of trees and corporation, the best interests of the current shareholders would be best served by clearcutting old groves as quickly as possible.

Rarely do we see a direct face-off of the conservative business approach (oriented to the long-term maximization of value from assets, the long-term competitive positioning of the company itself, and the continuity of its arrangements with suppliers, customers, and employees) and the radical grab-the-profits-and-run approach made famous in the 1980s. The Pacific North Coast gives us just such a confrontation in the story of the Pacific Lumber Company.

PACIFIC LUMBER: A SHORT HISTORY AND APOLOGIA

The early Pacific Lumber Company (until 1985) was a model of family style business enterprise. Run for three generations by the Murphy family, it was characterized by community service, environmental sensitivity, and the most scrupulous care of its workers. So successful was it as an old-fashioned paternalistic company that a pair of fascinated left-leaning sociologists (Hugh Wilkerson and John van der Zee) wrote a book about living in its employment and in the company-owned town—appropriately called *Life in the Peace Zone*.[17] From this chronicle emerges a unique story. The company and its headquarters, Scotia, were founded about 1869. For the first part of their history, there was no limit on the harvest; since (by the 1920s) it took four to five days for a team of men to cut down a single giant tree, and close to a week to complete its processing, not much damage was done to the forest by such lack of regulation.[18]

In the 1930s, the company adopted a policy of perpetual sustained yield: mature trees were marked for selective cutting, felled, snaked out by the "cat" tractor, and milled. With more light in the forest, the younger trees matured faster; where bare spots were left, the company reseeded. In theory, such practices should "keep the company supplied with redwood logs from its own lands in perpetuity."[19] The sustained yield policy is economically sound and kind to shareholders. Pacific Lumber's financial statements for the years through 1984 show small cyclical adjustments to demand, but steady earnings on its outstanding shares.[20]

It took just as good care of its workers:

> After he has put in ninety days on his mill job, [the worker] can get on the list to move into Scotia, where a comfortable one-bedroom company bungalow, with a garden and a lawn on a quiet residential street rents from under sixty dollars a month. Water and sewage and garbage removal are free. Every five to seven years, the company will repaint his house, inside and out, free. As he moves up in the company, or as his family grows, he can move to a larger house in another part of town . . . He has good accident and health coverage, and a choice of pension plan or an investment program. . . . And, in the remote future, as a Pacific Lumber employee, if his son or daughter qualifies for a four-year college, he or she will receive a thousand-dollar scholarship from the company.[21]

Further, Pacific Lumber hired any son of a worker who wanted a job, never laid off, rarely fired, and promoted entirely from within. The pension plan, overfunded past all worrying, was generous; a secure old age was certain. Workers could be forgiven a certain amount of complacency. Corky, one of the workers the sociologists interviewed in some depth, was happy with his job and everything else in his life. "Golly, for the rent, you can't match this." He was twenty-four at the time of the interview. "I got forty-one years to go, and I can't see any reason I'd leave."[22]

Conscientious efforts to find something outrageously wrong in this secure life availed the authors nothing. One schoolteacher pointed out that the children's conviction of utter security, in some cases buttressed by two or three generations at Pacific Lumber, was based on faith alone: "What they don't know is that PL could fold tomorrow. And then what?" But that seemed so unlikely, even to the authors, that they dismissed it: "Most people . . . recognizing that Pacific Lumber with its high-quality line of products and enormous timber holdings is not about to fail overnight, decide to . . . settle for the obvious rewards of a relatively comfortable and untroubled future."[23] Also: "What Scotia is really offering those dismayed with the world outside, the tie that pulls men back who vowed to leave, is not the promise of fulfillment but an assurance of moderation, the possibility of living a humane life in a humane community. And for that, there will always be a waiting list."[24]

THE HOSTILE TAKEOVER

And then, in 1986, came the hostile takeover, and Pacific Lumber failed them overnight. Charles Hurwitz, CEO of MAXXAM, seized control of Pacific Lumber (with $900 million in Drexel Burnham junk bonds) and immediately terminated the pension plan, accelerated the traditionally measured timber harvest, and told the employees about his "Golden Rule: He who has the gold, rules."[25] He used $55 million of the pension funds to pay down part of his buyout debt.[26] An insurance company controlled by Hurwitz, Executive Life, bought more than one-third of the junk bonds, and issued the "annuities" required by Federal law to replace pension funds when their managers deplete them. Executive Life collapsed when the junk bond market did, leaving the workers without pensions beyond what the truncated company was able to supply on a temporary basis.[27] Repayment of the same debt required that Hurwitz get money off the land as fast as possible, and Pacific Lumber's old-growth forest was certainly available for cutting. Immediately, forestry practices changed, the company began to attack groves that the old Pacific Lumber had been saving for the end of the century, to clearcut where selective cutting had been the rule, to speed up the pace of logging, and to abandon the costly projects of replanting that had insured the future harvest.

The selective cutting and replanting, besides providing for future harvests, had held the soil in place after logging, and prevented erosion of the steep slopes in the relentless rainfall of the region; under new management, the soil began to wash into the streams. As above, that erosion is bad for the slopes (which cannot then grow more trees), bad for the banks of the stream (which overflow with regular spring floods), and fatal for the salmon (which cannot breed when soil from erosion covers the gravel at the bottom of the streams).[28] These practices continued without limit until 1991, when U.S. District Judge William Dwyer declared a moratorium on the cutting of the old-growth habitat critical for the spotted owl.

Of course it was takeover time all over the industry; Sir James Goldsmith had acquired two forest products companies, and Rupert Murdoch had made a run at Regis, driving it into the arms of Champion International. Champion itself was protected by a substantial purchase of its stock by Warren Buffett, an investor with an interest in stabilizing solid managements; otherwise it too might have gone the way of Regis.[29] A lumber company's attractiveness to a raider is easy to understand: if it owns huge tracts of timber, as PL and the others did, those trees represent cold cash as soon as they are "monetized"—cut and sold—and that cash can be distributed to the shareholders. (Should there be different ways to evaluate such "assets," to make companies that protect the forests less vulnerable to such hostile actions?)

THE RATIONALE OF DESTRUCTION

However undesirable the results of the takeovers may seem, it should be pointed out that the only way a company can be taken over like that is by offering the shareholders more money for their shares than they could get otherwise. Hurwitz certainly did that, obtaining the cash to do so from the sale of the junk bonds and other loans against the assets of the company. The shareholders of record at the time of the takeover made out very well indeed. (Shareholders later in this sort of game make out somewhat worse.)[30] Hurwitz may have hurt the environment and the pensioners, but he enriched the shareholders.

Recall that the CEO's fiduciary duty is to the shareholders and the shareholders alone. How can we condemn Hurwitz for making the lives of retired employees miserable? If it was legal to terminate the pensions under the conditions Hurwitz terminated them, and very much in the shareholders' interest to do so (since it was the condition for the high price they received for their stock), then, it could be argued, Hurwitz was obligated to do it. As John Boland points out, "the only direct, clear legal obligation of corporate fiduciaries (beyond obeying civil law and contractual constraints in general) is to the corporate owners who pay them."[31] After all, the government will take care of the retired workers. Corporations are not in the business of running charities for pensioners.

As for the environmental concerns, those too, as above, are beyond the competence of business to decide. Everything Hurwitz did was within the law. If the American people, through their elected officials, wish to keep more of certain kinds of products (like trees) in the ground and away from the market, let them pass a law to that effect, and law-abiding businessmen will adhere to the law. But in a publicly held, profit-oriented corporation, it should not be management's obligation, or option, to look after the long-term fate of the trees. Pacific Lumber was in business to make money for the stockholders, not to act as unpaid trustee for the North Coast forest.

As for the laws to protect the trees, it should be added that a good businessman would regret, as a citizen, the loss to the economy that such a restriction would represent, and would feel obliged to bring to the attention of the citizens the potential cost in jobs, tax revenues, and so forth. In this effort, the company presidents, contemplating profits and prices per share, would be joined by the loggers, contemplating their jobs. As a matter of fact, the major initiatives to limit the effect of the Endangered Species Act, and to free more acreage of old-growth timber for cutting, have come from the workers and the small businessmen of the affected regions, with the major timber companies, Pacific Lumber included, taking a back seat. The loggers have very few options. Most of them were raised in the region, either in the Pacific Lumber family or in similar areas with similar expectations. They do not see themselves as having the skills to move elsewhere; for them, only a job cutting down trees (or milling them, or serving those who do) stands between them and permanent unemployment. "Jobs or woodpeckers?" their signs demand; their bumper stickers insist that they "Love Spotted Owls: Fried, Boiled, Barbecued. . .", or that "Loggers, too, are an Endangered Species." With such strong political alliance, it might be pointed out, the companies have little motivation to retrain them for other employment.

CAN WE RECLAIM THE REDWOODS FOR OUR OWN?

We have here a direct and serious confrontation of environmental value and a short-term economic imperatives—the imperatives that rest on the rights of private property and the responsibilities to shareholders. Adam Smith held that business enterprise of all kind is limited by supply and demand, and would have held out hope for the trees in the very saturation of the market. There is a demand for only so much redwood lumber, he would argue; ultimately, it will cost PL more to mill the logs it cuts than they will sell for, and then they will have to scale back logging until demand returns. But if the market includes players who are operating by different rules—the Japanese, say, who pursue long-term instead of short-term economic interests—that reasoning fails to apply.

For the lumber companies have by now disposed of their mills, as costly and unpredictable; they sell raw logs overseas, enjoy sales completely unlimited by domestic demand, and leave their workers to be taken care of by the government. [32] The closing of the mills, not the restrictions on the logging, seems to be the real cause of unemployment in the area.

Aristotle and Adam Smith both proved, in very different ways, that property (specifically, land and all resources for production) was better off, and more likely to be taken care of, in private hands than public. This assumption, that the private owner is the best caretaker, underlies the importance we attach to the right of private property. Is the assumption now, at least in these cases, false? The redwoods of Pacific Lumber are clearly not safe in Hurwitz's hands. Do we have a legal right, or structure, to take the land away from him? We know that under the doctrine of "eminent domain" we can seize the redwoods for a new park; but can we seize all that land just to continue a more conservative logging operation?

Pacific Lumber's trees could be protected under the doctrine of eminent domain only if the Federal Government condemned the land for a park, and compensated Pacific Lumber for its acquisition. This is a very expensive course of action. If we are going to spend that kind of money, we might simply offer to purchase the old groves. Charles McCoy, writing in *The Wall Street Journal* in August, 1993, gives us an account of just that proposal—offered by Charles Hurwitz himself. In a suggestion "that brings new meaning to the term greenmail," Hurwitz

> . . . wants the U.S. government to pay him hundreds of millions of dollars for 4,500 acres of the ancient redwoods, in a remote California grove known as the Headwaters Forest. Otherwise, he says, he will press ahead with his plans to cut the trees down.[33]

That acreage is only a small part of the 45,000 acre tract on which the ancient forest sits, and would probably not be adequate to preserve the habitat. Dan Hamburg, Democratic Representative to the U. S. Congress from California, has proposed a bill to purchase the entire tract; Hurwitz has expressed no interest in selling it all, demanding $600 million for the smaller piece alone. If he does not get his price, the trees die.

From two disparate sources comes another theory on which the American people might reclaim Pacific Lumber's remaining ancient forests—especially the Headwaters Forest. Environmentalist author G. Tyler Miller, in his ninth edition of *Living in the Environment,* and two Democratic Congressmen, George Brown and Pete Stark of California, in a joint Op-Ed in the *New York Times,* point out that Charles Hurwitz owes the taxpayers a very large amount of money, and that the old grove might be a proper repayment.[34] For Charles Hurwitz is primarily a financier, not a lumberman, and has a history of running financial enterprises, successful and otherwise. One of the least successful was the United Savings Association of Texas, a Savings and Loan institution that went bankrupt some years ago, leaving the taxpayers to pay back up to $1.6 billion, the amount on which USAT had defaulted. There seems to be no disagreement that the grove would be better off in public hands; could not Headwaters be a partial payment of the debt owed by Hurwitz to the American people? As Brown and Stark point out, Presidential action would be required to initiate such a "debt-for-nature" swap, since it involves the coordination of several executive branch agencies, including the Federal Deposit Insurance Corporation, the Department of the Interior, and possibly the Justice Department.[35]

Action will have to be soon and decisive: the statute of limitations is running out on the debt, as long as the trees remain in Hurwitz's control they are in peril, and Pacific Lumber has shown no interest in adhering to agreements, or even court injunctions that forbid the cutting of trees or destruction of habitat. In 1990, PL "reamed a broad, mile-and-a-half corridor into the middle of the Headwaters forest and called it, with a wink and a snicker, 'our wildlife-biologist study trail.'"[36] Two years later the damage was more extensive. Charles McCoy recounts the precedent of Owl Creek, a 465-acre stand of ancient redwoods, second only to Headwaters in its extent and home to the endangered marbled murrelet:

> In June and November of 1992, over weekends and holidays when wildlife regulators weren't working, Pacific Lumber cut down hundreds of redwoods and firs in Owl Creek—despite warnings from regulators that doing so might violate wildlife protection laws, and despite previous agreements that regulators insist committed the company to hold off logging.[37]

Particularly galling was the "renegade logging" of the November portion, the "Thanksgiving massacre": PL broke off ongoing talks with the state of California and the U.S. Fish and Wildlife Service to cut down as many trees as they could get to during the Thanksgiving 1992 weekend. The company claimed that Governor Pete Wilson had approved the cut, but a state appeals court brought it to a halt at the beginning of the next week. The environmentalists sued; Fish and Wildlife officers considered (but did not pursue) criminal charges. In February 1995 a Federal District Court judge ruled that PL's logging of Owl Creek was illegal, a threat to endangered species, and must be stopped. Immediately PL announced that it would begin logging the Headwaters tract and filed a new Timber Harvest Plan declaring its intention to do so. The only way to stop such plans is by further slow and expensive litigation, and the environmental organizations that bring such suits are running out of time and money.[38]

THE COMPANY'S POSITION

When asked to give an account of its running of Pacific Lumber, MAXXAM stresses continuity with the old firm as run by the Murphys—environmentally responsible, committed to a policy of sustainability into perpetuity, public spirited, and community oriented.[39] It insists that the spotted owl, the fish, and above all the trees, are flourishing under its administration, and that they will continue to do so into the indefinite future (it sees no natural limitation on redwood harvests). The company voluntarily runs a fish hatchery; it has performed at its own expense numerous studies of the marbled murrelet; it plants half a million seedlings on its land each year; it has nesting boxes for the northern spotted owl. It observes the spotted owl living comfortably in marginal new growth and nesting boxes supplied by the company, and disputes the observations of the conservation ecologists that the owl can only live in old growth. A separate White Paper is published on the Headwaters forest, with its position clearly stated:

> Valued by an independent appraiser hired by the U. S. Forest Service in 1993 at about $500 million (including a 1,500 acre buffer), Headwaters is zoned by the state of California exclusively for the growing of commercial timber used to make wood products. Accordingly, Pacific Lumber wants to manage Headwaters as a working forest.[40]

It is not being permitted to by crews of "environmental extremists and special interest groups," who raise "judicial and administrative roadblocks." [41] Conceding that Headwaters is the largest old-growth tract in private hands, the White Paper goes on to argue that Headwaters is inaccessible, surrounded by working tree farms, and therefore unsuitable for a park, even if the U. S. could raise the $600 million dollars the company would want to get for its purchase. Meanwhile, the company wants to harvest that old-growth wood, because, as it candidly admits, it can get a higher price for shipments of wood if some old-growth wood is enclosed with the newer, because the old wood is so rare and of such high quality.

For the bulk of the popular attacks on the company, PL simply argues that it is the victim of a bum rap: the takeover itself was legitimate because of the previous officers' "undermanagement"; the junk bonds were later turned to investment-grade bonds, and besides, Drexel Burnham didn't hit the skids for years after its association with PL; the Executive Life annuities replaced an "overfunded" pension plan, and no one knew at the time that it would go bankrupt, and besides, PL picked up the pension obligations for most of its workers until other arrangements were found; the acceleration of the tree harvest schedule was "to make up for past underharvesting." Profits are up, employment is up, and "were it not for the emotional nature of the redwood debate, the acquisition would be held as a model of a sound business transaction in which all sides won."[42]

On the whole, the company's image of itself is as an environmentally sensitive and conscientious property owner, understandably committed to its right to use that property, but cooperating with all reasonable parties to achieve the best for the community and the natural environment. Its image of its opponents is of committed radicals opposed to the institution of private property, or as immature sentimentalists who are irrationally attached to the nurturing trees, not noticing that the very tracts they write and newspapers they circulate depend entirely on the industry that they are trying to cripple.

Pacific Lumber is typical of American companies in any industry; it does not insist, Friedman-like, on some absolute right and duty to make all the profit it can, nor refuse to acknowledge the right of any nonshareholder to be taken into account. It takes the environment seriously and carries out many projects protective of that environment. It wants to see itself, and have others see it, as a company with a strong sense of social responsibility. This fact suggests another tactic, in addition to the debt-for-nature swap suggested above. We ought to take that desire very seriously, and see what can be done to construct a reality that will match.

THE ROLE OF GOVERNMENT

Even timber executives agree that in a competitive climate, government regulation will be necessary to limit environmentally destructive practices. Then by what means, and to what end, shall the government regulate? At various stages in the effort, Congress has opted for: (1) preservation of the woods for the people to enjoy forever, (2) conservation of the woods to support the timber industry into the indefinite future, and (3) protection of the right of private owners to cut all the wood they wanted, subject only to minimum regulation.

Preservation is administered by the Department of the Interior, which supervises the National Parks and Wilderness Areas. Wilderness is just what it sounds like: areas protected from any invasion at all. The Parks are a different matter: the values of wildness preservation and easy access for tourists will never sit easily together, and we will never be at peace over the way to love our parks. But in neither of those areas can the trees simply be cut for lumber. The National Forests, on the other hand, were established under Teddy Roosevelt by his chief Forester, Gifford Pinchot, for the express purpose of making sure that there would always be trees to cut for the timber industry (although even at the beginning there were other, recreational and educational purposes, thrown in). Here is where the trees can be cut, and here is where the controversy begins for purposes of this section.

The Forest Service, a division of the Department of Agriculture, is responsible for managing those National Forests, federally owned forest-lands that include some 36 million acres in northwest United States. From 1904 at its founding, until World War II, the Forest Service had no problem reconciling its two charges: to promote logging while preserving wilderness for study, watershed protection, recreation, and other uses. At that time, the major timber companies were cutting on private land and in fact were discouraging Forest Service timber sales as unwanted competition. With the war, however, came an abrupt increase in timber demand, at a time when much of the more accessible privately owned land had already been cut; and the transformation of the Service from "guardian, to arm of the timber industry" began.[43] In the postwar years the Forest Service's reputation as a "federal timber company"[44] grew, as logging on federal land began to exceed their own guidelines, with the warm approval of loggers, paper and pulp companies, lumber interests in general, and the congressional delegation of the Pacific Northwest.

Along with more extensive logging came technological "advances," in the form of giant machinery capable of clearcutting the woods; the economic advantages of clearcutting were immediately apparent to lumber companies, and the practice was widely adopted. National ambivalence on the justifiability of such a practice, felt by the lumber companies and their regulators also, is shown in the Forest Service requirement that "protects" the ordinary citizen from having to view it. "Visual protection corridors," a suitably broad band of trees left in place alongside highways, are required by Service regulations; the insiders call them the "fool-'em strips."[45]

Occasionally, the Forest Service's management of the National Forests suggests that it has become an auxiliary to that industry. It is supposed to sell the timber to the companies, and make a profit for the taxpayer in the bargain. It does no such thing. It runs at a loss. The price charged to lumber companies for the right to cut and sell the lumber on these lands has been historically, notoriously, low. Some economists estimate that the Forest Service loses up to $200 million a year. Financial horror stories abound: spending $3 million to log $40,000 worth of timber, a loss of 90 to 99 cents on every dollar spent by the Forest Service, selling trees so cheaply "that loggers would be foolish to say no. It [the Forest Service] builds roads, pays rangers, absorbs the risks of fires and insects, then sells at a loss."[46] Taxpayers may be expected to dislike this result. One way the Forest Service makes the situation look better is by amortizing the cost of roads over hundreds of years. One critic commented that, "It's as if the current Italian government was still paying for the Appian Way."[47]

Congressional action to halt the situation is unlikely. As reporter Jane Fritsch noted in the *Times,* Senator Frank Murkowski, chair of the Senate

Natural Resources Committee, which oversees logging in the National Forests, turns out to have a personal financial interest in the Ketchikan Pulp Company, which will profit enormously from the bill that Murkowski introduced to increase logging in the Tongass National Forest.[48] The same senator has been active in threatening appropriations bills if the executive branch does not interpret law favorably to the lumber industry.[49] While we tell our government to keep watch over private enterprise as it impacts the environment, who will watch the watchers?

The strongest indication that the Forest Service and its allied agencies in Federal government may not be the true villains lies in the work they do when the law asks them to think creatively about these forests and their future. Pursuant to MUSYA (the Multiple Use Sustained Yield Act of 1960), the Forest Service, BLM and USFWS were asked to describe ways that the owl might be saved and the trees might be put to work for the nation besides being cut down. They did a fine job: the combined report of the Forest Service and the BLM, "Actions the Administration May Wish to Consider in Implementing a Conservation Strategy for the Northern Spotted Owl" (May 1, 1990), recommends a drastic cutback in the old-growth harvest by forbidding export of logs, then recommends and describes extensive educational and retraining programs for the loggers put out of work by the ban. Technical assistance will make logging and milling more efficient (avoiding the extensive waste entailed by present practices); recreational facilities will make the forests better known and used (and create political pressure to conserve the trees). Even more impressive is the USFWS report, "Economic Analysis of Designation of Critical Habitat for the Northern Spotted Owl" (August 1991). Going beyond the multiple-use scenario, the report specifically addresses "Non-Use Values": the value to the nation just to have the forests *there.* "Estimates of recreation user demand, benefits of scenic beauty, and benefits of water quality represent only a partial estimate of society's total value for the spotted owl and its associated habitat. The public also is willing to pay for the option of recreation use in the future, the knowledge that the natural ecosystem exists and is protected, and the satisfaction from its bequest to future generations . . . The average willingness to pay higher taxes and wood product prices reported in a referendum contingent valuation format was $190 per year. The lower limit of the 98 per cent confidence range was $117 per household."[50]

These reports put the Federal government's environmental services in a new and better light—a much better light. On the whole, they have been open to serious criticism as the merest tools of the timber industry: ineffective in regulation even when it is attempted, and rarely attempting it. These reports suggest that the idealists who once joined government service to protect the nation's environmental heritage may still be there, waiting only for public opinion to catch up to them. A new agenda for the environment will require a trained corps of experts in science and policy to articulate a national environmental ethic and frame the plans for its implementation. In developing these reports, the Forest Service, BLM and USFWS have made an auspicious start.

TOWARD A FOREST FUTURE

Summary Reflections

The heart of the problem, from an environmentalist point of view, is the old-growth forest. From the loggers' point of view, it is jobs. The owl, the financier, and the alphabet soup of agencies and laws are bit players in an agonizing 20th century drama of loss and conflict. We need not search for villains. Once we all thought that the forests were unlimited. The timber industry's managers, who watched the old growth disappearing before their eyes, and did not know that it could not be restored—that once gone, it would be gone forever—were no more ignorant than their regulators, their customers, or their fellow citizens. The environmental movement is not the sole property of Eastern Elitists, as the loggers suspect, nor is the timber industry a series of tintypes of Charles Hurwitz, as the environmentalists are convinced. Protecting the forests will require the abolition of a way of life, one that has been honored and valuable in our immediate past. It will raise a series of questions that will not go away.

Are there new directions that the environmental movement should be taking? Should we abandon the "endangered species" approach and reorient itself to ecosystem integrity?[51] Or will that move succeed only in disorientation, discouraging followers by forcing an admission that previous efforts were wrongly conceived, and plunging them into indefinable terms and inchoate goals? The ESA has at least the virtue of clarity.

Meanwhile, quite aside from efforts to protect the owl, the current recession has lowered the demand for lumber and depressed the industry. About 50% of the cut forest has been exported to be processed in mills abroad, not in the United States.[52] Even if permission were granted to cut every last old growth tree, they would all be gone, and the jobs with them, in five to ten years. What then?

The ironies abound, not the least of which is the agencies-within-agencies fighting each other. But the most disturbing aspect of our political response to these dilemmas is the hypocrisy, of the United States urging Brazil and other Third World countries to halt the cutting of their tropical rain forests in the interest of preventing the worsening of global warming, while we cut ours at a rate of about twice theirs. To quote an official with the Oregon Natural Resources Council, "It's interesting that we're telling Third World countries, 'don't cut your forests' [while] . . . we're wiping out our fish runs, we're wiping out our biotic diversity, we're sending species to extinction . . . we're not a Third World country.

We're not so poor that we have to destroy our ancient forests. And we're not so rich that we can afford to."[53]

QUESTIONS FOR REFLECTION

+ What, for instance, are the business imperatives of a company that logs redwoods? Is it sufficient to replace 2,000-year-old groves with young stuff that can be harvested in 40 to 80 years?[54] Sufficient for what?

+ What, exactly, are we prepared to do to compensate and redirect the people orphaned by preservation? Or, on the other hand, are we prepared to spare ourselves that difficult decision by allowing the forests to be destroyed?

+ Once the trees are gone, the industry will die, and the workers will be unemployed, but then it will be their problem, not ours. How much are we willing to lose in order to avoid the pain of making a decision? Our history would suggest, quite a bit.

+ Are there environmentally friendly ways to carry on logging operations?

+ What problems present themselves when trying to strike a "balance" in the taking and consuming of an irreplaceable resource?

+ Can you present a rationale for saving *all* of the remaining old-growth forests, regardless of economic worth or other features? Can you present a rationale for saving *none* of them? Put together a debate along those lines. Then try to figure out a rule that will pick out a "happy medium" between those two positions. What ethical grounds would you base it on?

+ Is it time for a full-scale debate on private property? We have no private property in the ocean; why not? Is land, like air and ocean, somehow "given" to humanity collectively, not to be parceled out for private destruction for personal purposes?

Notes

1. Manuel Velasquez, "Ethics and the Spotted Owl Controversy," *Issues in Ethics* 4(1) (Winter/Spring 1991): pp. 1, 6.

2. Ted Gup, "Owl vs. Man," *Time* (25 June 1990): pp. 56–62.

3. *CRS Issue Brief*, "Spotted Owls and Old Growth Forests," Updated August 19, 1991 by M. Lynne Corn, Environment and Natural Resources Policy Division, Congressional Research Service, The Library of Congress, p. 2.

4. David S. Wilcove, "Of Owls and Ancient Forests," in *Ancient Forests of the Pacific Northwest* (Washington, DC: Island Press, 1990): p. 27.

5. Manuel Velasquez, "Ethics and the Spotted Owl Controversy," pp. 1, 6.

6. David S. Wilcove, "Of Owls and Ancient Forests."

7. Ibid., p. 78.

8. G. Tyler Miller, Jr., *Living in the Environment,* 9th Ed. (Belmont, CA: Wadsworth Publishing, 1996): p. 653.

9. *CRS Issue Brief,* "Spotted Owls and Old Growth Forests."

10. Ibid. "That habitat includes "specific areas outside the geographical area occupied by the species, . . . on which are found . . . features essential to the conservation of the species," and "areas outside the geographical area" at the time of listing, later deemed by the Secretary of the Interior "as essential to the conservation of the species" (p. 6).

11. Catherine Caulfield, "The Ancient Forest," *The New Yorker* (14 May 1990): p. 46.

12. Ibid.

13. Sallie Tisdale, "The Pacific Northwest," *The New Yorker* (26 August 1991): p. 54.

14. Hugh Wilkerson and John van der Zee, *Life in the Peace Zone: An American Company Town* (New York: Macmillan, 1971).

15. D. L. Thornbury, *California's Redwood Wonderland: Humboldt County* (San Francisco: Sunset Press, 1923).

16. Milton Friedman, "The Social Responsibility of Business is to Increase Its Profit," *The New York Times* (13 September 1970).

17. Hugh Wilkerson and John van der Zee, *Life in the Peace Zone.*

18. D. L. Thornbury has an excellent account of the industry in the early 1920s on pp. 38–41 of *California's Redwood Wonderland.*

19. Hugh Wilkerson and John van der Zee, *Life in the Peace Zone,* pp. 112–113.

20. In the third quarter of 1984, for instance, PL reported that its net earnings rose 50% over the previous year ($11,337,000, or 47 cents per share, compared to $7,547,000, or 31 cents per share, for the third quarter the previous year.) See Pacific Lumber annual reports, years 1981-1984.

21. Hugh Wilkerson and John van der Zee, *Life in the Peace Zone,* p. 45.

22. Ibid., p. 49.

23. Ibid., p. 83.

24. Ibid., p. 106.

25. Constance E. Bagley, "Pacific Lumber Company: Case Presentation" (presented at Commercial Real Estate Annual Conference, Lake Tahoe, Nevada, June 1991).

26. Gisela Botte and Dan Cray, "Is Your Pension Safe?" *TIME* (3 June 1991): p. 43.

27. Ibid.; also James Castro et al., "A Sizzler Finally Fizzles: In America's Largest Life Insurance Company Collapse, California Officials Seize Control of Shaky Giant Executive Life," *Time* (22 April 1991). *Nightline* (ABC) did a program on the dire straits of workers who have lost their pensions in the collapse of insurance companies in general, with special attention to Pacific Lumber, on June 18, 1991. The program featured interviews with aging retired workers, bewildered and frightened, demonstrating in the streets, demanding the return of their pension fund.

28. Grant Sims, "Can We Save the Northwest's Salmon?", *National Wildlife* (October–November 1994): pp. 42–48.

29. Forest L. Reinhardt, "Champion International Corporation: Timber, Trade and the Northern Spotted Owl," *Harvard Business School Case Study* 9-792-017 (15 March 1993).

30. Because the assets are spent down so quickly. For another account of how Hurwitz's financial dealings and shareholders work in the market, see William Barrett, "Aluminum Cow," *Forbes* (6 January 1992), detailing Hurwitz's handling of Kaiser Aluminum.

31. "More Controversy for Hurwitz," *The Wall Street Journal* (10 February 1988).

32. G. Tyler Miller, Jr., *Living in the Environment,* pp. 296–98.

33. Charles McCoy, "Cutting Costs: For Takeover Baron, Redwood Forests Are Just One More Deal," *Wall Street Journal* (6 August 1993): pp. A1, A6.

34. G. Tyler Miller, Jr., *Living in the Environment,* p. 296; George Brown and Pete Stark, "The Last Stand: Only Clinton Can save a Priceless Redwood Grove," *New York Times* (1 December 1995): Op Ed.

35. Charles McCoy, "Cutting Costs," p. A6; George Brown and Pete Stark, "The Last Stand."

36. John Skow, "Redwoods: The Last Stand," *Time* (6 June 1994): p. 59.

37. Charles McCoy, "Cutting Costs," p. A6.

38. "Owl Creek Victory Triggers Pacific Lumber's Plans for Revenge Cut," *EPIC* (Environmental Protection Information Center, PO Box 397, Garberville, CA, 95542) (29 March 1995).

39. For the information in this section I am indebted to Robert Irelan, MAXXAM's Vice President for Public Relations, and to Jim Noteware, President and CEO of MAXXAM Property Company.

40. Pacific Lumber company publication, "The Pacific Lumber Company and the Headwaters Forest: A White Paper."

41. Ibid.

42. Ibid., p. 7.

43. Jack Shepard, *The Forest Killers* (New York: Weybright and Tally, 1975): pp. 18, 19.

44. Ibid., p. 31.

45. Catherine Caulfield, "The Ancient Forest," p. 60.

46. "Taxpayers Pay for the Timber," *New York Times* (3 November 1991): p. E1.

47. "News of the Week in Review," *New York Times* (3 November 1991): p. 3.

48. Jane Fritsch, "Friend of Timber Industry Wields Power in Senate," *New York Times* (10 August 1995): p. B6.

49. John Cushman, Jr., "Court Fight Over Timber Starts Immediately After Law is Changed," *New York Times* (28 August 1995): A13; "New Law for Timber Industry," *New York Times* (28 August 1995): Editorial.

50. U.S. Fish and Wildlife Service, Department of the Interior, Washington, D.C. "Economic Analysis of Designation of Critical Habitat for the Northern Spotted Owl" (August 1991).

51. Kathie Durbin, "From Owls to Eternity," *E: The Environmental Magazine* 3(2) (March/April 1992): pp. 30–37.

52. Tim Hamach, "The Great Tree Robbery," *New York Times* (19 September 1991).

53. Catherine Caulfield, "The Ancient Forest," p. 53.

54. Jack Shepard, *The Forest Killers,* p. 33.

CHAPTER *10*

Legacy of War
The Nuclear Weapons Cleanup

QUESTIONS TO KEEP IN MIND

Why are the tanks at Hanford so dangerous?

Why didn't anyone know about that danger until a few years ago?

Why is it so difficult to find a place to store nuclear wastes?

What laws and agencies are in place to get the nuclear wastes cleaned up? What are we doing about the nuclear wastes?

THE TANKS OF MENACE

Horror stories, especially on film, play on our terror of the unknown—of that which is surely hideously dangerous, but which lurks somewhere beyond knowing. Somehow, we cannot succumb so completely to fear when we can see the danger in the daylight, analyze it, and face it squarely. Therefore, the danger waiting in the storage places for the waste products of our nuclear warfare industry is made for the horror film. All we need is a good screenwriter; the plot is already in place.

We will set the opening scene at the "tank farm" of the Hanford Nuclear Weapons Facility near Richland in Washington state, a reservation half the size of Rhode Island, bisected by the Columbia River. In business since 1942 under a variety of caretakers (including General

Electric, Rockwell International, and, since 1987, Westinghouse), the Hanford plutonium finishing plant (PFP) made plutonium for atomic bombs—to keep the United States safe and secure from its enemies. The work had the terrible urgency and secrecy of all acts of war, where speed is essential, and the worst danger is subversion by a foreign enemy. No one, except a very few of those who worked there, was ever told what was done with what was made, and what was done with the waste products. Secrecy was the rule: any exposure could lead to sabotage.

On Christmas Eve of 1992—three years after the last plutonium had been sent out from the PFP and three years after the plant had been put on "stand-by" status for safety concerns—Matthew Wald of the *New York Times* presented a grim report. Despite the warnings "that catastrophic explosions were possible at million-gallon waste tanks at [Hanford] the Department of Energy still does not know just what is in the tanks or how risky they are."[1]

> According to internal correspondence, Energy Department reports and outside analysts, the department and Westinghouse still have not determined exactly what is in the 177 tanks, which together hold 57 million gallons. . . .

Some of the initial ingredients are known:

> The tanks hold liquids left over from the production of plutonium for nuclear weapons. Complicating the problem, in the cold war years technicians added organic chemicals that were meant to make the most radioactive materials sink to the bottom of the tanks in a sludge; the remaining liquids, somewhat less dangerous, were then dumped into the dirt.

In this rich stew, the chemicals began interacting:

> . . . the organic chemicals, under intense heat and radiation, are undergoing changes that produce flammable and explosive gases and solids. And because of years of transfers among the tanks, no one is sure how much of each chemical is contained in each tank.

As the reactions continue, gases, especially hydrogen, are released; when the gas pressure builds up enough inside a tank, the tank tends to leak or "burp" it into the outside air, radioactivity and all.

> Energy Department reports show that 16 times since 1987, including seven times in 1991, workers have been exposed to toxic gas leaking from the tanks, and some have suffered permanent lung damage.

If workers can be injured, how about the rest of us?

> Experts say the questions of worker safety and public safety are closely related. Although the tanks are well inside the Hanford

> reservation, . . . the presence of uncontrolled gases that may be explosive is a bad indication for public safety, experts say.

Indeed. On more complicated matters, experts speak with less certainty:

> The problem even confounds experts. For example, just last year the [Department of Energy] realized it had grossly underestimated the amount of plutonium in the tanks, and it now monitors six tanks to determine if a nuclear reaction is likely.

There is apparently more than enough plutonium in the waste tanks to form a critical mass and start a chain reaction. There should be some indications of such a reaction, or of an impending explosion, in the temperature of the mix in the tank. But the scientists attempting to monitor the tanks can not be sure of the present condition in each stew. Usually, the temperature-measuring devices, where these are present at all, are mounted on a single pole in the center of the tank. Unless the mixture is stable and homogeneous throughout, they have no way of knowing if the conditions away from the pole are as safe as those at the pole—or immeasurably more dangerous. Some tanks can not be monitored at all (too dangerous to insert probes), and some very dangerous stuff is in there:

> Two dozen tanks contain ferrocyanides, compounds that pound for pound, the Department of Energy said last year, have about one-quarter the explosive power of TNT. . . .

And it is not sitting still:

> Videotapes made last year inside tank 101-SY, which has a hydrogen problem, show what looks like partly-cooled lava inside a volcano, seething and lurching as it burps noxious and explosive gases that are produced by chemical and nuclear reactions. The shifting wastes splash the walls and bend metal parts; a narrator describes "rollover events" in which the tank agitates itself.

Mixtures intensely hot, intensely radioactive, reasonably suspected of being explosive, churn themselves forever in these tanks, far too dangerous for the workers to reach, test, analyze, and control. In the heat of the wars, the engineers at Hanford secretly filled these tanks in order to dispose in secret of the wastes generated by their death-dealing products. Now the wars are over, the engineers are gone, but these brews continue the maleficent work on their own, in the darkness of the tanks, beyond human control, churning out the stuff of death. Produced by the U.S. Department of Energy, directed by our best private companies, with a cast of thousands—including all the citizens in the way of the toxic and radioactive plume that will follow a major explosion—we need only a good screenwriter for the horror film of the century.

How could we have come to this pass? How, in one of the most sustained efforts this nation had ever undertaken to secure the safety of its citizens from the worst threats our leaders could imagine, did we manage to produce one of the worst dangers any people have ever faced since the beginning of the human race? Keith Schneider, an environmental reporter for the *New York Times,* summed up the causes of the nuclear weapons industry's waste disaster as follows:

> A cold war curtain of secrecy, coupled with inattention by Congress and a succession of administrations . . . allowed poorly maintained nuclear reactors and dangerous nuclear processing plants to continue operating without any scrutiny.
>
> . . . The industry's lethal radioactive and chemical wastes were spread across miles of open ground in the West, poured into rivers and lakes in the East, and dumped where it was most convenient and least expensive throughout the 12 states where there are nuclear weapons plants and laboratories.[2]

How could this have happened? The short answer is: No one had foreseen the problems of disposal of nuclear wastes when the industry began.

SCIENTISTS EXPERIMENTING FOR THE GOOD OF THE NATION

In 1933, Dr. Leo Szilard, a Hungarian physicist, first contemplated the possibility of building an atomic bomb. Then, in 1939, physicists around the world learned that a uranium atom had been "split"—turning some of its matter into enormous amounts of energy—by physicist Dr. Otto Hahn. Between 1939 and 1941, some of the world's greatest scientists, many in the United States as exiles from Hitler's Europe, plotted, pondered, researched, and worried about German research on a nuclear bomb. These giants, many of them Nobel laureates, included Szilard and Hahn, Drs. Vannevar Bush, James B. Conant, Ernest O. Lawrence, Arthur Compton, Hans Bethe, Robert Oppenheimer, Edward Teller, Nils Bohr, Enrico Fermi, and even Albert Einstein. They were associated with the country's great universities—Princeton, Harvard, Carnegie Institute, Chicago, California at Berkeley.

Letters drafted by Szilard and others and signed by Einstein finally convinced President Franklin D. Roosevelt that research on a bomb should have top priority, and just prior to Pearl Harbor, in 1941, the "Manhattan District" (Project) was born. Construction of the famous nuclear pile in the Squash Court at Stagg Field of the University of Chicago began on November 16, 1941. By December 2nd it was large enough to be considered "critical" and the world's first sustained nuclear reaction occurred. Dr. Fermi was the project leader.

Then the project began in earnest, urged on by the British and fueled with fear that Germany might develop the atomic bomb first. The race to make the most destructive weapon of all time was in full swing. The choice was made to build it in the desert at Los Alamos, New Mexico, and Dr. Oppenheimer was chosen to lead the scientific effort with General Leslie Groves overseeing the operation on behalf of the military. They were the oddest couple ever: General Groves a strict, authority-oriented, disciplined military man; Dr. Oppenheimer (Oppie) was an acknowledged genius, a scientific dreamer, brilliant theoretician, and espouser of left-wing causes.

The secrecy was probably the most intense this nation has ever seen. Beyond the scientists and the President, only the Vice President, the Secretary of War, and the Army Chief of Staff were in the information loop. The hundreds of scientists recruited by Oppenheimer found Los Alamos practically a prison. There were 485 counterintelligence agents watching them, they had fake names and drivers licenses with numbers instead of names, their phone lines were tapped, and their mail went to a Box number in Sante Fe. Even their wives did not know what they were doing.

The first "gadget" was tested on July 16, 1945 at the Trinity Test site in Alamogordo, New Mexico, with great success—equaling the effect of 20,000 tons of TNT. The first bomb was dropped on Hiroshima, Japan on August 6th. With that nuclear bomb, and the one that followed close on its heels at Nagasaki, the war was over; but the nuclear terror had just got started. The Russians, who turned against us as soon as Germany surrendered, were well on their way to developing a bomb of their own, thanks to the very effective spying of Klaus Fuchs. The Cold War, with all of its nuclear secrecy, was begun.[3]

BY-PRODUCTS OF WEAPONRY

The Hanford nuclear weapons complex was built in 1942. By now, seventeen nuclear weapons facilities, all of them polluted, are scattered through 13 states. They are or have been operated by private corporations such as General Electric, Rockwell International, Westinghouse, and EG&G, all under contract first to the Atomic Energy Commission, now to the Department of Energy. For 45 years, they operated in total secrecy.

All activities were classified top secret, and workers often had no idea what they were doing. "The Cold War atmosphere encouraged an us-versus-them mentality, and any critic of the weapon-building process could be readily dismissed as siding with the enemy." As a result contractors flourished with no oversight and demonstrated behavior "that not only violated common decency, but frequently the law . . ."[4] No one was minding the store. The operations were exempt from the Occupational Safety and Health Administration (OSHA) oversight, Environmental Protection

Administration (EPA) regulations, environmental laws, the Freedom of Information Act, and had no congressional oversight.[5] According to then-Secretary of Energy Hazel L. O'Leary, "We were shrouded and clouded in an atmosphere of secrecy. And I would take it a step further. I would call it repression."[6] Seth Shulman in *The Threat at Home* compares our nuclear weapons facilities today to the pollution in post–Cold War Eastern Europe that resulted from industry that: (1) operated under one authority, (2) pressured production, and (3) maintained secrecy.[7] Most environmental laws, the laws that would have insisted on safe disposal of wastes, were passed in the early 1970s, but the Atomic Energy Act exempted weapons sites from compliance. Not until the late 1970s and early 1980s, when Senator John Glenn of Ohio began investigations into these facilities, did the pollution disaster details began to trickle out.[8] Only in the last few years has DOE become subject to the regulations and laws that govern the rest of U.S. enterprises. This means that however much worker safety remains a concern in these polluted sites, OSHA oversight is at least in place.

Every step in the process of manufacturing a nuclear weapon produces radioactive and chemical wastes, in varying amounts and variously lethal. One ton of uranium ore produces only a few pounds of uranium, the remaining "tailings" being mildly radioactive. Of that ore, only 1% is the U-235 isotope necessary to build a bomb, so it has to be "enriched," a difficult and expensive process that occurred at the Savannah River facility in South Carolina, Fernald in Ohio, Oak Ridge in Tennessee, and Paducah in Kentucky. Thousands of tons of the left-over material are stored at these plants. Because enrichment is so onerous, plutonium-239 became the preferred fuel. But plutonium is a man-made element obtained by bombarding uranium with neutrons. After the plutonium is separated, what remains is a radioactive stew containing many highly radioactive isotopes (fission products), as well as uranium and plutonium isotopes. For every pound of plutonium that is produced, 170 gallons of high-level waste and 27,000 gallons of low-level waste is produced.[9] This "reprocessing" procedure has resulted in 105 million gallons of radioactive and chemical waste—enough to fill a 1,000 foot supertanker.[10] Most of this waste is at the Savannah River and Hanford facilities, with some in Ohio and New York. Other bomb components were manufactured in Florida, Missouri, and Ohio, with the final assembly occurring at the Pantex plant in Texas (which now disassembles bombs), all contributing more waste. The grand total stands at:

403,000 cubic meters high level radioactive waste (from reprocessing);

2,600 metric tons spent fuel (not reprocessed);

107,000 cubic meters transuranic waste (mostly uranium and plutonium);

1,800,000 cubic meters low-level radioactive waste; and

780,000 cubic meters mixed chemical and radioactive waste.[11]

Three-quarters of these wastes have still not been completely identified.[12] During the Cold War, workers would frequently dispose of waste without sampling, labeling, or recording; as a result, many storage tanks have unknown contents.[13] Between 1943 and 1970, billions of gallons of radioactive wastes were just poured on the ground, leaching into ground water. The Columbia River at Hanford, the Clinch River at Oak Ridge, and the Savannah River at that complex are all radioactively contaminated. Spent fuel rods are stored in rusting containers, some of which are 50 years old, in unlined, cement pools. The worst case scenario is a "criticality" event, during which enough fissile material accumulates to allow a nuclear chain reaction to occur.[14]

THE EXTENT OF THE PROBLEM: HANFORD, ROCKY FLATS, AND SAVANNAH

The Hanford PFP, the oldest and largest of the facilities, presents the worst case for any cleanup. According to Seth Shulman ". . . all of the government's nuclear facilities are polluted—possibly beyond repair. . . . But none matches the scale of the problems at Hanford [which] . . . represents one of the most daunting environmental catastrophes the world has ever known."[15] The Hanford site contains enough radioactive waste to cover 15 football fields 3 feet deep.[16] Between 1944 and 1947, 400,000 curies of radioactive iodine-131 (a thyroid cancer threat) was knowingly emitted into the air, exposing 10,000 people to radioactive fumes. (For comparison, during the Three Mile Island accident, the public was exposed to 30 curies of I-131). This information was suppressed for 40 years. Over the years, 200 billion gallons of radioactive wastewater has been poured onto the ground and leached into groundwater. Concentrations of radioactive strontium-90 (a bone cancer threat) at 500 times the federal standard have been measured in the Columbia River.

Hanford is probably most notorious for that "tank farm" that began this account: 177 leaking tanks, some with a million gallon capacity, containing a total of 61 million gallons of mixed high-level radioactive and chemical waste. The earlier tanks were designed with a single lining, to last 25 years, since their designers were sure that some permanent solution to the problem of nuclear waste would be found by then. By now, some of them are 50 years old, and the lining has eroded; 67 of them are either known or suspected to have leaked up to a million gallons of waste. This includes nitrates, nitrites, chromium, mercury, cyanide, cesium-137, strontium-90, and iodine-129. Moreover, 24 tanks have been considered in danger of exploding in varying degrees. One, as described above, has been burping hydrogen, causing workers to fear even probing it to determine its contents. (A mixer has been installed to lessen the threat.)[17]

THE ROCKY FLATS TRIAL

The public's first real exposure to the problems of nuclear waste came after armed FBI agents invaded the Rocky Flats facility in June of 1989. The Rocky Flats plant is located 16 miles northwest of Denver, Colorado and manufactured the "triggers" for nuclear bombs from 1952 until it was closed in January, 1990. Rockwell International, the company that was managing the plant at the time the FBI arrived, had run the facility since 1975, taking over from Dow Chemical Company.

The FBI agents carried a search warrant that included accusations that Rockwell had dumped toxic wastes into drinking water sources, and that they had illegally operated an incinerator that had been closed for safety reasons. They seized thousands of documents, and a grand jury was convened. The jury heard some 100 witnesses, and had evidently reached a number of conclusions by March, 1992, when a settlement between the U.S. Department of Justice (DOJ) and Rockwell was announced. By that settlement, Rockwell pleaded guilty to 10 crimes and agreed to pay an $18.5 million fine—but the case would be closed, and none of the executives who made the decisions would be charged with a crime or brought to trial.[18] That was one of the conditions for the plea agreement.[19]

That deal gave us a measure of public outrage at the evidence of danger covered up by its caretakers. The members of the jury hit the ceiling at the self-serving cynicism of such an agreement. Federal grand jury deliberations are, by law, sealed. Nevertheless, some jurors leaked a part of the draft of their report to the press, in which they accused DOE of conspiring with Rockwell in violating environmental regulations. Not only that, the grand jury believed that violations were continuing, with the collusion of the DOE, even as they were deliberating the case.[20] They would have recommended criminal indictment of Rockwell and DOE officials. Later, one FBI investigator testified to a House of Representatives subcommittee that when he heard that no individuals in the case would be charged, "I physically got sick." The jurors, and the citizens who joined them, even wrote President-elect Clinton asking for a special prosecutor.

The plea agreement not only insured that no individuals would go to jail, but was noteworthy in the lack of any admission of guilt regarding release of toxic materials into the environment (which had been a part of the search warrant). Such an admission, given the plant's proximity to Denver, would have opened the door to civil lawsuits brought by nearby residents.[21] Despite juror and Congressional pressure, the first Bush

Administration's Department of Justice resisted requests to pursue the matter further. (One DOJ official offered that "Environmental crimes are not like organized crime or drugs. There you have bad people doing bad things. With environmental crimes, you have decent people doing bad things.")[22] However, in a memorandum that accompanied the Rockwell plea, the DOJ did chastise the DOE, saying that it "established a 'prevailing culture' that put production of plutonium triggers for nuclear weapons above any other concern, including care for the environment and public safety."[23]

The legal settlement took care of the problems experienced by the executives contemplating indictment. What did it do for Rocky Flats? Nothing: Rocky Flats was and still is a polluted "plutonium dump"[24]:

+ In 1957, a fire resulted in radioactive emissions equal to 16,000 times the level considered safe. No state or local officials were notified.[25]

+ Sludge containing cadmium, chromium, barium, lead, and silver was mixed with cement after it started to leak from the solar pond where it had been discarded. The resulting slabs were placed in a parking lot, but not having solidified, started to leak again. Workers had disposed of waste water by simply spraying it onto the ground—some 80 million gallons per year. When a 2,760,000 gallon chromic acid spill occurred and leaked to the sewage treatment plant, that too was sprayed around.[26]

+ Plutonium, unused due to the virtual halt of bomb manufacture, still contaminates the plant and is a serious threat to the clean-up workers.

+ Containers of plutonium have ruptured, contaminating workers.[27]

Hanford and Rocky Flats are by no means the only problems facing the Department of Energy. The Savannah River complex is generally considered to be second only to Hanford in concentration of contamination. Indeed, 96% of all of the DOE's high-level radioactive wastes are shared between the two. Savannah River was also a plutonium producer, and their tanks also leak into ground water. They also produced tritium, a bomb component, some of which has leaked into the Savannah River.[28] Among other wastes found there is ammonium nitrate, the stuff of which the World Trade Center bomb was made.[29]

There are others. At the Oak Ridge Tennessee Laboratory, for instance, which saw early work on the first bomb, 68 pounds of weapons grade uranium remains, 4.4 pounds of which has leaked. Fear of a nuclear chain reaction has been reported. According to the Oak Ridge Environmental Peace Alliance, ". . . they've got a nuclear pipe bomb in their backyard there."[30] The remainder have similar problems, but on a smaller scale.

What do we do now?

There seems to be no disagreement on the agenda for the nation in this appalling situation:

1. We must do whatever we can to prevent explosions that would spew toxic and radioactive wastes over the regions near the obsolete plants, and also prevent other sorts of deterioration and damage. We must keep these situations from getting worse.

2. We must find a way to neutralize and store all those wastes, in some setting that will keep them out of harm's way until they are safe.

3. We must arrange to pay for the security, the neutralization, and the evacuation of the wastes; we must carry out and pay for the transportation and storage for however long it takes. Just how we can fulfill this agenda, given the extent and novelty of the problems and the astronomical costs, is a separate question. Each of these items presents problems.

Security is the first problem. The Department of Energy must secure all the facilities in order prevent further leaks, explosions, terrorist attacks, theft, and radiation exposure to workers.[33] Only after security is established, by no means an easy task, the work of cleaning up these sites may be considered. But the situation is so dangerous now that the engineers in charge of the plants dare not even place monitors in the accumulated sludge. Secretary O'Leary gave worker safety top priority in the operation of these plants.[34] Additionally, O'Leary promised (and while she was in office, delivered) openness regarding DOE's present and past activities. These developments would seem to bode for a better future than the past, but that's not saying much. At least the law of the land now applies to these outlaw operations.

Finding some safe place for plutonium will also be difficult. Plutonium is considered by some to be the most toxic substance known—minuscule amounts inhaled can cause lung cancer. Additionally it ignites spontaneously, and storing it as part of spent fuel presents a problem, because just a few kilograms can constitute a critical mass and cause a nuclear reaction.[35] Compounding the problem is its half-life (the time during which one-half the amount becomes non-radioactive) of 24,000 years.

We're working on it. A $2 billion vitrification plant is being built at the Savannah River Plant; already it is rife with cost overruns and deadlines missed.[36] The plant is designed to mix high-level radioactive waste with glass (solidify it), after which it would be stored in impermeable casks that eventually would be transferred to a permanent geologic repository.

What permanent geologic repository? After extensive surveys of geological stability, Congress selected Yucca Mountain in Nevada as a permanent disposal site for high-level radioactive waste (of commercial origin). Opponents have successfully blocked implementation of the idea, claiming that the mountain may not be safe for the thousands of years required.[37] How long is *that*? Plutonium wastes, with a half-life of 24,000 years, will be radioactive for 250,000 years. That's more than four times as long as the time since the last glacier. That number of years is simply too long to think, so the government set the criterion for "permanence" of any site at 10,000 years. That's only as long as it's been since the origin of agriculture. There are worries that Yucca Mountain may not make it.

Another site, much further developed, is the Waste Isolation Pilot Plant (WIPP) in New Mexico, designed to absorb the wastes of our weapons plants. This site too has encountered problems (like pressurized brine reservoirs distressingly close to where the waste is to be stored); worst-case scenarios have been projected that have nuclear waste, in the form of liquid slurry, oozing out through the cracks and invading the water supply in neighboring regions. For the moment, by federal injunction, the site is not in use for storage; the remaining geological problems have to be solved before permission to store wastes will be granted. (It is still costing us $160 million a year to maintain it.)

Possibly the site will absorb a significant percentage of the wastes when it opens. But if they're going to be dangerous for tens of thousands of years, how shall we ever make sure that people stay away from it? Clearly what we need is some ultimately monumental "Keep Out" sign. But how shall we write it? To design the sign, the EPA assembled a blue-ribbon panel that met during the Fall of 1991 and the Spring of 1992 to design the monument that would warn the future. The problems that they encountered, while insurmountable, come almost as a relief after the horror scenes of Hanford and Savannah. There is a wonderful philosophical humor in the deliberations.

Who knows whether humans will speak English ten millennia hence-or whether the term "human" will still apply?[38]

We cannot assume the political ascendancy of our present government-dynasties thousands of times greater than ours have waxed, waned, and faded into the jungles—nor the persistence of our language, or any language now spoken. To last over the enormous timespan,

> what architectural model should the markers panel follow? Of the original Seven Wonders of the World, only one—Khufu's pyramid in Egypt—still stands, a mere 4,500 years old; Stonehenge is a thousand years its junior. The marker, too, must compete for uniqueness with all the monuments yet to rise and fall; the millennia of liberty and civil war statuary, the carcasses of shopping malls, the innumerable legs of stone both vast and trunkless.[39]

The physicists and astronomers of the panel suggested a "black hole" approach: a covering of black asphalt which, in the desert sun, would get too hot for anyone to approach. The artists suggested a design called Forbidding Blocks, "one square mile of massive, irregularly carved boulders, laid out in a tight grid like some Flintstonian Manhattan."[40] Others included the Landscape of Thorns, the Rubble Landscape, the Spike Field, and the team favorite,

> Menacing Earthworks: an expansive empty square, surrounded by 50-foot-high earthen berms jolting outward like jagged bolts of lightning. And at the center of the square, a 2000 foot-long walk-on map displaying all the world's nuclear dumps, including this one.[41]

We have never really taken on the need to communicate with future generations on matters of urgent importance. How might it, in the end, be done?

More immediately, the costs simply boggle the mind. For starters, we must pay the companies that are running these sites now, and they charge very high rates; the price tag charged to the U.S. taxpayer continues to grow. The DOE spends about one-third more than industry does to their contractors.[42] When Hazel O'Leary was Secretary of Energy and nominally in charge of these contracts, she appeared to be "getting tough"; for example, Westinghouse was denied a bonus after a steam pipe rupture killed a worker at Hanford. Nevertheless, Westinghouse was paid $5.4 million from April to September 1993.[43] Although DOE refused to pay the court costs to Rockwell for the case described above, documents reveal that the United States has reimbursed Rockwell for other civil cases brought by near-by residents and employees.[44] The contractor that followed Rockwell as plant manager, EG&G, is not meeting contract obligations, according to the *Rocky Mountain News*. Therefore it lost its $9 million *bonus* for the second time![45] EG&G and the DOE have since parted company. They also lost a contract with the DOE's Idaho Engineering Laboratory that had been netting them $5 billion every 5 years for 18 years. EG&G's departure is also credited to O'Leary's determination to hold these firms accountable for performance.[46] And of course the cost to establish real security—to render those tanks harmless to the region, if nothing else—will cost much more.

Then there are, will be, the costs of the cleanup. All those deadly substances have to be vitrified or otherwise rendered inert, packed in trucks and taken to that place that we will, by then, have decided is safe to keep them for 240,000 years, or at least 10,000 years. How much is this going to cost? 1989 estimates put it at $92 billion; even then Senator John Glenn attacked the figures as a serious underestimation.[47] Since then, cost estimates have gone through the roof; DOE documents predict the cleanup will cost somewhere between $230 to $500 billion over the next 75 years just to "stabilize" the sites.[48] Hazel O'Leary, who has done more than anyone else to bring these waste sites to public attention, despairs of actually cleaning up all of them. We quote: "Are we going to clean-up each one of these sites so they become greenfields where young children can picnic with their families? There's not enough money in the country to do that. There's probably not enough money in the world to do that. So we will go after the worst messes first."[49]

There may not be enough money in the world to do those; and then, what about the rest? DOE itself says that *after* the job is completed the sites will need "continued guarding and monitoring," and that in some contamination cases "no effective technology is yet available [for remediation]."[50] During the 1980s the military and the DOE suggested that the Hanford facility might become a "national sacrifice zone"; that is, just fenced off and abandoned forever, as an area too contaminated to clean up.[51] Have we come to this? How will we ever explain this to our children?

The only certainty is that we will have to muster a steady national will to engage this cleanup. To quote a DOE publication, "The Cold War is over, but its legacy remains. Solving the waste management and contamination problems of this legacy will take decades and enormous resources . . . one thing is clear: the challenges before us will require a similar—if not greater—level of commitment, intelligence, and ingenuity that was required by the Manhattan Project."[52] Are we still capable of achieving such a level? The nuclear waste problem will surely answer that question.

QUESTIONS FOR REFLECTION

One source points out that beyond being a toxic and radioactive waste disaster, Savannah River happens to be located in a "heavily African-American area of South Carolina."[53] Was this fact part of the planning? What is the significance of the choice of sites for "bad neighbors" like nuclear weapons plants?

Is the problem of waste disposal sufficient proof that we ought not to use nuclear energy? Why or why not?

For fun: try your hand at scripting the horror movie. How will the legacy of the Cold War figure in your script?

"Security" has traditionally been interpreted as a matter of weapons directed at foreign powers. Yet nuclear wastes pose a threat to our security that has nothing to do with either—ironically, in this case, generated by efforts to provide for national "security." What other areas of environmental degradation might pose large-scale national safety hazards and threats to security?

How would you structure a debate on whether or not to clean up Hanford? Try to frame a solid argument that we should spend not one penny on that site, but should just fence it off and abandon it until those chemicals run out of energy, nuclear or otherwise. What are the drawbacks to that solution?

Was there any human wrongdoing, as far as you can tell, in the generation of this embarrassing and dangerous situation? Should the companies in charge of operations have foreseen the end, and taken steps to avert it? Is the fact that the private corporations who administered this site for the government were publicly traded corporations responsible to their shareholders to make a profit—or at least, not to incur losses—relevant to our judgment of their oversight?

Notes

1. Matthew L. Wald, "Hazards at Nuclear Plant Fester 8 Years After Warnings: Little Has Been Done to Ease Fears of Catastrophic Explosions," *The New York Times* (24 December 1992): p. A11. The remainder of this section comes from this article.

2. Keith Schneider, "Wasting Away," *New York Times Magazine* (30 August 1992): p. 45.

3. The major portion of the material on the history of the bomb was taken from Peter Wyden, *Day One Before Hiroshima and After* (New York: Simon and Schuster, 1984); and corroborated by "Always the Target?" by Arjun Makhijani, *The Bulletin of Atomic Scientists* (May/June 1995): p. 23.

4. Linda Rothstein, "Nothing Clean About the Clean-Up," *The Bulletin of Atomic Scientists* (May/June, 1995): p. 15.

5. Pamela Murphy, "Coming Clean," *The National Voter* (4 March 1994): p. 14; Seth Shulman, *The Threat at Home Confronting the Toxic Legacy of the U.S. Military* (Boston: Beacon Press, 1992): p. 95.

6. Pamela Murphy, "Coming Clean," p. 14.

7. Seth Shulman, *The Threat at Home Confronting the Toxic Legacy of the U.S. Military*, p. 94.

8. John F. Ahearne, "Fixing the Nation's Nuclear Weapons Plants," *Technology Review* (July 1989): p. 24.

9. Pamela Murphy, "Coming Clean," p. 14.

10. United States Department of Energy (DOE) Office of Environmental Management, *Closing the Circle on the Splitting of the Atom* (Washington, DC: Government Printing Office, January 1995): p. 18.

11. Linda Rothstein, "Nothing Clean About the Clean-Up," p. 34.

12. Ibid.

13. DOE, *Closing the Circle on the Splitting of the Atom*, p. 31.

14. Linda Rothstein, "Nothing Clean About the Clean-Up," p. 34.

15. Seth Shulman, *The Threat at Home Confronting the Toxic Legacy of the U.S. Military*, p. 95.

16. Pamela Murphy, "Coming Clean," p. 14.

17. The numbers of tanks and gallons vary from source to source; the major sources used are: Matthew L. Wald, "Hazards at Nuclear Plant Fester 8 Years After Warnings"; Linda Rothstein, "Nothing Clean About the Clean-Up," p. 34; Seth Shulman, *The Threat at Home Confronting the Toxic Legacy of the U.S. Military*, p. 97; DOE, *Closing the Circle on the Splitting of the Atom*, p. 7; Matthew L. Wald, "Uranium Rusting in Storage Pools Is Troubling U.S.," *The New York Times* (8 December 1993): p. A1.

18. Keith Schneider, "U.S. Takes Blame in Atom Plant Abuses," *The New York Times* (27 March 1992): p. A12.

19. Matthew L. Wald, "Bomb Plant Draws More Fire," *The New York Times* (2 November 1993): p. A18.

20. Matthew L. Wald, "New Disclosures Over Bomb Plant," *The New York Times* (22 November 1992).

21. Matthew L. Wald, "Justice Department Called Too Lenient in Bomb Plant Case," *The New York Times* (5 January 1993).

22. "Lets Hear the Rocky Flats Jurors," *The New York Times* (1 November 1993): Editorial.

23. Keith Schneider, "U.S. Takes Blame in Atom Plant Abuses."

24. Len Ackland, "A Dump Called Rocky Flats," *The Bulletin of Atomic Scientists* (November/December 1994).

25. World Resources Institute, *The 1993 Information Please Almanac* (New York: Houghton Mifflin): p. 141.

26. Linda Rothstein, "Nothing Clean About the Clean-Up," p. 34.

27. Len Ackland, "A Dump Called Rocky Flats," p. 12.

28. *The 1993 Information Please Environmental Almanac*, p. 141.

29. Matthew L. Wald, "At an Atomic Waste Site, the Only Sure Thing is Peril," *The New York Times* (21 June 1993): p. A1.

30. Matthew L. Wald, "Uranium Leak at Tennessee Laboratory Brings Fears of an Accidental Chain Reaction," *The New York Times* (25 November 1994): p. A18.

31. Linda Rothstein, "Nothing Clean About the Clean-Up," p. 15.

32. Ibid.

33. DOE, *Closing the Circle on the Splitting of the Atom*, p. 6.

34. Matthew L. Wald, "Worker Peril Seen in Waste Clean-up," *The New York Times* (10 March 1993).

35. DOE, *Closing the Circle on the Splitting of the Atom*, p. 40.

36. Linda Rothstein, "Nothing Clean About the Clean-Up," p. 34.

37. John F. Ahearne, "The Future of Nuclear Power," *American Scientist* Vol. 81 (January-February 1993): pp. 24–35.

38. Alan Burdick, "The Last Cold-War Monument: Designing the 'Keep-out' Sign for a Nuclear-waste Site," *Harper's Magazine* (August 1992): p. 66.

39. Ibid., p. 63.

40. Ibid., p. 64.

41. Ibid.

42. John H. Cushman, Jr., "U.S. Pays More Than Industry for Atomic Clean-up," The New York Times (30 November 1993): p. A30.

43. Matthew L. Wald, "Manager of No. 1 Nuclear Site is Rebuked by U.S.," The New York Times (9 December 1993).

44. "DOE Picks Up Court Cost Tab for Rockwell," *Denver Post,* (20 September 1993).

45. Katie Kerwin, "Rocky Flats Contractor Gets 2nd Bad Review," *Rocky Mountain News* (3 April 1994).

46. Steve Bailey, "Saying So Long to Uncle Sam: Veteran Cold War Contractor E G & G Marches into the Commercial Market After Turning Its Back on the Energy Department," *The Boston Globe* (11 September 1994), p. B5.

47. Philip Shenon, "Atomic Cleanup Is Seen Costing U. S. $92 Billion; Some Say Energy Dept. Still Underestimates," *The New York Times* (5 January 1989): p. A16.

48. Linda Rothstein, "Nothing Clean About the Clean-up," p. 34.

49. Andrew Lawler "As O'Leary Struggles to Preserve Energy Department," *Science* (19 May 1995): p. 965.

50. DOE, *Closing the Circle on the Splitting of the Atom*, p. 9.

51. Seth Shulman, *The Threat at Home Confronting the Toxic Legacy of the U.S. Military*, p. 94.

52. Ibid., p. 9.

53. Karl Grossman, "Environmental Racism," in *People, Penguins and Plastic Trees* (Belmont, CA: Wadsworth, 1995): p. 39.

Epilogue
Projections of Despair and Hope

The foregoing chapters give us few grounds for hope for the natural environment. While small bits of progress can be discovered (the banning of DDT; the American Chemistry Council's "Responsible Care" initiative), all lines projected from the cases terminate in environmental devastation. The genetically modified organisms, for instance, do not seem to pose any threat to the environment, at least in comparison to most of the other situations documented. But the controversy over the "Frankenfoods" gives us a perfect example of a bad fit between environmental activism and the problem it attempts to address. As we write, the population problem grows worse; there is no morally acceptable way of dealing with it, and as long as it is there, nothing else will work in any field. Global warming is increasing. We are watching the ice caps melt and lakes form in the Arctic, and an anti-environment administration has only now admitted that it might be a problem. While tens of thousands protest, the slaughter of the apes continues; as with the Taliban's destruction of the giant ancient statues of Buddha, the horror felt by the civilized world seems to have no effect on mindless destroyers. Bhopal continues to appear in the news, as again a machine turned on once, propelled by vengeance and greed, seems impossible to stop. Pesticides flourish, even without DDT; the organochlorines of which they are made are poisonous, persistent, and widely blamed for the deterioration of the fishing stock in the Great Lakes. Antibiotic resistance, a condition unheard of a few decades ago, now threatens lives all over the world, raising the ghosts of ancient diseases we thought conquered and dead. The fisheries continue in decline. Logging continues in the national forests and the last reserves of the ancient redwoods. And right now *no* plan to clean up the seething tanks of nuclear waste at Hanford seems to make any sense.

This is surely not the time to back away from the mandate to preserve the natural environment. We must discover and implement those methods of commerce and manufacture that can be carried on indefinitely, with the same or slightly larger population on the earth, without using up the earth. "Sustainable" economic activity, developmental or otherwise, has to be the goal of research and policy now and into the foreseeable future. Yet just at this point, the national (and international) effort to preserve environmental gains seems to be running into a wall of opposition. It is difficult to believe that only nine years ago we elected an administration whose Vice-President had written a major book on the need to preserve the environment. Environmental initiatives undertaken at the outset of the Clinton administration died aborning, and a national mood of "deregulation" set in, sweeping environmental protections toward oblivion. The present administration's first environmental initiative was an attempt to open the Arctic National Wildlife Refuge to oil exploration.

Why this sudden check in the commitment to environmental preservation? The explanations are legion; most have to do with the change in the priorities of the middle class. The first job of the head of the family is to make a living. Charities and long-range obligations, like those to the natural environment, come second. A skillful politician can make it appear that environmental initiatives are a threat to jobs, which they sometimes are in the short run, and improve his or her own position in the polls by siding with "jobs" and against "treehuggers." Along with fears of unemployment, resentment of "government regulation" lies close to the surface of the American mind, and no one wants to pay the taxes that support public initiatives and agencies. In times of economic and political uncertainty, there is political gold in opposition to expensive and job-threatening environmental regulations. Ideologues and politicians have discovered this gold; historians writing the story of the last decade of the 20th century will document an ugly mood in an ungenerous electorate, impatient with all centralized attempts to regulate for the common good in the long run.

If there is a note of hope in the generalized downward trend of the environmental initiatives, it comes from a strange new angle. These cases are too nascent to write about, but as we try to include some good news in each edition of *Watersheds,* we will keep an eye on these for the future:

Rocky Mountain Institute has a building as its headquarters where bananas and tropical flowers are grown, in the Colorado cold that reaches 47 degrees below zero Fahrenheit. It has no furnace. How does it do this? By special insulating windows that receive all light and hold all heat, and by orienting these windows intelligently to the sun. You don't need a government subsidy to build such a headquarters. It saved them its cost in heating bills the first years of its operation. We could build all our houses this way. If we put photovoltaic cells on the roofs of those houses, we could make electricity. Houses could be like trees, producing more energy than they consume. If all of us did this, the energy crisis would be over, now and forever.

Technology Today, alumni magazine of MIT and hardly a radical sheet, featured an article on the fuel cell cars of the future. Only, the future is now—prototypes are zipping around the roads now. They're not ready for prime time, the author of the article thinks; like most brand new technology, they cost too much to build to sell them at a price acceptable to the average consumer and still make money. But they'll get there, probably very soon.[1]

Many European nations have introduced the concept of "extended producer responsibility" to address the problem of solid waste and trash. If you make it, goes the concept, it's yours. When whomever you sold it to is through with it, you'll get it back. You'd better, therefore, make it: (1) biodegradable, (2) reusable after upgrade (this especially for computers), (3) recyclable or reusable after reassembly with other parts—or you will have a very large trash disposal bill. If there is, God forbid, lead in your product (as there is in many cathode-ray tubes (CRTs) from computer monitors), your trash bill for toxic waste will be astronomical. People will learn how to make CRTs differently, or prepare to recycle all of them. Most hopeful in this new concept of environmental regulation is the powerful incentive it gives all manufacturers to design for sustainability—to design each product with its end use and disposal in mind, knowing that it cannot put any further burden on the earth.

These items and others are discussed in *Natural Capitalism,* by Paul Hawken and Amory and L. Hunter Lovins, the prime movers of Rocky Mountain Institute, mentioned earlier. There is the hope—although, in the light of the chapters foregoing, we'd best not fall in love with it—that with minimal government intervention, private enterprise will remake itself in an environmentally sustainable mode. Maybe it will, maybe it won't. Stay tuned.

Note

1. Peter Fairley, "Fill 'er Up With Hydrogen," *Technology Today* (November-December 2000): pp. 56ff.

Further Readings

Attfield, Robin. *The Ethics of Environmental Concern*. New York: Columbia University Press, 1983.

Berry, Thomas. *The Dream of the Earth*. San Francisco: Sierra Club Books, 1988.

Brooks, Paul. *The House of Life: Rachel Carson at Work*. Boston: Houghton Mifflin, 1972.

Callicott, J. Baird. "Animal Liberation: A Triangular Affair." *Environmental Ethics* 2:311–38 (1980).

Callicott, J. Baird. *In Defense of the Land Ethic: Essays in Environmental Philosophy*. Albany: SUNY Press, 1989.

Callicott, J. Baird. *Beyond the Land Ethic: More Essays in Environmental Philosophy*. Albany: SUNY Press, 1999.

Carson, Rachel. *Silent Spring*. Boston: Houghton Mifflin, 1962.

Cummins, Ronnie, and Ben Lilliston, *Genetically Engineered Food: A Self-Defense Guide for Consumers*. New York: Marlowe & Co., 1999.

Daly, Herman E., and John B. Cobb, Jr. *For the Common Good: Redirecting the Economy Toward Community, the Environment, and a Sustainable Future*. Boston: Beacon Press, 1994.

Dobbs, David. *The Great Gulf: Fishermen, Scientists, and the Struggle to Revive the World's Greatest Fishery*. San Francisco: Island Press, 2001.

Easterbrook, Gregg. *A Moment on the Earth: The Coming Age of Environmental Optimism*. New York: Penguin Books, 1995.

Eisenberg, Evan. *The Ecology of Eden*. New York: Alfred A. Knopf, 1998.

Elkington, John. *Cannibals with Forks: The Triple Bottom Line of 21st Century Business*. Stony Creek, CT: New Society Publishers, 1997.

Epstein, Richard A. *Takings: Private Property and the Power of Eminent Domain*. Cambridge, MA: Harvard University Press, 1985.

Freeman, Martha, ed. *Always, Rachel: The Letters of Rachel Carson and Dorothy Freeman.* Boston: Beacon Press, 1995.

Goodpaster, Kenneth E. "On Being Morally Considerable," *Journal of Philosophy* 75:308–25 (1978).

Graham, Frank, Jr. *Since Silent Spring.* Boston: Houghton Mifflin, 1970.

Haimson, Leonie, and Billy Goodman, eds.; Michael Oppenheimer, David S. Wilcove, and Michael J. Bean, contributors, *A Moment of Truth: Correcting the Scientific Errors in Gregg Easterbrook's A MOMENT ON THE EARTH.* New York: Environmental Defense Fund, 1995.

Hargrove, Eugene C. *Foundations of Environmental Ethics.* Englewood Cliffs, NJ: Prentice-Hall, 1989.

Harris, David. *The Last Stand: The War Between Wall Street and Main Street Over California's Ancient Redwoods.* New York: Times Books/Random House, 1996.

Hawken, Paul, Amory Lovins, and L. Hunter Lovins. *Natural Capitalism: Creating the Next Industrial Revolution.* Boston: Little, Brown and Company, 1999.

Lear, Linda. *Rachel Carson: Witness for Nature.* New York: Owl Books, 1997.

Leopold, Aldo. *A Sand County Almanac and Sketches Here and There.* Commemorative Edition with an Introduction by Robert Finch, New York: Oxford University Press, 1949, 1987.

List, Peter C. *Radical Environmentalism: Philosophy and Tactics,* Belmont, CA: Wadsworth, 1993.

Lovins, L. Hunter, and Amory B. Lovins, with Seth Zuckerman. *Energy Unbound: A Fable for America's Future.* San Francisco: Sierra Club Books, 1986.

Lucas v. South Carolina Coastal Council. U.S. June 29, 1992; 22 *Environmental Law Reporter* 21104 (September 1992); *Lucas v. South Carolina Coastal Council.* S.C. Nov. 20, 1992; 23 *Environmental Law Reporter* 20297.

McCay, Mary A. *Rachel Carson.* New York: Twayne Publishers, 1993.

McKibben, Bill. *The End of Nature.* New York: Random House, 1989.

McKibben, Bill. "Not So Fast: The Environmental Optimists Are Wrong..." *The New York Times Magazine* (16 July 1995).

Miller, G. Tyler. *Living in the Environment.* Belmont, CA: Brooks/Cole (ITP) Publishers, 11th Edition 2000.

Oelschlager, Max. *The Idea of Wilderness: From Prehistory to the Age of Ecology.* New Haven: Yale University Press, 1991.

Orr, David W. *Ecological Literacy: Education and the Transition to a Postmodern World.* Albany: SUNY Press, 1992.

Passmore, John. *Man's Responsibility for Nature: Ecological Problems and Western Traditions,* London: Duckworth, 1974.

Quammen, David. *The Song of the Dodo: Island Biogeography in an Age of Extinctions.* New York: Simon & Schuster, 1996.

Regan, Tom. *The Case for Animal Rights.* Berkeley: University of California Press, 1983.

Rolston, Holmes, III. *Environmental Ethics: Duties to and Values in the Natural World.* Philadelphia: Temple University Press, 1988.

Sagoff, Mark. *The Economy of the Earth: Philosophy, Law, and the Environment.* New York: Cambridge University Press, 1988.

Simon, Julian L. *The Ultimate Resource*. Princeton: Princeton University Press, 1981.

Singer, Peter. *Animal Liberation: A New Ethics for our Treatment of Animals*. New York: New York Review Press, 1975.

Sterling, Philip. *Sea and Earth: The Life of Rachel Carson*. New York: Thomas Y. Crowell, 1970.

Stone, Christopher D. *Should Trees Have Standing? Toward Legal Rights for Natural Objects*. Los Altos: William Kaufman, 1974.

Switzer, Jacqueline Vaughn. *Environmental Politics: Domestic and Global Dimensions*. New York: St. Martin's, 1994.

Taylor, Paul W. *Respect for Nature: A Theory of Environmental Ethics*. Princeton, NJ: Princeton University Press, 1986.

Weir, David. *The Bhopal Syndrome: Pesticides, Environment and Health*. San Francisco: Sierra Club Books, 1987.

World Bank 2000. *World Development Report 2000–2001*. Oxford University Press, 2001.

Index

Bold indicates chapter